THE LIFE OF
LORD ALFRED DOUGLAS

For Oscar from
Bosie
Feb 2 1894.

AT TWENTY-THREE

THE LIFE OF
LORD ALFRED DOUGLAS

SPOILT CHILD OF GENIUS

by

WILLIAM FREEMAN

F.R.S.A., Fellow of the Institute of Journalists

LONDON
HERBERT JOSEPH LIMITED

FIRST PUBLISHED IN 1948

PRINTED IN GREAT BRITAIN BY
ODHAMS (WATFORD) LTD., WATFORD, HERTS

TO

MY FRIEND

HARFORD MONTGOMERY HYDE

"*Poor race of Men!*" *said the pitying Spirit*
"*Dearly ye pay for your primal fall—*
Some flowerets of Eden ye still may inherit,
But the trail of the Serpent is over them all!"

TOM MOORE, "Paradise and the Peri."

CONTENTS

LIST OF ILLUSTRATIONS

AUTHOR'S NOTE

The critical reader will observe that, although the qualities of Douglas as a poet are assessed, no specimens of his poetry are included.

I regret the fact acutely. The omission is due to one cause only, and that beyond my control.

The laws of copyright impose restrictions upon the biographer. These can be, and frequently are, relaxed. But in this case no relaxation was attainable.

ACKNOWLEDGMENTS

LET me say at once that it is impossible to thank adequately the many people whose interest in Douglas helped me to write this book about him.

When I began it, I had no conception of the number of friends he had possessed, some whose intimacy dated from early days, some who had known him only in his old age; sympathetic and critical and kindly, and all alike anxious that the portrait should be a fair one.

I can do no more than tender my gratitude to a few of these—to Lord Queensberry, present head of the House of Douglas, who, as well as furnishing information, allowed me to inspect the extraordinarily interesting collection of letters that passed between his uncle and Mr. Bernard Shaw; Lord Tredegar, to whom I am indebted for an account of Bosie's last hours and other family matters; to Mr. Gerald Hamilton, Mrs. A. M. Sherard and Miss Alice Head, all of whom knew him long and intimately; to the family of the late T. W. H. Crosland, for their invaluable collection of Press cuttings; to Mr. Hesketh Pearson, Mr. Hugh Kingsmill and Mr. Hector Bolitho; to Mr. Montgomery Hyde, for his generosity in putting his unique collection of Wilde-Douglas literature at my disposal; to the Executors of the late James Agate, to Mr. Ivan Bright, library assistant at the National Liberal Club, for his unwearied helpfulness and for the loan of so many books from his private library, and finally, heaviest debt of all, to my wife.

As for the Bibliography I originally meant to include, it threatened to expand into an interminable list covering not only almost all the well-known works on Douglas, Wilde and their contemporaries, but many books containing personal references that extended to only a page, or even a sentence, while at the same time supplying valuable intimate details not recorded elsewhere. In addition, I have had access to several unique collections of privately printed editions and pamphlets, and to quantities of Press cuttings and letters.

My formal "Bibliography," therefore, comprises the merest handful of authorities. But with it should be included *The Times* and *The Daily Telegraph*, whose contemporary pages were invaluable in supplying details of law cases mentioned, and *Who Was Who*.

W. F.

Spring, 1947—Summer, 1948

INTRODUCTION

EVERY biographer, in common with his literary blood-brother, the historian, from whom he differs only in telling the story of a people instead of that of a single individual, finds himself confronted by certain linked and inescapable problems.

He has to decide what his attitude in general is going to be towards his subject; he has also to decide what selection from the vast mass of detail which goes to make up any human existence he will make, not merely as essential, but as his own justification for that attitude. He must, in other words, exhibit simultaneously the qualities of the industrious anthologist and the well-informed and clear-headed critic—the latter because no biographer worth his salt sits down to his task with the unimpassioned detachment of a compiler of *Bradshaw's Guide* or *Whitaker's Almanack*.

It is an obvious truism to say that each individual is, in the literal meaning of the word, unique. But the life of Alfred Bruce Douglas exhibits that uniqueness to an outstanding and challenging degree. To the qualities which for centuries made the family of which he was a member conspicuous in history for many virtues (but rarely that of thrift), and many vices (but never that of cowardice), he added physical beauty and immense personal charm.

It is equally a truism to say that most individuals possess a dual nature. There are, the friends of such a man say tritely, " two sides to him." Where genius is concerned, these incongruities are liable to become acute. Douglas was indubitably a genius of a minor order, and in his case this schizophrenic cleavage makes a balanced estimate of his character extremely difficult to achieve.

To that was added the impact of another character, also that of a genius, and even more divided against itself, an impact so powerful that one can only compare it to the collision of two planets, their fusing, and the subsequent changing of their orbits. One star dimmed, and only nine years after the collision passed into final darkness. But the second remained an altered star. And that star was Alfred Douglas.

For these reasons he remains, from the biographical standpoint, an extraordinarily difficult person to visualize in the fair and impartial light which is the ideal of every portrait painter, whether his medium be paint or words.

From the moment of his first meeting with Wilde to the end of his own life his personality was coloured by the older man's. It is for that reason that Wilde, with all that made him the figure he was, occupies so large a share of this book. Indeed, to a certain extent he dominates it.

What career Douglas would have made for himself if the two had never met is purely conjectural. He might have taken his place as a mere aristocratic *flaneur* of his generation, a late-Victorian equivalent of Beau Brummel. His talents, developing in a healthier, more normal environment, instead of amid that strident, restless crowd, might have soared to universally recognized greatness. Or he might still have been his own worst enemy. *Quien sabe?* As it is, I have done my best to present a portrait which shall be clear and undistorted against a background drawn and coloured in true perspective.

It is common enough for a gifted man to do his best work in his youth, and, living to a considerable age, to lapse into mediocrity, if not obscurity. The history of English literature is haunted by such evanescent geniuses—Fanny Burney, Wordsworth, Swinburne and De Quincey are examples.

It is common enough, too, for gifted men to achieve fame on the strength of a single novel, a single poem, a single play, written sometimes in old age. Defoe and de Morgan belong to that rarer company. Douglas did his best work in his early and middle years, while continuing to challenge a world which would have been glad to forget the central incident of his early life.

He was seventy-four when he died. In those seventy years England changed perhaps more comprehensively than in any past century. He watched the changes, and changed with them. But not greatly.

" I doubt if I even existed ! " records the delicious Evelina, swooning, when Lord Orville has dropped on one knee to ask her to marry him. One doubts if Alfred Douglas ever " existed." He was fundamentally a poet, and poets do not exist, but live, vividly and passionately and self-consciously, so long as the flame burns.

CHAPTER I

FAMILY ALBUM

1

THE family of Douglas is one of the oldest and most distinguished in Scotland. Indeed, it is inconveniently old and distinguished from the biographer's point of view, since its ramifications go back so far and its members have played so large a part in history that it is impossible to deal with either in detail, or to assess their historical values.

To *The Complete Peerage* and *The Dictionary of National Biography,* both nobly monumental in their scope and volume, I am indebted for much of my information concerning Douglas's remoter ancestors. Nearly a hundred and twenty pages of the *D.N.B.* are devoted to the Douglas family, while the *Peerage* occupies thirty-three pages with its titles, starting with the earldom of 1358, though in point of fact the records go back at least five centuries earlier.

Few noble families in the United Kingdom can have acquired (and lost) more favour with the reigning sovereigns, or have acquired (and lost) more vast territorial possessions. "Noble," indeed, is the appropriate word, since the Douglas titles have at one time or another included four dukedoms — one Scottish, one English and two French — a French countship, three marquisates, and an incredible collection of lesser earldoms, viscounties and baronies, both English and Scottish, the creations, forfeitures, surrenders, attainders and extinctions of which, in conjunction with the fantastic irregularities with which some of these honours were bestowed, involve complications enough to baffle the most expert and devoted genealogist.

Since every recorder of family history must decide upon his starting-point, I have made a beginning with the younger son of a knight who possessed the doubtless appropriate nickname of Longleg.

He was SIR WILLIAM DE DOUGLAS, himself nicknamed " the Hardy." The date of his birth is unknown; what is known is that he held lands from his long-legged father in 1286, and that in 1287, in defending an attack against one of his manors, he was so severely wounded that one lurid account of the fray says that his head was " all but cut off." Not entirely, however, since he recovered, and from then onward until his death, in 1298, lived a life packed with incredibly thrilling adventures. These include his storming of a Haddingtonshire manor, and his carrying therefrom a lovely young widow, a ward of the English sovereign—he himself was a widower at the time—marrying her, and afterwards being captured by officers of the enraged King and imprisoned in Leeds. From this he was, however, soon released and sentenced to pay what seems a very reasonable fine of £100. Incidentally, he never paid it.

He was as dashing a soldier as a lover. When de Baliol, the Scottish King, abdicated, Douglas was left in command in Berwick. The town was besieged and captured by the English, the civilian inhabitants were massacred, but the garrison was allowed to go free with the exception of their leader. He was, however, released on swearing fealty to Edward. He broke his oath, was captured again, and died a prisoner in the Tower.

His eldest son, SIR JAMES DOUGLAS, " Lord of

CHA

Succ
Duk
Cr. Baron

ARCHIBALD WIL
b. 1818, d. 1858, as the
Styled Viscount Dru

JOHN SHOI
b. 18
Styled Viscoun

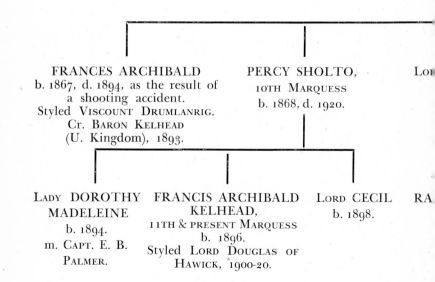

FRANCES ARCHIBALD
b. 1867, d. 1894, as the result of
a shooting accident.
Styled Viscount Drumlanrig.
Cr. Baron Kelhead
(U. Kingdom), 1893.

PERCY SHOLTO,
10th Marquess
b. 1868, d. 1920.

Lor

Lady DOROTHY
MADELEINE
b. 1894.
m. Capt. E. B.
Palmer.

FRANCIS ARCHIBALD
KELHEAD,
11th & present Marquess
b. 1896.
Styled Lord Douglas of
Hawick, 1900-20.

Lord CECIL
b. 1898.

RA

OUGLAS, K.T., 6TH MARQUESS
  b. 1777, d. 1837.
n the Death of his Cousin,
eensberry (" Old Q."), in 1810.
OF KINMOUNT (U. Kingdom), 1833.

JOHN, 7TH MARQUESS
b. 1779, d. 1856.

P.C., 8TH MARQUESS
of a shooting accident.
from 1837 to 1856.

H MARQUESS
900.
LANRIG, 1856-58.

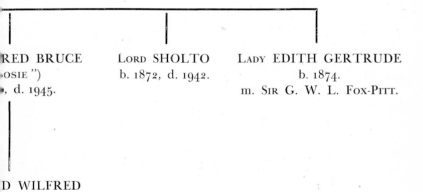

RED BRUCE
OSIE ")
, d. 1945.

LORD SHOLTO
b. 1872, d. 1942.

LADY EDITH GERTRUDE
b. 1874.
m. SIR G. W. L. FOX-PITT.

D WILFRED
OLTO,
1902.

Douglas," known as "the Good" (1286-1330), succeeded him. During his father's imprisonment he was sent to France; when he returned, it was to find that the estates he should have inherited had been assigned to Sir Robert Clifford. He tried to regain them by offering to swear fealty to the English King, failed, and allied himself to Robert the Bruce. A succession of raids, skirmishes and sudden, fantastically devised attacks (Sir W. Scott has something to say about these in *Castle Dangerous*) culminated in his being placed in command of a wing of the Scottish army at Bannockburn, and being knighted by the Bruce on the field of battle.

For the next thirteen years Douglas, combining magnificent daring, military genius, and the prestige always acquired by a leader who pays no regard whatever to disparities in the numbers of the enemy's forces and his own, harassed the armies which the second and third Edwards sent against him, the high spot in those excursions being the night when, with only five hundred horsemen, he nearly succeeded in capturing the English King himself.

Edward eventually decided to make peace with his nightmare enemy. Under the terms of the treaty, all the Douglas estates were restored, and added to those which had from time to time been given to Sir William by Bruce.

His end was splendidly typical.

Bruce had vowed that when his fighting days were over he would go on a pilgrimage to the Holy Land. A fatal illness—leprosy—made that vow impossible to fulfil. He begged that when he was dead his heart might be carried there. Douglas accepted the mission. With the heart enclosed in a golden casket, he set out. Reaching Spain, he offered to the King his knightly services against the Saracen King of Granada. They were accepted. In the great victory that followed, Douglas and a few companions pursued the flying Moors. The little party, inadequately supported, went too far; the enemy turned, and the good Sir James was borne down in a final mêlée, and slain.

SIR ARCHIBALD DOUGLAS (1296-1333), second Lord of Douglas, succeeded his brother, in spite of the fact that Sir James had left a son, and there was a surviving elder brother, Hugh. But Hugh resigned, and the nephew apparently acquiesced in his uncle annexing the estates.

Sir Archibald carried on the family tradition of warring against the English and inconvenient rivals of his own nationality with cheerful impartiality. This he did with the added prerogative of royalty, as he was, in 1333, appointed Regent of Scotland, David, the King, being a minor.

He totally defeated de Baliol, who had been crowned as rival King of Scotland, at Annan in 1332, but lost the Battle of Halidon, where his impetuosity seems to have exceeded his skill, a year later. He and many companions, including the son of Sir James, were left dead on the field of battle.

Sir James, " the Good," died in 1330, and left two sons, William (legitimate), already mentioned; another, Archibald (illegitimate). The bend sinister, however, can rarely have mattered less. The churchly Hugh, having already made way for Archibald, his legitimate brother, now made way for his illegitimate nephew, also named Archibald, and had his nephew " inserted " in the entail of the Douglas estates. He, presenting his claim to the Scottish Parliament as Lord of Galloway, was obligingly accepted.

ARCHIBALD, THIRD EARL OF DOUGLAS, born about 1328, is known as " the Grim," or alternatively as " the Black." He served under his cousin William, the surviving son of the Sir Archibald who was killed at

Halidon,* and later, to vary the monotony of fighting against the English, accompanied him on a Continental expedition on behalf of the English against the French. At the Battle of Poictiers he had the bad luck to be wounded and captured. He escaped imprisonment, however, after another English knight had explained to the French captor that Sir Archibald was merely a servant who had dressed himself up in his master's armour. This elementary specimen of fourteenth-century guile was believed, and the prisoner set free on payment of forty shillings.

When, in 1388, preparations were made to invade England, the third Earl commanded the larger portion of the Scottish army. His kinsman, the Earl of Douglas, led the other, and won a brilliant victory and lost his life at the Battle of Otterburn.

Sir Archibald succeeded to his estates. Peace with England and his own recognition as Earl of Douglas followed. He took part in yet more fighting, and in the preparation of a legal code to govern the Marches in war. He lived to see matrimonial alliances with the royal family, and the addition of yet further estates to the already vast ones he possessed. He contemptuously refused a dukedom on the grounds that the older earldom was more honourable. But it is as a " bonnie fechter " that posterity remembers him.

He died about 1400. And with his death it was said that the glory of Scotland departed.

The fourth Earl, his son Archibald, born about 1370, was appointed Lord Warden of the Marches on his father's death, and commanded a Scottish army which invaded England a year later. At the disastrous battle of Homildon Hill (1402) he was wounded five times, lost an eye, and was taken prisoner—such are Time's revenges—by Harry Hotspur. The fact did not

* The career of William, who founded the other branch of the family, and who was created the next Earl of Douglas, is dealt with later on.

prevent his subsequently joining Harry Hotspur in the rebellion against the English King, Henry IV. Wounded again, and captured again at Shrewsbury, he remained a prisoner in England until 1408.

Four years later he set out for Paris. Hostile weather drove his ship back three times, but (adds the legend) he made an offering to St. Columba, who, in return, obligingly sent a wind that blew him all the way to Flanders. Returning, he pursued what the historians tactfully term " an ambiguous policy "—in plainer English, negotiating and fighting simultaneously with his enemies. Eventually he agreed to accept a pension of two hundred pounds a year in return for the services of as many horsemen. After that, still continuing his ambiguous policy, he crossed the seas again with ten thousand men to support the French against the English who were paying him his pension. He was immediately appointed a lieutenant-general in the French army, was created Duke of Touraine, and took the oath of fealty. His new dignities were rounded off by his appointment as a canon of the cathedral.

But in the following summer the pitcher which had been so many times to the well made its last journey. At the Battle of Verneuil the stubborn English archers, under the Duke of Bedford, triumphed over a Franco-Scottish army. Four thousand men of the allied forces fell; Douglas, his second son James, and his son-in-law, Lord Buchan, were among them.

The Earl was buried at Tours. It was said of him that " personal courage, a quality common in that age, he possessed. But ambition was the keynote of his character."

His son ARCHIBALD, the new Earl, followed faithfully the family tradition. He, with a Scots army, fought victoriously in 1420 in France, and the King created him Count de Longueville. The French nobles were less appreciative, and sneered at the Scottish leaders as " wine-bags and mutton-gluttons." The Earl himself was not in France when Verneuil was fought and his father died, which was unlucky; a rumour of his death led the French King to transfer the Touraine estates to a royal nephew, and although Douglas continued to use the ducal title, it was without its revenues.

But in any case he found plenty to do in his native land. He was one of the ambassadors sent to bring James I of Scotland home from his English captivity. James's reactions were prompt, but hardly grateful. He arrested Albany, his own relation, and nearly thirty other Scots nobles, Douglas among them; and followed that up by a welter of executions.

But the executions did not include Douglas. He was set free—to function as a member of the assize which tried his colleagues.

In 1437 the ungrateful James was murdered. Douglas was suspected. But his character " being less inclined for war than other members of his house " saved him from anything more than suspicion. He was made one of the Council of Regency, and, as Lieutenant-General of Scotland, summoned its Parliament. In 1439 he died of a fever, leaving two youthful sons, William and David.

WILLIAM, the elder, a boy of about fifteen, succeeded him. Magnificent titles, vast estates and powers greater, say the historians, than that of any other subject, led to a reckless defiance of the Government, a charge of high treason in which his younger brother, David, was included, and the beheading of both, after a short trial, in Edinburgh Castle in 1440. The connivance in this tragedy of their great-uncle, James, younger brother of the first Duke of Touraine, was suspected.

Of William's titles, his French honours became extinct; so, too, did some of his Scottish titles. But the lordship of Galloway was allowed to devolve on the Earl's sister, and the earldom itself, with other property, to pass to the nearest male heir, in this case James.

JAMES accordingly succeeded as seventh Earl. He was nicknamed " the Gross," or alternatively " the Fat," and a contemporary adds unflatteringly that " he had four stone of tallow in him," an incubus to the fighting powers of even a Douglas. But it left unaffected his flair for acquiring landed property and any titles attached thereto.

He died in 1443.

His son WILLIAM succeeded. His career began promisingly. For six years or so he was in high favour with the King, and as Lieutenant-General of Scotland twice defeated the English. He married his cousin Margaret (" the Fair Maid of Galloway "). His end was, however, tragic. Joining the opponents of the powerful court party, he was treacherously stabbed by the King himself at Stirling Castle in 1451.

His brother JAMES was his heir. His record as Earl is almost as dramatic. A reconciliation with the King took place, but within two years he had allied himself with the English, and later openly accused the Scottish King of the murder. Treacheries and desertions, however, dispersed his army. The Earl fled, losing all his honours and estates.

The end, however, was not yet. The ex-Earl escaped into England, and there, surprisingly, he received a grant from Henry VI of £500 a year until he should recover his possession " taken by the self-styled King of Scots." He was also made a Knight of the Garter.

His native Parliament was not impressed. They offered a reward for his capture and death.

He joined the Duke of Albany in an invasion of Scotland, was defeated and captured, and died a prisoner in Lindred Abbey in 1491, and was buried there.

But another branch of the Douglas family still

flourished—that springing from William, the son of the Sir Archibald who had been killed in the Battle of Halidon in 1333.

He came back from campaigning in France in 1348, a hardened warrior of about twenty, and immediately started a vigorous campaign to recover his Scottish possessions. He expelled the English from Douglasdale, captured Roxbourgh Castle, and restored Ettrick Forest to the Scottish Crown. He reduced Galloway, and made its chief swear fealty to Scotland. Then, turning aside to indulge in a purely personal feud, he killed his godfather and kinsman, the Knight of Liddesdale, in Ettrick Forest, principally, insists History, because the Knight was intriguing with Edward III, and not, as Romance would have it, because Douglas was intriguing with the Knight's lady.

The years that followed were crowded with fighting, in which the actual causes seem to have mattered little and the nationalities of his enemies even less. He was created Earl of Douglas, and when he married a lady who was Countess of Mar in her own right, added her title as well as the territories to his own. He died of a fever in 1384.

JAMES, his only son, succeeded him. Froissart describes the new Earl as " a fayre young childe "; he was certainly an important child, for the King, on his accession in 1371, had knighted him and contracted the boy in marriage to his daughter Isabel.

He proved himself a warrior of parts, for in a raid against the English seven years later he was knighted a second time for valour. And there is the story of a later raid in which he, thirty French knights and about fifteen hundred " other ranks " defeated an army under two English earls, and returned to Scotland " with great spoil of goods and chattels."

In 1385 the French landed in Scotland with 2,000 men, 1,400 suits of armour, and a promise of 50,000 crowns in cash to help Douglas against the common enemy. Differences almost immediately arose, one of the chief being Douglas's insistence on the visitors being subordinate to the native army. The French knights saw no honour and little profit in the campaign, and Douglas eventually released them. But not before the 50,000 crowns had been paid in full.

The Battle of Otterburn, otherwise Chevy Chase, ended his career. Hotspur, son of the Earl of Northumberland, made a night attack on the Scots camp. He and his brother were killed. So was Douglas. He was only thirty when he died.

He left no legitimate heirs, and from this point onward the Douglas pedigree becomes almost hopelessly complicated. His cousin, nicknamed " the Grim," succeeded, and distinguished himself in fighting against the English in England, and with them in France, having played a knightly part in the Battle of Poictiers.

2

With its holder's attainder in 1455, the famous Douglas earldom became extinct. The family of Douglas, however, was far from extinct. In 1611 WILLIAM DOUGLAS, Earl of Angus in the peerage of Scotland, succeeded his father, " whose stately hospitality is said to have exceeded that of any other noble." Having resigned his claim to the privilege and prerogative of being the first to sit and vote in the Parliament of June 13th, 1633, he was, on the following day, created Marquess of Douglass, Earl of Angus and Lord Abernethy of Jedburgh Forest in the same peerage.

He joined Montrose's rebellion in 1644, was captured and imprisoned in Edinburgh Castle, but bought his release in 1647. Cromwell's not conspicuously gracious "Act of Grace" fined him another £1,000 in 1654.

He died at the age of seventy, and was buried at Douglas.

ARCHIBALD, his eldest son, born about 1609, succeeded him.

Though for a time he commanded a regiment in France, he was a courtier rather than a warrior, and spent most of his time in Scotland. He was Scottish High Chamberlain at the Coronation of Charles II, and was by him created Scottish Earl of Ormond, but owing to Cromwell's invasion of Scotland, the patent of the peerage never passed the Great Seal, and was consequently non-effective. Cromwell, adding injury to insult, fined him also £1,000 under the Act of Grace.

He died in 1655, and his grandson became the second Marquess.

His separation from Jane, his first wife, is immortalized in the ballad of " Oh, waly, waly, up the bank," and History further records that he appears " to have been morose and peevish, and incapable of managing his own affairs, for which purpose he was, indeed, a year before his death, to appoint a commission."

He died, after selling a considerable portion of his estates, at the age of fifty-three.

JAMES, only son of his father's first marriage, succeeded him. Known throughout his life, for no very obvious reason, as the Earl of Angus, his chief claim to fame is that, in 1689, at the age of eighteen, he raised and commanded a regiment of 1,800 men, today known as the 26th Foot, or Cameronians.

He was killed at the Battle of Steinkirk in his twenty-first year.

A half-brother, son of the second marriage, died an infant, and William, the youngest and only surviving son of that marriage, and born in 1694, became the third Marquess.

He, too, was known as the Earl of Angus.

But in 1703, "in consideration of his ancestry," refined gold was gilded and he was created Duke of Douglas and Marquess of Angus and Abernethy, with four lesser titles to follow. He helped the Government in the Rising of 1715, fought at the Battle of Sheriffmuir, and died, childless, aged sixty-six. His lately acquired honours became extinct, but the earlier one devolved upon his cousin.

History paints an unattractive portrait of the first and last Duke of Douglas. "A person of the most wretched intellect," comments one observer, " proud, ignorant and silly; passionate, spiteful and unforgiving." " Passionate " seems probable, for in 1725 he either murdered or killed accidentally his brother-in-law's son, who had been visiting him at Douglas Castle, and immediately afterwards fled to Holland. A rather kindlier note is struck by the statement that he possessed " an eccentrick and coarse manner (not devoid of wit), a manly courage and a most enterprising temper," whatever that may mean. It tells us, too, that the Duke was " good-looking, though not handsome."

The cousin who succeeded him in his Scottish titles was already equipped with a dazzling collection, derived from his great-great-grandfather, the third Duke of Hamilton. He was also Duke of Brandon.

Eight other Douglas baronies—surely a record— were created between 1628 and 1875. Of these, four are now extinct, one was resigned and re-granted, and the remainder are now merged in other titles.

The peerage from which the present (Scottish) marquisate is directly derived goes back only to Sir WILLIAM DOUGLAS OF DRUMLANRIG, " son and heir of Sir James of the same, himself knighted before he succeeded to his father's estates."

His career, combined with high achievements and distinctions, was governed, one feels, predominantly by discretion. He held a long succession of offices under

the crown, acquired by charter three baronies, enter-
tained King James I at Drumlanrig, continued in
favour with Charles I, and on the occasion of Charles's
visit to Scotland was crowned Earl of Queensberrie.*

JAMES, the second Earl, also held a number of public
offices, including that of a commissioner for the
apprehension of Papists. He, however, was ill-advised
enough to side with Charles in the Civil War. Taken
prisoner and shut up in Carlisle in 1645, he was fined
180,000 marks (60,000 was remitted) and again fined—
this time £4,000—by Cromwell, his total penalties for
backing the wrong horse being estimated at nearly
£235,000, a colossal sum in those days.

WILLIAM, third Earl and first Marquess, more than
restored the family prestige and wealth. He was
appointed one of a commission to apprehend English
rebels escaping into Scotland, a commissioner to
suppress crime on the borders, and eventually the Lord
Justice-General for Scotland. In 1681 he was created
Marquess, and three years later Duke of Queensbury,
with a further spate of new lesser titles, including the
Marquisate of Dumfriesshire. The tide turned
abruptly in 1686, in the course of which year he was
stripped of all his offices and forbidden to leave
Scotland. The tide turned again, however, when King
James graciously testified to the council that he " had
given satisfaction "—a phrase quaintly suggestive of a
kitchenmaid's references—and he regained all his lost
ground.

James's kindly patronage did not prevent the Duke
from supporting William III in the exciting dynastic
switch-over of 1698, and from swearing allegiance to
the Dutch-born King.

He died in Edinburgh in his fifty-eighth year.

JAMES, his eldest son, born in 1662, succeeded him
in 1695. The list of offices he held in Scotland and of

* Also spelt Queensbury, and, of course, later Queensberry.

the distinctions conferred upon him is too long to
quote. They were not, however, the result of conspicuous loyalty to the sovereign. At twenty-three he
was sent to court to congratulate James II on his
accession. In 1688 he deserted to the Prince of Orange,
and as colonel of Scottish Horse Guards fought in his
own country against his own former commanding
officer. " The first Scotsman," comments Lockhart,
" notwithstanding King Charles and King James's
goodness to his family, that deserted over to the Prince
of Orange, and thereby acquired the epithet (among
honest men) of Protorebel." He deserted at Andover,
and embarked with the Duke of Ormond and other
persons of quality for Flanders to campaign with the
army there.

Followed a dazzling and meteoric rise to place and
power, checked for a brief time in 1704, but resumed—
though Queen Anne privately detested him—in 1705.
She created him Duke of Dover and Marquess of
Beverley, and granted him the privilege in perpetuity
of exporting gold, silver and all other metals found in
the Dukedom of Queensberry duty free.

His Grace received a snub when the House of Lords
raised an objection to his voting at their general
election of Scottish peers on the ground that he was
now a peer of Great Britain.

He died of colic, in 1711, in his forty-ninth year.

Regarding the part played by the " Union Duke," as
his contemporaries nicknamed him, in the Act of
Union, Sir Herbert Maxwell pointed out that " the
statesman who should undertake this formidable task
had need not only of moral fortitude and conviction
but of personal courage." And it is certain that while
he had many enemies, he had also warm friends. A
fellow Scotsman, Sir John Clark, records that " His
Grace was a compleat courtier, and partly by art, and
partly by nature, he had brought himself into a habit

of saying very obliging things to everybody. I knew his character, and therefore was not much elated by his promises. However, I found afterwards that there was nothing that he had promised to do for me but what he made good." And here is another contemporary vignette: " He is a Gentleman of good estate, of a fine natural Disposition, but apt to be influenced by people around him, hath a genteel address, much in the Manner of a Man of Quality, of very easy Access, thin, of a black complexion."

His eldest son died when an infant; his second son was a congenital idiot with, if a certain ghastly story is to be believed, cannibalistic tendencies. Kept in close confinement, he died, mercifully, when he was seventeen. He was passed over so far as his accession to the dukedom was concerned.

THE THIRD DUKE OF QUEENSBERRY (also Duke of Dover) was born in 1698. He was known as Lord Charles Douglas until he was seven, when he was given a fresh batch of peerages, of which the Earldom of Solway was the chief, with a special remainder in favour of his younger brothers. The death of his father in 1711 brought him the Scottish Dukedom of Queensberry and the English Dukedom of Dover.

His career thereafter was worthy of this rank. He was lord-lieutenant of three counties, a Lord of the Bedchamber, Vice-Admiral of Scotland, a Commisioner of Claims for the Coronation of George II, a Gentleman of the Bedchamber to Frederick Prince of Wales, and Lord Justice-General for Scotland. He travelled extensively, and while staying in Italy in 1718, the titular Duke of Mar did his best to obtain his support for the Old Pretender. It was uphill work, however, and it failed.

His wife's exclusion from court affected his career a little, but only a little. She was the illegitimate daughter of Lord Carleton, friend of Gay, and has been

described as "witty, warm-hearted and beautiful."
With these attractions went a large fortune left her by
her father.

She died, aged seventy-six, in 1777. The Duke himself
died a year afterwards, as the result of an accident when
getting out of his carriage. The Dukedom of Dover and
other English titles conferred on his father became
extinct, for his two sons had predeceased him. The
other Scottish titles and the vast Douglas estates went
to a cousin, WILLIAM, Duke, Marquess and Earl of
Douglas, and the ultimate holder of an incredible
collection of lesser titles.

"Old Q," immortalized by Thackeray as the
Marquess of Steyn, was born in December, 1725, and
for six years, until the death of his father in 1731, was
known as Viscount Peebles. Then he became the Earl
of March. His mother had been Countess of Ruglen in
her own right. She died in 1748, and he added her title
to his father's.

For a short time the small, precocious Earl was under
the guardianship of an uncle. The uncle, dying, left
the task of fitting the boy for his place in the world to
be carried on—so far as it could be said to be carried
on at all—by a cousin, the third Duke of Queensberry,
whom "Old Q" eventually succeeded. But the
succession to a string of magnificent titles, and equally
magnificent estates, did not take place until 1778, when
he was fifty-three. And into those fifty-three years, into
his boyhood, youth and middle age, the then Earl of
March crowded every experience that the Parisian shop-
keeper understands under the title of "le High Life."

Destined to be a great landowner, no man ever cared
less for a great landowner's life and duties. Nor,
although his life was passed in the most brilliantly
intellectual circles of the time, did he take even a
superficial interest in learning. He was practically
uneducated in the academic sense of the word.

While still an impecunious youth he established himself in Edinburgh, and there began a career almost legendary in its variety. He was a boxer, a jockey and, above all, a gambler—a triple combination which, against his eighteenth-century background, should have justified any moralist in prophesying a career as brief as it was ruinous. But Providence has a disconcerting habit of deserting from the camp of the virtuous in support of the daring, the dashing, the amusing. William, Earl of March and Ruglen, might be a gambler and roué of the first water; he was also cool-headed, patient and scientific in his gambling; his bets were made with an apparent rashness that camouflaged a mental equipment that had surveyed, analysed and provided for every risk in advance. A raffish young aristocrat who backed himself to pull off what appeared to be fantastic impossibilities, and who conveyed a general impression of being a pigeon merely waiting to be plucked, seldom had to wait long in the eighteenth century. What the would-be pluckers were apt to over-look was that the wagers of the reckless Lord March did not include clauses stipulating how soon those wagers should be carried out. He could take his time, and mature his plans to the smallest detail. The result was a succession of bets that he won at extremely profitable odds. One was that he would produce a man who would run faster trundling a carriage wheel than an opponent's candidate running entirely unencumbered; another, that he would convey a letter a distance of fifty miles within an hour (he actually did this in just over thirty minutes by including the letter in a cricket ball thrown from hand to hand by a team of experts). Yet another, that he would produce four horses that would draw a four-wheeled vehicle, containing a man, at a speed of nineteen miles in an hour.

By the time the raffish young aristocrat was twenty-five he had created a formidable reputation as an expert and authority on sport.

Elsewhere, however, he had one failure. He put in a claim to the title of Earl of Cassilis and the estates which went with it, as the heir-general of his mother's mother. He could hardly be surprised when the claim failed. He had, however, titular compensations. He was made a Lord of the Bedchamber in 1760 and held the office for nearly twenty years. A year later he was elected a representative peer, and served as such in five Parliaments. In 1763 he became a Knight of the Thistle. From 1776 until 1782 he was—irony of ironies!—First Lord of the Police.

In 1778, when he was nearly fifty-three, his cousin and ex-guardian died, and he found himself fourth Duke, also Marquess and Earl of Queensberry. In 1786 he was given a barony of Great Britain, and thenceforward could no longer act as a Scottish representative peer.

Two years later he was among the members of George III's household who opposed the Government on the question of the Regency, holding that the King could not permanently recover his mental health. He was, of course, right. But the King did temporarily recover and—not surprisingly—dismissed him from office. He was described by his enemies as " a Rat who had deserted his Master to hobble after a young Prince."

The young Prince, at any rate, appreciated the friendship. And the Rat himself probably found it a relief to turn from the court to other spheres in which his heart really lay. From 1748 onward Queensberry's horses had been running under Jockey Club rules; they continued to run until 1805. He had a high reputation for honesty where betting was concerned, and according to an anonymous member of the Jockey Club was " a far better jockey than any of us." He was, too, a lover of music. And, in spite of a reputation for ultra

careful spending, he could prove a generous friend
when his feelings were stirred.

His passion for gambling was merely typical of his
class and times, while the scandals that linked his name
with innumerable mistresses are probably given undue
prominence in a career that dazzled his little world for
so long. In the last few years of his life he drifted,
"labouring under a multitude of infirmities," including deafness and the loss of one eye, between his
house at Richmond and his London mansion. But his
mind was still active. There were times when the aged
dilettante's inescapable enemy, boredom, overtook
him. "What is there," he commented bitterly once, as
he surveyed the Thames from his window, "to make
so much of? I am quite tired of it. There it goes, flow,
flow, flow, always the same!" And as an antidote, he
gave endless suppers and concerts and card games to
emigrés who had escaped to England from the horrors
of the French Revolution.

Of his last years one commentator (Wraxall) says:
"He pursued pleasure in every shape and with as much
ardour at fourscore as at twenty. After exhausting all
the gratification of Human Life, he sat down at his
residence at Hide Park Corner, where he remained a
spectator of that moving scene. His person had then
become a ruin, but not so his mind; he possessed all
his intellectual faculties, including his memory. Never
did any man retain more animation, or manifest a
sounder judgment." Of him the Princess of Wales
(later Queen Caroline) wrote, when she heard of his
death: "I had a weakness for him, and I believe he
had for me."

He never married. When a young man he had fallen
deeply in love with the daughter of Henry Pelham, the
Prime Minister. But the lady's father's "No" was firm
and final; the Queensberry reputation for dissipation,
even for those broadminded days, was too well known.

He died " of a severe flux " in his Piccadilly home, and was buried under the communion-table in St. James's, Westminster. The fortune which he left shared the fate of his titles, and was split up. For a century the Dukedom of Queensberry had been held by only two people; thereafter it was merged for ever in the sister Dukedom of Buccleuch.

The Marquisate and Earldom, with lesser titles, went to a cousin, Sir Charles Douglas, born in 1777. His career was as unspectacular—and respectable—as " Old Q's " was the reverse. He became a Lord of the Bed-chamber, and was given an English baronage which became extinct when he died, aged sixty, in 1837, leaving no children.

JOHN DOUGLAS (his brother) succeeded as seventh Marquess, adding his mother's estate of Lockerbie to the Queensberry possessions. Beyond founding the Dumfriesshire Hounds, and acting as second in a duel in which his principal was mortally wounded, he " did nothing in particular and did it very well."

He died, aged seventy-seven, in 1856 in Edinburgh, leaving an only son.

ARCHIBALD WILLIAM, known during his father's life-time as Viscount Drumlanrig, was born in 1818. He went to Eton. He held a commission in the 2nd Life Guards, which he retained until he was twenty-six. He made an early marriage. He was appointed Lord-Lieutenant and Sheriff-Principal of Dumfriesshire—the offices were almost traditional—and Controller of the Household. He resigned the Controllership because Palmerston refused to revive the Solway barony in his favour. He was, however, made a Privy Councillor in compensation.

Then, at the age of forty, came the tragic finale.

He had gone out alone rabbit shooting, on the family estate of Kinmount. He did not return; a search party found him lying dead, his double-barrelled gun, one barrel of which was discharged, beside him. The assumption was that it had gone off accidentally while he was reloading the second barrel.

But less charitable experts insisted that the wound could only have been self-inflicted. A contemporary evening paper commented: "In sporting circles a belief is expressed that the death was not accidental; he had lately sustained severe losses."

And there the matter must be left.

JOHN SHOLTO DOUGLAS, who had also been known by the courtesy title of Viscount Drumlanrig, succeeded.

His character and career are sufficiently remarkable to deserve a separate volume. He was an epitome of the qualities of a race whose members had in the past eight centuries reigned as regents, deputized as kings, and married into kingly families; who had been warriors, nobles and landowners powerful enough to challenge royal authority; who had developed in the past the qualities which almost inevitably accompany unfettered power and dominance, and shown themselves violent tempered and recklessly vindictive, with a conviction that they were above and beyond all normal laws and conventions.

Yet the career of the eighth Marquess began conventionally enough. Born in 1844, he came into the title in 1858. The next year, as a boy of fifteen, he entered the Royal Navy. From there he left to spend two years at Magdalene College, Cambridge—an odd change of environment. He matriculated when he was twenty, and at twenty-two fell in love with and married a girl whose face and character were alike beautiful, the daughter of Alfred Montgomery, a commissioner of Inland Revenue and descendant of a family with a history almost as old and picturesque as Douglas's own.

The future seemed endowed with all that the Fates could offer. He was young, immensely wealthy, owning a family seat with which went an estate of nearly thirty thousand acres and a yearly rent roll of over twenty thousand pounds, to say nothing of a second great house, Torthorwald Castle, and lesser properties. His position in society appeared to be unchallengeable. His private tastes and predilections and eccentricities seemed scarcely likely to affect it.

His education, in the academic sense of the word, had been negligible. He did not care for literature, nor, indeed, any of the arts, though it is on record that in 1881 he published a " meditation " in blank verse on " The Spirit of the Matterhorn." To the end of his life his knowledge of music was limited to a capacity for picking out tunes on the piano with one finger. Science in any form was entirely beyond him. The life of a country squire, which traditionally and providentially absorbs the surplus energies of so many men of his type, made no appeal to him whatever. Yet there were occupations to fill the vacuum.

His tastes were almost entirely sporting, a fact demonstrated at Cambridge, where he spent most of his time hunting and steeplechasing. But it is in connection with boxing that he is most honourably remembered.

His interest in the prize ring dated from his 'Varsity days, if not before them. And he was still only twenty-one when, accompanied by John G. Chambers, a professional boxer and lightweight champion, he went to America with the entirely laudable object of raising boxing from the disreputable level to which it had fallen and converting it into a sport cleanly and effectively controlled, and one which a gentleman could patronize without loss of reputation.

His plans seem to have been nebulous; what concerned him most was that the two countries should find common ground for discussion, agreement and action. The result of that visit was the acceptance of the

Queensberry Rules—fourteen of them—which to this day are accepted as valid in every organized prize ring in the world.

He had accomplished, had he realized it, his best work. The passing of the Rules carried him to the summit of popularity, and probably of happiness into the bargain. He returned to England still a very rich man, though extravagance had already fretted away some of the splendid inheritance. He had a wife who had married him for love. She had borne him an heir—another Viscount Drumlanrig. In course of time there were to be three more sons and a daughter.

And for a time the Victorian conventions did seem to lay a steadying hand upon the Marquess. He allowed himself to be elected a representative peer for Scotland. He accepted the appointment to the command of the 1st Dumfriesshire Rifle Volunteers. He was made a deputy-lieutenant of the same county.

It has been said of the Japanese that they are a " but also " race; that their sound civil and social instincts are cancelled out by other disconcertingly negative qualities. In Queensberry's case, a strange spiritual coarsening, an intensification of all that was most primitive and ignoble in his nature, seemed to set in. It first manifested itself in his openly expressed contempt for religion. In 1880 he ceased to be a representative peer, the reason being that by then (I quote *The Annual Register*) " he had become notorious as a supporter of Bradlaugh and secularism." Notoriety is inevitable when a man in his position not only attacks Christianity in public, but refers to the oath of allegiance to the Queen—involved in his election—as " such religious tomfoolery."* His political career was at an end. Her Majesty was incapable of forgetting and unlikely to forgive.

* The Queensberry title is, incidentally, the only one of its rank which, possessing no lesser British title as an alternative to election, does not admit its owner from the Upper House.

Few people, one imagines, could have cared less. He was still young, still rich, still influential enough to indulge in whatever vocation had a stronger appeal. In this case, of course, it was sport.

After the death of his father he had become Master of the Dumfriesshire Hounds. He moved, however, from Scotland, and took a house in the neighbourhood of Worcester, and was for two years thereafter Master of the Worcestershire Foxhounds. But his reputation as a gentleman rider mattered far more to him than hunting. Over and over again he rode his own horses in the Grand National. In 1886 he expected and hoped to ride Old Joe—not his own horse this time, but a cousin's—to victory. At the last moment the cousin decided that Queensberry was too old. The horse, with a professional jockey up, was a winner at forty to one, and a lifelong ambition failed to materialize.

Later, the Fates struck far more heavily. But by now he was in process of degenerating into a violent and eccentric tyrant, his especial victims being his own family.

One form this change took was a continual restlessness. He disposed of most of his ancestral Scottish properties, and acquired instead what has been termed " a surfeit of residences " in or near London — in Buckingham Gate, Cromwell Road and Cadogan Place—as well as a large rambling house in Berkshire. His wife and children saw less and less of him, and as the years passed their natural affection, to say nothing of the hero-worship due to a hunter, rider and lightweight boxer of international authority, changed into indifference, contempt and, at least in one instance, into bitter hatred.

His third son referred to him as an inhuman brute with a mania for persecuting his wife (herself an angel and a saint), and who for twenty years neglected and ill-treated his children. Bernard Shaw comments drily: " He seems to have earned his son's opinion of him very thoroughly. He was a Scots Marquess, Earl, Viscount and Baron, with a fourfold contempt for public opinion, an ungovernable temper and, after his divorce, a maniacal hatred of his family. . . . He was, when irritated, so foully abusive that his second son, Percy, was provoked to punch his head in broad daylight in Bond Street, and when the two were bound over to keep the peace, nobody was surprised, for that was the sort of man the Marquess was supposed to be."

Frank Harris gives a clear-cut little picture of the Marquess.

" Queensberry," he says, " was five feet seven in height, broad and strong, with a plain, heavy, rather sullen face, quick, hot eyes, a taste for side-whiskers and bowler hats. He was a man of self-conceit, all bristling with suspicion, and in regard to money, prudent to meanness. Under a rather abrupt, but not discourteous, manner he had an irritable, violent temper. He was combative and courageous, as very nervous people sometimes are when they happen to be strong-willed. His insane temper got him into rows at the old Pelican Club more than once."

Before he died, aged fifty-five, in 1900, he had become obsessed by the poverty complex. " I am," he would assure his family, " a very poor man."

Drumlanrig, his eldest son, was born in 1867, within a year of his parents' marriage. He was educated at Harrow and at Sandhurst; at twenty became a lieutenant in the Coldstream Guards, the same year in which Lady Queensberry divorced her husband. (She lived until 1935, dying in Hove in her ninety-first year.)

While his father's character deteriorated, Lord Drumlanrig's career appeared to be shaping conventionally and successfully. As a Liberal, he was, in 1892, appointed assistant private secretary to Lord

Rosebery, then Premier. In 1893 he was created a peer of the United Kingdom as Baron Kelhead of Kelhead, and appointed a lord in waiting. The world, social and political, that his father had abandoned, seemed at the new peer's feet. But on October 18th, 1894, came tragedy. What a friend described as " that amiable, excellent little man " was found dead at Quantock Lodge, Somerset, a hunting lodge belonging to the Stanley family. The coroner's jury returned a verdict of death from the accidental explosion of his own gun.

His next brother, Percy, became heir to the title. He married, but the Marquess, who himself had taken a girl of nineteen as his second wife and been divorced again within a few weeks, disapproved so violently that he refused to attend either the wedding or the baptism of his first grandson, the present Marquess of Queensberry.

Reference here may be made to another member of the family, who combined general eccentricity with a flair for achieving sudden and startling publicity. The Lady Florence Caroline Dixie, née Douglas, daughter of the seventh and sister of the eighth Marquess, deserves, if not a book, at any rate a chapter, on her own account.

Born in 1857, she married, at eighteen, Sir Alexander Beaumont Dixie, eleventh Baronet, of Bosworth Park, Leicestershire. One of her two sons had the Prince of Wales for his godfather. She wrote verse—reams of it. (One poem, written when she was twelve, begins: " Metropolis, gay licenser of sin.") She also wrote a blank verse tragedy, "Abel Avenged," of which one critic said ambiguously, " It supplied what Milton omits," books of travel, and ballads, which included " Why I kissed the sailor boy." Marie Corelli found her poems very fascinating, Ouida was much affected by their beauty and pathos, while an anonymous sailor announced that he had become a total abstainer after reading "Drink's Curse." She went to Patagonia in 1878, to California in 1879, and acted as a special correspondent of the *Morning Post* in Zululand and the Transvaal.

She also wrote novels, in one of which the heroine, aged twelve, goes undetected to Eton; then—later, of course—to Oxford, where he, or rather she, comes in first in six events in the Melton Hunt Steeplechase. The zenith of this hero-heroine's career is reached when she enters the House of Commons, to become Prime Minister at twenty-eight.

Lady Florence appeared at Ascot in a cool white boating-costume, upon which occasion the Prince of Wales, with perhaps a shade less than his usual tact, inquired if she was wearing a nightgown.

But it was while she was living in a riverside villa called The Fishery, between Windsor and Maidenhead, in March, 1883, that society learned that a dastardly attempt had been made by two tramps, dressed as women, to murder Lady Florence while she was picking flowers. One of these miscreants seized her by the neck; the other struck her twice with a knife. The whalebone of her ladyship's stays, however, stopped the blade, whereupon the first tramp pushed a large handful of earth into her mouth and nearly choked her. Rescue, however, was near. A moment later her large and powerful St. Bernard dog broke through the wood and dragged off assailant number two. After which Lady Florence heard a confused rumbling of wheels and remembered no more.

This story created a terrific excitement. The Queen sent her confidential servant, John Brown, to make inquiries, and was later rewarded by " an autographed [*sic*] portrait of Hubert, the dog, photographed by Mr. Snooks, of Windsor."

Sir Henry Ponsonby conveyed the Court's congratulations, messages came from the Prince of Wales, the Duke of Edinburgh, the Empress Eugenie, and the Mayor of Windsor. The papers were full of the story; *The Times* indulged in a leading article. Irish Fenians were suspected of being responsible, though why was not obvious; so also were gipsies, poachers, escaped convicts and soldiers. Mr. Gladstone was asked in the House if he could give any information about the attempted assassination of Lady Florence. The answer was in the negative. Nor could Sir William Harcourt or Mr. Parnell assist.

Nor, in fact, could anyone else, though the police and other authorities went through the ancient routine of exploring every avenue and leaving no stone un-turned. The sensation died down. The only reasonable explanation of the mystery, in view of a complete absence of any confirmatory evidence, seems to be that Lady Florence either suffered from hallucinations or invented the whole story because she wanted to create a sensation. She indubitably succeeded so far as the sensation was concerned. When she died in 1905, the world, in view of her other admirable qualities—she was the originator of seaside camps for poor children—had forgotten all about it. Possibly she had forgotten, too.

Her eldest sister, Lady Gertrude, left the ranks of Society at the age of forty to carry out what the *Pall Mall Gazette* described as " an experiment in a sort of Christian socialism," by marrying " a respectable man of humble position," a baker employed at a refuge by one of her brothers, who had become a Roman Catholic priest.

Her brother, Lord Francis, was involved in an adventure that was wholly tragic. On July 13th, 1865, when only nineteen, he and three other members of the Alpine Club with three guides set out from Zermatt, under the leadership of the great Edward Whymper, to attempt the hitherto unscaled summit of the Matterhorn. They succeeded, but on the return journey one of the party slipped and fell, snapped the connecting rope (a rumour persisted that one of the guides cut it) and precipitated himself, Douglas and two others four thousand feet on to the Matterhorn Glacier.

The body of Douglas was not recovered until some time afterwards.

CHAPTER II

VICTORIAN LANDSCAPE

THE decade 1870-80 was one of smug, inglorious ugliness. It opened with a Continent restless under an unstable peace, while in England there had already begun the rumblings of future warfare between those who were comfortably well off and those who were uncomfortably poor. It was an England which would seem to the alert and critical eyes of today almost as remote, physically, socially and psychologically, as the England of the Middle Ages.

Victoria, now past fifty, had been on the throne for over thirty years. The sovereign, once radiantly young, if never beautiful or even pretty, had subsided into chubby, stolid middle age, vaguely suggestive of a widowed seaside landlady who has seen better days, and still determinedly surrounds herself with full mourning paraphernalia. It had been hoped that by now she might have recovered sufficient spirits to open Parliament in person. As nearly nine years had passed since the Prince Consort's burial, the assumption seemed reasonable. But she found the effort too much for her; she could not even bring herself to open the Victoria Embankment.

Bertie, otherwise the Prince of Wales, having given up all hope of being allowed to take any active part in affairs of State, had resigned himself to the less responsible career of the First Man About Town, and was filling the rôle with a gusto and absence of formality that exasperated his illogical and formidable

44

mother. To elaborate the boarding-house metaphor, he was occasionally allowed to receive the less important visitors and to interview the tradesmen, but never to inspect the books.

The Liberal Party had been in power for six Parliaments in succession, with Mr. Gladstone at its head and the enigmatic Mr. Disraeli, lean, yellow, and incorrigibly dandified, snapping vindictively on its flanks.

" Swells " wore billycock hats with coloured bands, and carried sticks with tassels. Ladies wore bonnets and unbelievably voluminous skirts. Old clo' men went about with three hats piled on their heads.

The streets and houses were lit by gas. Domestic servants were lucky if their wages were five shillings a week.

Postmen wore kneebreeches and black silk stockings. Dustmen wore kneebreeches and white stockings. Policemen, whiskered and bearded, wore high, varnished helmets with " combs," and were equipped with rattles. London cabmen hoisted little flags when their vehicles were disengaged. Fashionable women walked with a limp, because the Princess of Wales had sprained her ankle, and a limp was consequently *de rigueur*. Nigger minstrels were at the height of their popularity; the can-can, and the arch naughtiness of its implications, were all the rage. " Black-eyed Susan " was holding the stage, Henry Irving establishing his reputation.

Tennyson, Browning, Matthew Arnold and Swinburne were writing poetry; Ruskin, majestically if a little unsteadily, was laying down the laws of Literature, Art and Morality. Carlyle, George Eliot, James Payn, William Black, Mark Twain, David Christie Murray, Wilkie Collins, Miss Braddon and Mrs. Henry Wood, and the Reverend George Macdonald were writing prose. Millais, Leighton, Holman Hunt, Alma Tadema and Watts were painting pictures; Harry Furness, Edwin Abbey, Linley Sambourne and "Kiki" du Maurier were drawing them. The pre-Raphaelites as a group were striving, with passionate, humourless sincerity, to rescue England from the horrors of Victorian philistinism.

A gawky, red-haired Irish youth of fourteen named Shaw was showing a precocious interest in music. Herbert Wells (English) and James Matthew Barrie (Scottish), aged ten, were two other lower-middle-class schoolboys who later were to enchant or exasperate their readers. Anthony Hope Hawkins, aged seven; John Galsworthy, aged three; Arthur Conan Doyle, aged eleven; and Rudyard Joseph Kipling, aged five, were all too young to do more than dream of Ruritanian romances, family sagas, super-sleuths or sublimated Jingoism.

Arthur Sullivan was composing music for the Albert Hall and the Victorian drawing-room, and at the same time beginning that unique collaboration with William Schwenk Gilbert, which, with the co-operation of Mr. D'Oyly Carte, was to produce large fortunes for all three and knighthoods and fame for two. London, already with thirty-odd theatres, was about to add three more; there were also over forty music halls. *Punch's* ironic prophecies included a train that could either fly or swim direct from London to Paris. Mr. Plimsoll's Bill for making footwarmers compulsory in railway compartments was thrown out by 152 votes to 32. Daring young men rode on penny-farthing bicycles, the less daring on tricycles. Dashing young couples rode in hansoms, as an alternative to dingy, straw-carpeted growlers. "The Metropolitan Railway," it was announced, "will now take visitors into the very heart of London."

The Royal Aquarium still existed; Jack-in-the-Green still danced in the London streets.

After much agonized doubt, Parliament had granted married women the right to possess property of their own. The Suez Canal had only lately been opened; the Panama Canal was still no more than an engineer's dream.

Italian boys sold plaster images; a horrible old crone who hawked bootlaces on Waterloo Bridge was popularly supposed to be the widow of Burke the murderer. The cries of " Buy my fresh lavender " and " Who'll buy a broom? " were still heard, so was the cheerful clang of the muffin-man's bell. A grey-bearded man dressed like a Druid was tried for cremating his daughter's body on a Glamorgan hill-top. He was acquitted.

There were no " popular " tea shops; only confectioners, where one's choice was limited to bath buns, three-cornered puffs, jam tarts and sponge cakes.

Minute private steam yachts, with funnels nearly the length of the boat, were popular on the Thames. Penny steamers were also running. The buses were ramshackle affairs, with plain wooden seats. The fare over Waterloo Bridge was a ha'penny.

There were speaking-tubes, but no telephones. (The first public exchange to open, with twenty-one enterprising subscribers, was in New Haven, Connecticut.)

The telegraph existed, under the old manual dot-and-dash methods of transmission. Regarded by the populace in general as a herald of personal and horrific disaster, its orange-coloured envelopes were received with trembling fingers and blanched cheeks. Electric communications between Europe and America had still the aura of the miraculous. Although since the beginning of the century there had been scientific dabbling in moving pictures, public exhibition in any form was still to come. Even the photographic film was unknown. Taking any photograph was an impressive ritual that began with a massive mahogany camera, and proceeded to its mysterious conclusion through Stygian darkness to exposures in wooden frames and other nerve-racking technicalities.

Tennyson's *Promise of May,* enlivened by Douglas's father, the eighth Marquess, arriving with a bouquet of vegetables intended for the leading lady, was produced.

The gayest, jolliest shows were at the Strand Theatre, but the cup-and-saucer dramas, *Caste, School* and *Ours,* with the Bancrofts at the old Prince of Wales Theatre, were also scoring their greatest triumphs. Forbes Robertson and Grossmith were in process of abandoning art for the stage; Bernard Partridge, the stage for art.

The penny plain and twopence coloured prints, as seen and loved by Stevenson, were still immensely popular.

Salvani was appearing as Othello at Drury Lane.

A remarkable number of illustrated weeklies, of a type now extinct in this country, enlivened the 1870's. They specialized in crude personalities, and had usually a violent political bias in one direction or another. Among them were *The Tomahawk* (edited by Arthur à Beckett, later to become editor of *Punch*), *Figaro in London, The Mask, The Owl,* and *Fun* (in which originally appeared W. S. Gilbert's *Bab Ballads*).

The claim of Arthur Orton, ex-butcher of Wapping, to the Tichborne baronetcy and estates, provided (in 1871) a prelude to what was to prove the longest trial in English history. It began on April 23rd, 1873, and ended, after 188 days of what the Lord Chief Justice rightly termed "investigation," on February 28th, 1874, with a sentence of fourteen years' penal servitude for the claimant.

Doctor Livingstone was "discovered" by Stanley in November, 1871. The doctor died in May, 1873.

The year 1870 itself was destined to include rather more than its share of minor and major excitements, with one predominating tragedy colouring its final months—the ruthless pulverization of French power by the newly allied German states under Prussia's leadership.

The Education Act was passed, ensuring that all juvenile England should have at least an elementary knowledge of the three R's.

January saw the burning down of the old " Star and Garter " at Richmond.

A porter in a Finsbury hotel was battered to death " with a tumbler or candlestick "—one would have thought they could have discovered which—by a hot-tempered lady he had secretly introduced into the house, and who was subsequently given a life sentence. The s.s. *Bombay* collided at Yokohama with the American warship *Oneida,* who, it appeared, had hailed its destroyer three times with a cry of " You've cut us down!" before sinking stern-first with 140 officers and men. The *City of Boston,* en route from Halifax to Glasgow, made an even more dramatic exit a few days later, when, with nearly two hundred people on board, she vanished without trace.

A meeting was held at the Mansion House to promote national emigration.

In February, Mr. Ruskin delivered his inaugural lectures as Slade Professor at Oxford, the Irish Land Bill was introduced by Mr. Gladstone, and the first Negro senator took his seat in the United States Senate.

In March, Texas was admitted into the Union, and Negro suffrage ratified. There was also held in London the first meeting of a Society for Organizing Charitable Relief and Repressing Mendicity.

In April, a proposal to move the Blue Coat schools from Newgate Street into the country was rejected. A

condemned murderer named Rutherford was respited
" owing to a malformation of the neck," while further
afield four English travellers were killed in cold blood
by Greek brigands.

An alligator, "alive but much exhausted," was
caught swimming in the Thames.

The Budget struck a pleasantly optimistic note.
Income Tax was reduced from sixpence to fivepence
in the pound, while hawkers' licences, the impress
Newspaper Tax, the Railway Tax and hail-and-cattle
insurance were all abolished. Halfpenny postcards and
book post were introduced.

A clergyman named Huelen and his housekeeper
were murdered by one Miller, who concealed the
gentleman's body under a stone floor. The lady's he
deposited in a wooden box, " said to contain a variety
of goods." He was duly hanged. Murder on a bigger
scale took place at Denham, where the Marshall family
of seven were slaughtered by a tramp " in their humble
roadside dwelling."

Mark Lemon, a founder of *Punch* in 1841 and its
editor since that date, died, and the Thames Embankment Railway was opened.

On June 9th Charles Dickens died; on the 14th
he was buried in Westminster Abbey, " at the feet of
Handel and at the head of Sheridan." When, a few
weeks later, his furniture was sold, it fetched extraordinary prices. (The stuffed body of " Grip," the
raven, went for 120 guineas.)

A " telegraphic evening party " was given by Mr.
Pender, chairman of the British Indian Submarine
Telegraph Co. The Prince of Wales and the Duke of
Cambridge were among the guests; a corner of the
saloon was fitted up as an office, in which Sir James
Anderson officiated, and a number of distinguished
people cabled messages of goodwill to numbers of other
distinguished people, including the Viceroy of India,

President Grant of America, the King of Portugal and the Khedive of Egypt.

When the Prince and Princess of Wales laid the foundation of a new college at Reading the Princess, after listening to a long address from the town clerk—incidentally she wore a dress of pink silk with a white muslin skirt—was presented with another address on her own account. It is stated to have been " in a very novel form." It was. The address, " reduced by photograph," was appended to a carved mother-of-pearl fan. Attached to the fan was a solid gold vinaigrette with the coronet and monogram of the Princess, who " appeared much pleased." On the 7th she left London to visit her parents in Denmark.

The Duke of Newcastle was adjudged a bankrupt. There was also a panic on the Stock Exchange.

In the meantime, the shadow of a conflict between France and Prussia and her allies was growing steadily darker and darker. England made tentative efforts to avert hostilities, but the most pacific efforts stood no chance in the face of Bismarck's long-term planning. On July 19th France formally declared war; the King of Prussia telegraphed to the King of Bavaria: " By an unheard-of presumption we have been driven from the most profound peace into war." On July 28th the Emperor and the Prince Imperial left for the front, leaving the Empress in Paris as Regent.

On the 13th the Prince of Wales, with Princess Louise, opened the Thames Embankment, which had been begun in 1864. It had been fully expected that the Queen would perform the ceremony, and three miles of gaily decorated seats had been provided. " Her Majesty's absence," says a chronicler, " told greatly upon the attendance." Becoming still more candid, he adds: " The State portion of the procession was not particularly imposing, but the shabbiness and ill-assorted carriages of the members of the Board of

Works introduced an element of the grotesque which rendered the whole almost ridiculous."

Sarah Jacobs, a Welsh girl, who, dressed as a bride, pretended to the crowds who visited her that she could exist without food, finally proved that she exaggerated by dying. Her father and mother, arrested for manslaughter, were given twelve months' and six months' hard labour respectively.

Six children sleeping in two beds were burnt to death in a fire that broke out in the Waterloo Road.

August opened ominously for the French, whose armies suffered four defeats in the first week. The Germans crossed the Rhine on the 8th, and invaded Strasburg on the 10th.

The murderer of Mr. Heulin and his housekeeper was executed seated on a chair, since he refused to stand. A week later, the tramp who had murdered the Marshall family was also hanged. His last remarks on the scaffold exhibited what must have been a unique mental lapse. He said: " My friends, I am going to die for the murder of Charles—what *is* his name? I forget."

A drunken schoolmaster, of Bath, named Prankard, shot two of his daughters with a revolver and then committed suicide. The elder, who had annoyed him by planning to go abroad, he " struck in the right ear with one bullet and in the left temple with the other." The second daughter, badly wounded (she died later), " fell on a long school desk, which was swimming in blood." It " presented a fearful spectacle." A third daughter, luckily for herself, was in the kitchen.

September 2nd brought the surrender of the French Emperor with a hundred thousand men at Sedan, and, two days afterwards, the end of the Empire. The Empress sailed for England and joined the Prince Imperial at Hastings.

On September 6th England's newest and most

formidable warship, the *Captain*, of 4,272 tons, ignominiously turned turtle with five hundred men on board and foundered in a squall off Cape Finisterre. She had already made successful voyages to Vigo. A few—very few—men were saved. She had been built, said her detractors afterwards, " in deference to public opinion."

In October a London firm of gunmakers was fined twenty pounds for trying to send two thousand cartridges to Paris, "under the pretence that the packages were filled with vegetables." Mr. Ruskin wrote to *The Daily Telegraph* pointing out that "neither the French people nor their Emperor had brought on the war by any present will of their own." Mr. Carlyle wrote to *The Times* declaring—"that the noble, deep, pious, patient Germany should be welded into a nation is the hopefullest public event that has occurred within time."

A monument to the author of *Robinson Crusoe,* subscribed for by the children of England in answer to an appeal through the columns of *The Christian World,* was unveiled at Bunhill Fields.

Margaret Waters, before being executed for murdering five foster-children, uttered in Brixton, in calm and composed tones, a beautiful extempore prayer. George Chalmers, on the other hand, hanged for killing a tollhouse keeper, insisted on declaring his innocence despite unusually persistent efforts from the officiating clergyman "to relieve those present from the very distressing position in which they were placed."

The distress could hardly have been limited to the spectators.

The Anchor liner *Cambria,* an iron-screw steamer of 1,312 tons, was wrecked off Inistrahull with the loss of 170 lives.

Into what the late Cornelius Whur so adequately

described as " this imperfect gloomy scene of complicated ill " was born, on October 22nd, 1870, Alfred Bruce Douglas, third son of the eighth Marquess of Queensberry.

CHAPTER III

EARLY DAYS

ALFRED BRUCE DOUGLAS, commonly known as Lord Alfred, was born at Ham Hill, a house near Worcester.

The family had migrated southward, and its head, as already stated, had become Master of the Worcestershire Foxhounds. Later, when the great Scottish properties of Torthorwald and Kinmount had been sold, properties which for centuries had been associated with the name of Douglas and all that it stood for, their exile became a permanent one.

But before that happened the boys did return for a time to Scotland, and at Kinmount the happiest hours of their lives were spent.

There they played and quarrelled, and explored the countryside and refought their ancestors' battles with wooden swords made for them by the estate carpenter. One combat nearly resulted in Percy putting out the eye of Francis, his elder brother, the heir whose place he was to take after the tragedy of a fatal gun accident a few years later. Frequently they visited Ecclefechan, that mecca of lovers of Carlyle.

Alfred acquired very early in his life the nickname of " Bosie,"* a corruption of the diminutive " Boysie " that his mother called him. Unlike the majority of these childish nicknames, it extended far beyond the

---

* Interestingly paralleled by Dickens's " Boz." This was a corruption of " Boses," in turn derived from the " Moses " of the *Vicar of Wakefield*, originally a nickname of Dickens's younger brother.

family circle, clung to him throughout life, and was used by him when writing to his friends.

A photograph of him when he was five hints, but only hints, at the physical beauty and grace which played so large a part in making him an almost literally magnetic figure later on. In the childish poise, as well as in the challenging eyes and imperious mouth, one can see the man who to the end of his life was a fighter against what he despised and disbelieved. Often, far too often, he despised and disbelieved through prejudice and anger. But his courage was unflagging.

He and Percy were inseparable friends up to the time when the elder boy, following his father's first steps, went into the Navy.

From lovely Kinmount, when the exile had become permanent, the Douglases moved to the desperately conventional and formal Cromwell Road, and afterwards to Number 18 Cadogan Place. By then the family had become hopelessly disrupted. Its head had ceased to live with his wife and children, and had taken rooms in James Street, Buckingham Gate, and the children rarely saw him, either in London or at their mother's country house, The Hut, three miles from Bracknell, in Berkshire, to which they all moved for the summer months. His absence must have been an aching humiliation, if not a privation, to his wife and sons; it is possibly for that reason Douglas dwells so briefly upon it in his *Autobiography*.

But concerning his mother he is less reticent. Indeed, there is no need for reticence. In her long life she passed from brief happiness, through years that included griefs that would have left a woman of less noble character bitter, reckless and disillusioned, to a serene and saintly old age. She and her sister, Mrs. Finch, children of Mr. Alfred Montgomery and a daughter of the first Lord Leconfield, were, Douglas tells us, so beautiful that when as young married women they went out driving in the park, sightseers stood on chairs to watch them pass. (A scene reminiscent of the days when George III allocated an escort of soldiers to protect the beautiful Miss Gunnings from the embarrassing admiration of eighteenth-century crowds.) The sisters were painted by Watts as children. One was dazzlingly fair, the other dark. Lady Queensberry, according to her son, continued to look like a girl until she was over forty, possessing a gentle, sad, proud, tiny flower-like face and head (the sadness is easily comprehensible), with a slim figure like a Tanagra statuette. Incredibly good and sweet and kind and patient, she was also the most valiant and loyal woman that ever drew the breath of life. She was to need, Heaven knows, all her sweetness and patience and valiance in the course of her long, agitated life, not only on account of the infidelities and cruelties of her husband, but in looking after a family, of which the adored and adoring Bosie was not the least difficult member. She turned from Low Church Protestantism to the Catholic Church in her eightieth year. Her husband had become an agnostic of the most vociferous and offensive type.

Bosie's education began, almost inevitably at that period, with the installation of a governess. His mother had always spoilt him; the governess, a Scotswoman named MacCormick, did her best to neutralize the result. He described her as dour and old-fashioned, an inflictor of primitive punishments that included the use of the cane and the back of a hairbrush. After the dismissal of this she-dragon came a succession of milder governesses—a pessimistic Miss Holland, a Miss Swift who told Bosie and his brother delightful fairy tales, a Miss Humphreys; and, for French, a Mlle de Souburan. To both of these latter ladies the Douglas boys were devoted.

When Bosie was ten, governesses ceased from troubling, and he was sent to Lambrook, a private school with what Lord Macaulay would call " aristocratical " connections. Francis, the eldest boy, at the same time left the same school for Harrow; Percy, the second son, was studying at another school at Portsmouth with a view to entering the Navy.

Lambrook was, to use Douglas's own adjective, " classy " enough not only to include two of Queen Victoria's grandsons, but to induce Her Majesty herself to come down more than once to see the boys play cricket—a conspicuous example, it may be safely assumed, of a sense of grandmotherly duty triumphing over boredom.

But Douglas had been there about a year when some unspecified trouble broke up the school. From Lambrook he went to Wixenford, whose headmaster was named Arnold, a tall, dark, black-bearded man with a terrifying resemblance to the " tall Agrippa " of *Struwwelpeter*. Sholto, the youngest of the four Queensberry boys, went with Bosie to Wixenford.

Douglas, according to his own account, was appallingly sensitive. He was also appallingly spoilt. He naïvely explains the reason. He was, he says, a very pretty child, and had captivating ways, and his mother could not, or did not, resist him. The consequence was that he suffered proportionately more at school. Unfortunately, the Agrippa-like Mr. Arnold was entirely uncaptivated by childish prettiness linked with childish spoiling. He punished with verbal scarifying rather than the cane, and Douglas's life, like the Gilbertian policeman's, was not a happy one. A few trivial incidents, islets of memory rising above the seas of oblivion that wash over long-past days, are recorded in his autobiography: the excitement that ensued when young Leveson, son of Lord Granville, distinguished himself by swallowing half a crown while

giving an amateur conjuring entertainment and distinguished himself even more by being none the worse
afterwards; visits to Walmer Castle; the quaint accent
of an American boy who re-nicknamed Bosie " Puppy-
dog."

But a darker cloud than any school troubles over-
shadowed the boys' lives. Their father's interest in and
affection for his home and family, never deeply rooted,
steadily withered. They and their mother saw less and
less of him; when at rare intervals he did appear, he
was neither an example nor a guide. He was not even
a friend.

Douglas was sixteen when the last pretence of a
united family life came to an end; and in January,
1887, Lady Queensberry was goaded into applying for
a divorce by her husband's threat to introduce a
mistress as a permanent member of the household. She
had no difficulty in obtaining the divorce; the whole
process, indeed, occupied only fifteen minutes. She
never remarried. Lord Queensberry did. His second
marriage, as already stated, was soon annulled.

Douglas left Wixenford for Winchester a little before
his fourteenth birthday. He had wanted to go to Eton,
and his mother had supported his wishes. Probably for
that reason, Lord Queensberry, who incidentally knew
nothing whatever about Eton, violently negatived the
idea at the last moment. He would never, he insisted,
illogically and a trifle obscurely—mental clarity was
never one of his outstanding qualities—have his sons
turned into " Belgravian loafers." Winchester, which
presumably did not produce loafers, was the alternative.

Says one of E. F. Benson's characters, apropos of the
English weather, " It would be grovelling flattery to
call it beastly." To a highly strung boy like Douglas,
Winchester *circa* 1880 might have been described in
exactly those terms. He compares it to the Rugby of
Tom Brown's Schooldays, complete with a bully of the

Flashman type, and adds that his first eighteen months there were " pretty much of a nightmare." The school was a sink of iniquity in which perished all of the purity, truth and beauty that his mother had watched so proudly and tended so devotedly. His ideals were trampled in the mud and slime by boys to whom morality and decency meant less than nothing. When he left he was one of them, no better, no worse, " a finished young blackguard, ripe for any kind of wickedness," with no kind of moral sense whatever. To this appalling and doubtless exaggerated statement he adds a faintly apologetic postscript to the effect that he did not mean that he, any more than his school friends, had lost all that they had learned at home, but that they had superadded to it all that the much-vaunted English public schools could teach. His closest friends in those disillusioning days were Lord Encombe, who afterwards shared his rooms at Oxford, and George Wyndham, son of his great-uncle Percy and Madeline Wyndham —a delightful couple to whom he was devoted, and to whom he pays generous tribute in his *Autobiography*.

He learnt little worth learning at Winchester. But he did develop an unsuspected talent for athletics. He was futile at cricket, and only fairly good on the football field. But he was light and spry; a born runner. He won the school steeplechase—two and a half miles across country—in 1887, when he was sixteen, and would probably have won it in the following year, his last at Winchester, if a severe cold had not intervened.

In a letter from Mr. George Milsted (chief partner in Messrs. Duckworth, the publishers, a firm which later produced several of Douglas's books), a junior at Winchester in 1889, I have been given an interesting glimpse of Douglas in his athletic days. He writes: " Lord Alfred Douglas, who was at Magdalen College, came to play football—we play, you know, a game of our own—for old Wykehamists against the School.

On this occasion it was a game of 'sixes,' a very fast game with only six men on each side. It was played in 'canvas' close to Meads Wall, where the ground was exceptionally heavy after rain. Lord Alfred had forgotten to put his footer boots in his bag with the rest of his kit, the result being that he had to play 'hot watch,' a position calling for a fast runner, in the patent-leather button boots he had put on before taking the train at Oxford that morning. I can't remember the result of that game, but I recollect that the onlookers outside 'canvas' enjoyed the young man's exhibition of athletics and fleetness of foot in spite of his handicap and lack of proper equipment."

At Winchester he began his career as a writer. What he wrote was humorous verse, and it appeared in 1888 in a school magazine called *The Pentagram,* which was published weekly. Under the triple editorship of Douglas and two other boys, it was, he says, a tremendous success. Perhaps. But it lasted only three months.

Douglas discusses his looks when he was a boy with the disarming frankness of Yum Yum in *The Mikado.* " There is no object in pretending that I was not rather exceptionally good-looking as a boy," he says, " and it is a fact that I went on preserving my looks and youthful appearance in a truly remarkable way right up till the time I reached the forties." To this he adds an anecdote about the attendant refusing him admission to the Casino at Monte Carlo, when he was nearly twenty-seven, on the grounds that no one under age was allowed to enter. Douglas, finding argument useless, went in search of his mother, who testified to his eligibility, the upshot being grovelling apologies from the official, who himself, it appeared, had a son of sixteen who looked much older than Milord.

Until he was forty he could, and frequently did, pass himself off for a boy. At thirty-one he was complimented by the aged Baronne de Rothschild on his French accent, and asked if he was at school in France.

He left Winchester at Christmas, 1888. Most of the next year was spent on the Continent with a tutor, Gerald Campbell, who later became a member of *The Times* staff. An authentic eighteenth-century grand tour atmosphere seems to have pervaded that vacation —or was it no more than the continuation of the Winchester tradition? It included, at any rate, an *affaire* with a divorced countess, from whose clutches Douglas, wearing what reporters still persist in referring to as " night attire," in this case provided by the divorcée, was eventually rescued by the scandalized Mr. Campbell.

OXFORD

In October, 1889, he went up to Magdalen.

He found it on the whole a pleasanter, more adult continuation of his later phases at Winchester. Writing many years later, he says that the morals there, especially in connection with one particular vice, were no better than at Winchester, adding that had he been a Catholic from childhood, it is a thousand to one that he would have passed unscathed through it all.

There he continued his running, coming in second in the two miles race in his first year, and first in the following year, as well as winning the one-mile handicap. His chances in the three miles race in 'Varsity sports, the only occasion upon which he entered, were wrecked by a combination of ignorance and sheer bad luck. With a slightly swollen vein behind one knee he went the day before the race to a doctor for treatment. The doctor, an incredible ignoramus, said he would " fix up the knee with a bandage." The bandage was one of stiff plaster; it did not appear to occur to either him or his victim that its rigidity would shorten the boy's stride and ruin any chance of his winning.

He dropped out exhausted, exasperated and bewildered, after the second mile, twenty-five yards behind the leader. And thereafter ran in no more races.

He also rowed, and one winter of exceptional severity he recklessly crossed the Thames on floating blocks of ice, and still more recklessly attempted to recross it, in consequence of which he fell into the water and was nearly drowned.*

In less energetic moments he cultivated a passion for church music and wrote verse in considerable quantities. In his second year at least one of the contributions to *The Oxford Magazine* (" Autumn Days ") reached true poetic level, and at the end of 1892, he became an editor again, this time of *The Spirit Lamp*.

" THE SPIRIT LAMP "

The periodical itself was published in Oxford for the proprietor by James Thornton, of the High Street. It was, within its limited range, a typically challenging affair, with all the stigmata associated with youthful intelligentsia. Douglas himself refers to it as the most distinguished undergrad. paper ever produced at Oxford, and adds that he quadrupled the circulation. In its first incarnation, it had lemon-yellow covers of glazed paper on which was a picture of the Tower of Magdalen. The size was octavo, the price sixpence, and the contributors included Lionel Johnson, Wilde, Lord Queensberry—of all people! (" Lines suggested by Fred Leslie's death "), John Addington Symonds and Charles Kains Jackson.

There was also "Answers to Correspondents," some of whom may have been imaginary, in the best under-

* We have Douglas's own statement for this, with the addition that " a coach and four was frequently driven down the river right past the row of college barges." But *the* great frost was in the winter of 1894-95.

graduate vein. " The title of your poem is very beautiful, but I don't like the poem." " Your poems are tainted with ethics. I suspect you of being a don." " You should certainly give up poetry. Why not emigrate? Literature is unknown in the colonies."

The March number had, in addition, an apology from the editor for the fact that he had been compelled to fill up the paper with his own articles, the approaching end of the term being held responsible for the falling off of suitable prose contributions, though there was no lack of poetry.

The May number introduced changes. The *Lamp* had become a more sober and expensive affair, a monthly quarto, minus all advertisements, with blue-grey covers and priced at a shilling. But the spirit within burnt even more brilliantly. The number included a letter written in prose poetry by Mr. Oscar Wilde and translated into rhymed poetry by " a poet of no importance," the translation being into French and the writer Pierre Louys; an essay (" Beethoven concerto in E Dur ") by Symonds; and a brief emotional " In Memoriam " appraisement of the author by Douglas as editor (Symonds had died at Rome on April 19th, after a two-day attack of pneumonia). There was a lengthy excursion into fiction, entitled " How we lost the Book of Jasher," signed merely " R.," but actually by Robert Ross. Douglas himself also contributed a critical review of Wilde's *Salome,* an essay " Concerning Rulers," and, in addition, "A Sicilian Love Song," which concludes with the lover's suggestion of " a bridal bed down in the cool, dark dingle."

The contents of the succeeding (June) number were of even greater interest. Wilde contributed " The Disciple," Douglas two poems, Gleeson White an article, " In Praise of Idleness." Another, " The Incomparable Beauty of Modern Dress," his first article to be printed and published, was by H. M. Beerbohm,

AT TWENTY-FOUR
(*From a silver-point drawing*)

later on to be doubly famous, as writer and caricaturist, as " Max."

The names on the covers of those slim volumes— themselves so dated, so determinedly stylistic, so representative of their editor, read like part of the programme of the drama that made up its editor's life. Symonds—the first to drop out of the cast—Wilde, Kains Jackson, the father whom Douglas was to hate so intensely, Ross whom he was to hate even more, Sir Max Beerbohm. " The tribe of Tegumai, they cut a noble figure then." But " of all the tribe of Tegumai who cut that figure, none remain." No, one, the little knight Wilde once referred to as a man to whom the gods had granted the gift of eternal old age, Max, in his retreat at Rapallo.

CHAPTER IV

WILDE

1. SUNRISE

THE Aesthetic Adventure—so Mr. William Gaunt has entitled his eminently readable book (the phrase, I feel, is hardly fair, now that it has become almost synonymous with " superficial ") on the movement which first manifested itself in a series of Continental tremors nearly a century ago.

It is an adventure that has its place here, because it included among its adventurers not only Douglas and Wilde, but an extraordinarily large number of famous, semi-famous and—to plagiarize the advertisement of Madame Tussaud—infamous people who swirled, dawdled, gyrated and posed and postured; who were worthily prominent or unworthily notorious; who possessed genius, talent, or nothing more than pretentions to either and sufficient effrontery to support those pretentions.

Of the reputations that flickered or blazed in the atmosphere of that strange little Renaissance, so hectic and so brief, some survive. But Time has extinguished many.

There is no space here to deal with them. Much has already been written of the incongruous company, which included the pontifical Ruskin; Whistler, gamin of genius who had a laugh so fiendish that Irving borrowed it for the stage; the great Jowett, a personal admirer of Wilde; and Pater, that old-maidish dabbler in eroticism who said he would give ten years of his life to be good-looking and compromised on an outsized moustache.* The aesthetic ménage is as various and amusing as the contents of a child's Noah's Ark.

It was inevitable that it should include people whose assessment of moral values varied enormously—men and women who were frankly and unashamedly degenerates, and others who deliberately slipped beyond the social pale; or, alternatively, were not utterly non-moral, but mere amateurs in the craft of experimental decadence, potentially vicious rather than qualified practitioners of vice.

Frank Harris, whom Douglas had only recently met, deserves special mention as the most melodramatically incredible member of Wilde's circle of friends. Born in 1856, he was the son of a captain in the Merchant Service. He himself stated that he ran away from home when a boy and went to America, where he earned his living as a page in a hotel, a cowboy, an advertising canvasser and a journalist. A rich man sent him to some university or other—or, to be more exact, "American, French and German universities" (I quote from his autobiographical notice in *Who's Who*). He came to England, and was for a time a master in a Brighton school.

Reverting to journalism, at twenty-eight he was editor of *The Evening News*. Later, he became in turn editor of *The Fortnightly Review*, editor of *The Saturday Review*, founder and editor of *The Candid Friend*, and owner and editor of *Vanity Fair*.

His writings include a play the credit for whose plot is due to Wilde, a novel of some credit to himself, and a book of reminiscences which, as a specimen of erotic imaginings, reflects no credit on anybody.

* Douglas was introduced by Wilde to Pater, of whom Wilde had an immense opinion; he spoke of him always as the greatest living writer of prose. Douglas tried hard to like Pater, but, apart from the fact that Pater had practically no conversation, he did not care for his prose, which he regarded as artificial and finicky.

But whatever may be said against Harris—and a great deal has been said, much of it indisputably true—he had one quality which lifted him above the level of the mere adventurer who lives by his own wits and the credulity of other people: a lifelong passion for and understanding of Shakespeare.

He married twice, but had no children. The end of his life was passed at Nice; there, not long before his death in 1931, he was visited by Bernard Shaw, his friendship with whom dated from the long-ago days of the '80's when, as editor of the old *Saturday*, Harris paid five pounds a week to G. B. S. as dramatic critic.

It was of Harris, whom Wilde began by disliking and ended by tolerating, that someone remarked that Frank was being invited everywhere nowadays.

" Yes," commented Oscar. " Once! "

A vivid, pathetic little picture is given by the late Alexander Woollcott of Harris's last days in his villa at Nice. But they may have had their compensations. Under " Recreations," Harris completed his *Who's Who* entry with : "A lover of books and men, who takes pleasure in the past by travelling, and in the future by dreaming."

The two decades 1870-90 covered a period which, so far as the average Englishman was concerned, might be labelled stuffily complacent. Over-petticoated, over-flounced, over-corseted women, and over-dressed, bewhiskered men surrounded themselves with over-upholstered furniture in over-furnished rooms. It was all intolerably suffocating by modern standards. An aesthetic revolution was overdue, a rebellion inevitable; the tragedy was the tragedy of every rebellion, in that too many of the rebels remained rebels after the revolution had become a *fait accompli*. Hence, the naïvely timid and the boldly sensual; the honest, though frequently muddle-headed, worshippers of blue-and-white ginger-jars, bowls and plates, and Oriental screens and prints and fans. Hence the ardent seeker after the beautiful, and the equally ardent seeker after the other seeker's cash.

The Yellow Bookery of the '90's was one minor manifestation of discontent. It was able to take itself seriously because its priests and prophets spoke in a language which their followers understood too little to translate into plain English. It was a great deal easier to fool some of the people some of the time seventy or eighty years ago than it would be today. The Education Act, the popular Press, the cinema and the radio have all had their uses in cramping the style of the eccentric, the egocentric and the plain degenerate.

There were, of course, critics, vitriolic or merely astringent. Robert Buchanan's frenzied attack on the Fleshly School of Poetry was of the first type; George du Maurier, with a nimbler weapon, ridiculing the movement's poses and pretences in *Punch,* and W. S. Gilbert striking the shrewdest, deadliest blow of all in *Patience,* were of the second.

From the earliest records of human relationships there have been stories of intense, if not inevitable, affinities, sometimes between members of the same sex, sometimes between men and women. And almost invariably—the " almost " is probably a superfluous qualification — there has been a definitely pre-dominating personality. Nature, it would seem, abhors not only a vacuum, she also abhors human equality in partnership.

Sixteen years before Douglas was born, an Irish couple of considerable distinction produced as their second son a child whom they christened grandilo-quently Oscar Fingal O'Flahertie* Wills. The phrase " considerable distinction " does not, in fact, do them justice. They were remarkable to the point of incredibility.

* Frequently—and wrongly—spelt " O'Flaherty."

The father was Sir William Robert Wills Wilde, M.D., surgeon-oculist to Queen Victoria in Ireland and Knight of the Swedish Order of the North Star. Photographs of Sir William suggest whiskered, self-righteous small-scale professional respectability, a Mr. Bultitude of a man. But the brilliance of his reputation as an oculist was dimmed by personal recklessness in his behaviour towards his patients, and towards one patient in particular.

His wife, Francesca Agnes Speranza, *née* Elgee, was in her own right an outstanding figure. A poetess, as well as an essayist of considerable charm, the receptions in her house in Dublin were a rendezvous for the Irish intelligentsia of the mid-nineteenth century.

The elder son, William (Willy), developed into a journalist who, while possessing considerable ability, also possessed too many of those Bohemian characteristics, so flatteringly regarded as inseparable from the artistic temperament, to stay the course. He married money, drank to excess, and died before he was forty.

There was also a sister, Isola. She did not survive childhood.

Oscar—he abandoned his other encumbering names early in his career—passed through his precocious infancy in a household in which brilliance and eccentricity were accepted as normalities. His mother spoilt him; it is also alleged that, until her daughter was born, she used to dress him up in girls' clothes.

At the age of eleven he left home to become a boarder at the Portora Royal School, Enniskillen. He was not liked there by either masters or boys. He seems to have lacked nearly every quality that makes for popularity. He was hopeless at mathematics and at drill.

He played no games; cricket he objected to on the ground that " the attitudes assumed were so indecent." Reserved and aloof, he used his already very considerable capacity for irony ruthlessly—and irony is non-contributory where popularity is concerned. Over-tall and bulky for his age, he was untidy, and, to mis-quote Dr. Johnson's pronouncement, " had no passion for cleanliness." But he dressed well, so conspicuously well that he was the only boy in the school who wore a top-hat. His manner towards his brother Willy was " superior," which may have contributed towards Willy's own considerable popularity.

To his credit stood the indisputable fact that he had an unusually mature knowledge of literature. He read omnivorously and with extreme speed. So, it may be added, do thousands of people with shallow brains and the novel-a-week habit. But Oscar's interest was the English classics—and he remembered what he read. In his last year he won the Portora Gold Medal for an essay on the Greek comic poets, with twenty-five per cent marks ahead of his nearest competitor. (It was a medal which had the advantage of being pawnable at any time—a fact of which he was to avail himself frequently in the years to come.)

Just before his seventeenth birthday he left the boarding-school for Trinity College, Dublin. There he remained three years, known as an awkward, good-humoured, generous fellow, liable to attacks of melancholy, and with a weakness for poetry and none at all for recreations that normally appealed to the undergraduates of the '70's.

From Trinity he won a demyship worth £95 a year that took him to Magdalen College, Oxford. He matriculated in October, 1874. While his reputation for intellectual brilliance increased, his personal reputation, so far as the authorities were concerned, did not increase. His attitude towards them was in-sufferably casual, frequently insufferably insolent. His laziness was ingrained and persistent, except when some special urgency stimulated him into action.

He came under the influence of J. P. Mahaffy,

Professor of Ancient History, later Provost of the College. Mahaffy contributed unofficially as well as officially to Wilde's education. He was a snob—indeed, a super-snob—and to Wilde's natural predilection for the classics, his gift of expression in his own tongue, and an entirely admirable desire for popularity, Mahaffy added a veneer which at its best was amusing, and at its worst a combination of toadyism and bad taste.

There were few people at Oxford whom he ungrudgingly admired. John Ruskin, Slade Professor of Art, was one of them. Pater was another. But Wilde, beginning to realize his own powers, his own possibilities and, above all, his own splendid right to indulge in whatever his tastes dictated, aspired to lead rather than to follow other leaders.

And so he led, beginning with that half-preposterous wholly pathetic world of adolescently passionate poetry, blue china, sunflowers and lilies, and all the other ingredients that combined to distinguish the Aesthetic Movement from all the other movements.

Hence, it was not his academic triumphs which interested, firstly, his little circle at Oxford, then London, and finally society at large. It was the Oscar Wilde of the long hair, strange clothing, and limpid, didactic, epigrammatic speech. His three rooms were considered the best three in college; they soon became three of the most famous. His qualifications as a connoisseur were negligible and superficial, but he nevertheless succeeded in posing as one whose judgments in art and literature were firm and unchallengeable. The story that during one vacation he studied art in Paris was probably baseless; it was demonstrably true that he could neither paint nor draw, while his literary contributions had been limited to Dublin-printed magazines, *The Month*, *The Catholic Mirror*, *The Irish Monthly* and to *Time*.

It was his blazing conversational effrontery and wit, added to his personal charm, that created his reputation, and sustained it, poor and broken though it became, to the end of his life.

Of Wilde in his Oxford days, and in the decade following, there are innumerable portraits. He was, indeed, a figure to invite portraiture. One college contemporary, the late Sir Frank Benson, describes him as " a lumbering, long-haired, sallow-faced individual, wearing a greeny-brown coat and a yellow tie. No one thought much of him, but he thought a great deal of himself."

He often went about when in London, says another friend, in a velvet coat, knee-breeches and a loose shirt. He was not a handsome man, says a third. He had not a single good feature. His eyes were large and rather protruding under heavy lids. He wore his hair artificially waved. His talk was a monologue—but it was real talk. He watched his listener closely, reacted to his replies, studied his mood, and adapted himself to it. His voice was exquisitely flexible, capable of softening the worst wounds that the razor-edge wit could inflict. His smile, his laugh were delightful enough to make it easy to forget and forgive.

Other observers, on other aspects of Wilde:

He was kind-hearted, but not large-hearted. He probably never cared for anyone as much as some cared for him.

The human, and still more the humanitarian, element is practically lacking in his writing.

He was not afraid to strike, but unwilling to wound. He was so lacking in vindictiveness that he was astonished at the storm of hatred and execration which struck him when he was down.

He could ignore what he disliked, what hurt him, or what did not suit him. " Ugliness," he said, " I consider a kind of malady, and illness and suffering always inspire me with repulsion. A man with the toothache ought to have my sympathy; he fills me with nothing but aversion. He is tedious, a bore; I cannot stand him, I cannot look at him."

He disliked realism in art or life. Even after his downfall, he saw the world through a romantic haze. Until his own tragedy overcame him, he made no attempt to come to close quarters with the bitter aspect of life. As a natural corollary, he had no instinctive sympathy with suffering.

Of colours, magenta filled him with horror; of places, he loathed Bayswater.

The late James Agate, whose brilliant and incisive English dealt body-blows to so many reputations, wrote, a month or so before he died:

" Wilde was a magnificent talker and a superb wit, but possessed neither a distinguished name nor a high social position; they were pegs for snobbery of the worst type. Photos show him as inseparable from top-hat and fur coat, with an unhappy leaning towards astrakhan. He could rant about the philosophy of art in an amateurish way, but to say that he ' altered the mind of men ' is just nonsense.

"Apart from his wit, he was bogus. He knew very little about the arts. In the matter of pictures Whistler was constantly putting him right. Music? He makes one of his characters say, ' Dvorak writes passionate, curiously coloured things.' No person with any knowledge of music could have written this. He sneered at Kipling as a genius who drops his aitches. ' Kipling,' he said, ' knows vulgarity better than anyone has ever known it. Dickens knew its clothes and its comedy, Kipling knows its essence, its seriousness. He is our first authority on the second-rate.' The truth is that there is more knowledge of life in six pages of Dickens or Kipling than in the whole of Wilde's scented output. He was a borrower, and his show pieces were lifted from the French. The atmosphere was taken straight from Maeterlinck, and the French from Ollendorff. Wilde was a fifth-rate poet with one first-class ballad to his credit. He wrote the wittiest, lightest comedy in the language; the other pieces are stilted, wholly insincere society dramas redeemed by their wit."

A damning indictment which echoes the comment of Frank Harris:

" Wilde was a snob as only an English aristocrat can be a snob. Douglas is one of the few good names in British history with the gilding and romance about it. To the last the mere name rolled on his tongue gave him extraordinary pleasure."

"Who wants an immovable washbasin in one's room. Hide the thing!" he said, when shown over the new Ritz Hotel in Paris. " I prefer to ring for water when I need it." Nor had he any use for lifts. They moved too fast to suit him.

His pose was that appropriate to a character of the Italian Renaissance, or of Elizabethan England. But from the point of view of the English gentleman there was something a little wrong with him everywhere—in his appearance, his manners, his clothes. He never looked well-dressed; he looked " dressed-up." The best tailor in London could not have made him look well-dressed. He had neither the build nor the knack of wearing clothes to be the dandy he aspired to be. In the upper reaches of society it was not the men, who mostly did like him, but the women who disliked him. He had all the qualities that make a successful politician—brazen self-confidence, an impervious skin to ridicule and an inexhaustible flow of language.

But he took no interest in politics.

His rooms, overlooking the Cherwell, were, in contradistinction to the dingy and shabby ones he had occupied at Trinity, notorious for what one observer called their exotic splendour. They were, in fact, a faithful mirror of the movement, contemptuously and with a considerable element of truth sneered at by the Philistines as a craze, of which Wilde was to become the High Priest, and eventually " the Master." When he went to London he was described as a " Professor of Aesthetics and Art Critic."

During vacation in 1875 he paid a visit to Italy. The beauties of Florence, Padua, Milan and—above all— Venice overcame him. The atmosphere, coupled with his friendship with a fellow-student named Blair,* who had lately joined the Church of Rome, carried Wilde a considerable distance towards accepting the same beliefs. But not all the way. The coldly prosaic fact that if he were to become a Catholic his father would indubitably cut him off with the traditional shilling was, he hinted, the main impediment.

Blair, still optimistic, suggested a visit to Rome in the following year. They went, and Wilde achieved an interview with the Pope, Pius IX, and received his blessing. But that marked the end of his spiritual explorations. In 1877 he went with Mahaffy and two others to Greece.

Sir William, his father, of whom he always spoke with affection, while despising his mere knighthood, had died in the previous year, leaving nearly £20,000. Of this Oscar received a small property worth about £4,000. So far as its value as a permanent source of income was concerned it might as well have been four thousand pence.

He left Oxford in 1878 in what one biographer terms " a blaze of glory," which glory arose from his winning the Newdigate Prize, the subject being " Ravenna."

It was the climax to three years in which he had deliberately built up a reputation, in the course of which he reached that state of near-humourless self-

*Later the Rt. Rev. Sir David Hunter Blair. See page 275.

absorption common enough and normally brief among brilliant adolescents in English universities.

Wilde's aestheticism, however, did not fade and wither in the cruder air of the outside world. Perhaps it was because it was not entirely humourless. Or even because it was not entirely genuine. It survived, and, indeed, found nourishment in the jostling of Gilbert's Philistines, even as it had survived the physical protests of scoffing undergraduates.

The death of his father had made essential some sort of profession, or at any rate some definite career. He came to London, where Lady Wilde and his brother already were. He did not live with them, but in Salisbury Street, running from the Strand down to the Embankment. His rooms, on the first floor, overlooking the river, were furnished with the same expensive " artiness " as those he had occupied at Magdalen. It was inevitable that he should entrench on his capital, and should soon be borrowing from his friends and from his widowed mother.

(The statement made by a biographer that he " loved money for the pleasure it commanded " was probably true, though not necessarily creditable; Wilde's own airy pronouncement that " I have no sense of property " might obviously apply—as in the last phases of his life it indubitably did apply—to other people's property as well as his own.)

There is a side to his character which developed rapidly after his 'Varsity days, and which I think is insufficiently stressed when dealing with his eternal money troubles. He had a passion for luxury in every material form—in food, in drink, in travelling, in his lodgings. And in such surroundings he required to complete his satisfaction titled people, or at any rate people of distinction and position, as his companions. In the company of such, his unassailable egotism, his arrogance, became at times intolerably offensive. He

laid down the law in a manner that outraged his elders
and frequently his betters; he arrived late for dinners
with preposterous excuses that outraged the feelings of
his hostesses.

It was not unnatural that society at large should
show a tendency to reserve judgment, and to view his
declamations and epigrams with distrust and his
sartorial extravagances with distaste. Conservative
extremists went further, and detested him and all that
he stood for.

They would have added contempt to their hatred if
they had known that his settled income was a mere two
hundred a year.

In 1881 there was published a selection of his poems
previously printed in a half-guinea volume. But
the book was not even a *succès d'estime*. *The Saturday
Review* damned it as " neïther good nor bad." *The
Athenaeum* accused him of flagrant plagiarizing.
Punch referred to the type as being " utterly too ! " and
added :

> "Aesthete of aesthetes
> What's in a name?
> The poet is wild
> But his poetry's tame."

Sir Henry Newbolt records that when Wilde
presented a copy of his poems to the Oxford Union
Library, its rejection was moved on the ground " not
that the poems are thin—and they *are* thin; not that
they are immoral—and they *are* immoral; but because
for the most part they are not by their putative father
at all, but by a number of better known and deservedly
reputed poets."

It must have been a period of considerable bitterness
and humiliation.

But there were compensations. He was beginning to
know people who mattered. Among the earliest was

Whistler, later to become his wittiest rival, later still
his most caustic enemy. Accepting some nebulous or
entirely non-existent invitation to breakfast with
" Jimmy," Wilde met Watts-Dunton at the same time.
Watts-Dunton afterwards predicted that within a year
Wilde would know ten people to every one his host
knew. It was a shrewd prediction. Wilde could not
be said to gate-crash—but he was an expert at oiling
locks and turnings keys. He was the social climber
in excelsis, with all the social climber's readiness to use
society's shibboleths and futilities and weaknesses to
his own ends. Beau Brummel in his 'prentice days
could have taught him nothing.

Later came the pre-Raphaelite leaders (Ruskin, of
course, he already knew).

On Christmas Eve, 1881, he set out for America to
begin his first lecture tour.

The engagement was due to a financial inspiration
on the part of D'Oyly Carte, who had recently produced *Patience,* Gilbert's brilliant skit on the Aesthetic
Movement. In that opera rival aesthetes replaced
Gilbert's original conception of rival curates — a
merciful modification. Swinburne and Pater and
Whistler had been in the running for the model upon
which the egregious Bunthorne was to be based,
but Wilde, with Whistler's celebrated lock of white
hair, was finally chosen.* What better advertisement
could there be for the opera, already playing to
packed houses in the States, than the presence of
Wilde in person?

Considering the devastating irony and the cata-
strophic effect of the play upon the movement, and the
roughness and toughness of many of his audiences, it
is an extraordinary tribute to the personality of Wilde

* Although when *Patience* was first performed it was assumed that
Grosvenor was intended for Wilde. It was not until later years, when
Wilde had become literally " fleshier," that the public identified Bun-
thorne with Wilde.

that his lectures—he gave no fewer than two hundred
—were both a financial and personal success. Americans
liked his bigness, his geniality, his charm. There were,
of course, flies in the ointment—bizarre, incalculable
incidents which seem inescapable during American
tours—friction with the Y.M.C.A., and a claim by them
for $200 damages, a friendly game of poker which left
him penniless, his failure to produce his play, *Vera*—
subsequently a hopeless flop. (It had already appeared
in book form in England.)

From America he went to Paris, meeting, among
other celebrities, the lovely Lily Langtry and the genius
Sarah Bernhardt. There, we are told, " he pleased, he
amused, he astounded." Under Parisian influences he
exchanged the aesthetic eccentricities for the last word
in fashionable extravagance. Also, to invent a phrase,
he dabbled in what is comprehensively termed
" decadence " in much the same spirit as a dangerously
spoilt, dangerously clever child misbehaves himself in
ways which he knows will not merely anger but
shock his relations. He absorbed and identified himself
with courses of action which were universally considered then, and are still largely considered, unwholesome and poisonous. His speech and writing grew more
brilliant, more paradoxical. And he spent too much of
his comparatively small income in extravagant eating
and drinking.

He came back to England, this new edition of
Magdalen's most famous son, physically heavier, but in
wit lighter, more sophisticated, and more insolent. He
kept his old friendships; he made new ones; he also
made new enemies. He was perennially hard up, but
still posing; lecturing in London and in the provinces
on " The House Beautiful "; pawning his gold medal
when he had no other assets available.

Then, in 1884, came his marriage to Constance
Lloyd, beautiful, gentle, and with the additional

henri Gaudier Brzeska 13

IN THE CAFÉ ROYAL

This extraordinary portrait, reproduced from the original drawing by permission of the owner, Mr. A. L. M. Cary, has an extraordinary history.

The artist was Henry Gaudier, a natural genius born in 1891, son of a French carpenter and his wife. In the spring of 1910, while studying at the St. Geneviève Library in Paris, Gaudier made the acquaintance of a Pole named Sophie Brzeska, plain, highly neurotic, and twenty years older than he, but with an immense personal magnetism. The attraction seems to have been immediate and mutual. " I am too old to live with you," she said, " but I will be a mother to you." She migrated with him to England on those terms at the end of 1910. (He had been there several times before.) She had had various other *affaires*, but this, the strangest, strongest, most devastating of them all, was to be the last.

In England they lived accordingly most of the time in acute poverty. And there gradually the realization of the qualities inherent in Gaudier's work, which he loyally signed with Sophie's name hyphened to his own, was realized. The first World War came to shock civilization and to interrupt the partnership. Gaudier left the security of London and went to the French front. He returned, but went out again. By January, 1915, he had been promoted to corporal, a little later he was sergeant. On June 5th he was shot dead during an attack on Neville St. Vaast. He was then twenty-three. Sophie struggled on for a time. But neither mind nor body recovered from the shock, and some years later she died in a mental home.

The drawing was made at a table in the Café Royal, frequented by Douglas at the time. A friend screened Gaudier with a newspaper while a series of lightning sketches were made. From these the final portrait was built up.

Had he lived, there is no doubt whatever that Gaudier-Brzeska would have ranked with the greatest artists of his century. His genius had already been recognized by Rodin and others, and today his works are among the treasures of the galleries of London and the Continent.

attraction of being an heiress. A honeymoon in Paris followed and, after that, a house in Tite Street, journalism, and more lecturing.

In October, 1887, he was offered, and accepted, the editorship of *Woman's World*. He remained in that incongruous, but not, one imagines, altogether unpleasing capacity for nearly two years, contributing a regular monthly article as well as other matter.

The biographer stumbles upon a good many coincidences in the course of his work. Wilde's editorship of *Woman's World* is curiously paralleled by Arnold Bennett's brief editorship of *Woman* a few years later. Bennett and he, superficially utterly unlike, had a number of points in common. Both were passionate believers in *le mot juste*; both treated authorship as a fine and distinguished craft; both lived in France, had a natural affinity for the French people, and read and admired French authors. Bennett, in his anonymous book, *The Truth About an Author* (a series of articles appearing in *The Academy* in 1903, shortly before Douglas had begun to edit it), gives a picture of what it means for a male journalist to be responsible for a feminine journal which might have been written by Wilde himself.

"There was no discipline and no need for discipline," he records. "Parcels were constantly arriving—books, proofs, process blocks, samples of soap and corsets. From time to time well-dressed and alert women called to correct proofs, to submit drawings or to scatter excuses. In each case I was, of course, introduced as the new assistant editor; they were adorable, without exception. At one o'clock, having apparently done little but talk and smoke, we went out, the editor and I, to lunch at the Cri. . . .

"Journalism for women, by women, under the direction of men, is an affair at once anxious, disagreeable and delicate for the men who direct. It is a

journalism itself, apart from other journalisms. . . .
I learnt a good deal about frocks, household management and the secret nature of women. Especially the
secret nature of women."

It was a period in which Wilde approached nearest
to the steady-work-at-a-regular-income ideal. It was also
a period of social growth. He moved extensively in
" the best circles."

His reputation increased. His personality could
dominate any company—and he knew it. It did not
always charm; swift and unanswerable repartee is no
friend to friendship, even when uttered in an exquisitely musical voice and accompanied by an infectious
smile. His enemies—he had many, Whistler by now
prominent among them—had keen eyes for the weak
joints in that armour of splendid effrontery which he
wore as no one else of his day wore it, or has worn it
since. Among other charges was the old one of
plagiarizing greater and better men. And the charge
was true.

In 1888 came his first real literary success, *The
Happy Prince and Other Stories*. The book is an
example of the charmingly precious type, now so dated.
Vincent O'Sullivan, in his *Aspects of Wilde,* says that
Oscar was not at all pleased if one praised his fairy
stories at the expense of the rest of his work. But up
to that date there had been only one play, *Vera,* already
mentioned, a failure. Another play, *The Duchess of
Padua,* written in 1883, also produced in America,
proved also a failure. *The Picture of Dorian Gray*
was a crude thriller to which a dash of ambiguity
and another dash of the supernatural added extra
thrills.

In the summer of the same year he met Alfred
Douglas.

The man responsible for the introduction was Lionel
Pigot Johnson, a close friend of Douglas. Three years

his senior, Johnson's academic career had been
dazzling—Winchester with a scholarship, prizes for
English literature and for an English essay, a gold medal
for verse, the editorship of the school paper; a
scholarship to New College, Oxford, the Goddard
scholarship there for the Classics, a second class in
Classical Mods, a first in the Humanities.

A poet of more than considerable promise as well as
a brilliant scholar, Johnson was also an eccentric, with
a dislike of keeping what our grandfathers called
" respectable hours " equalled only by a weakness for
alcohol that, as Douglas says, his small and childlike
frame could not withstand. He left Oxford for
London, to become a critic and reviewer as well as a
poet, and one of a little group of writers and artists
whose work was of serious value.

His health steadily deteriorated and, in September,
1902, he was brought to St. Bartholomew's Hospital,
having fallen in Fleet Street and fractured his skull.
He died without recovering consciousness.

But in 1891 he had only recently come to London.
There he met Oscar Wilde; to Wilde, Johnson
suggested a meeting with his own particular friend and
protégé, still at Magdalen. Oscar agreed. And one day
during the vacation he called at Lady Queensberry's
house in Cadogan Place for Douglas, and took him
along to Tite Street.* Whether he or Wilde realized
it or not, that encounter was the most tremendous event
in the lives of them both—tremendous in its immediate
effects, in its later repercussions, and in its sequels,
appalling as they were in the case of the older man;

---

* Robert Sherard, in a letter to *The Daily Telegraph* in 1935, recorded
one or two interesting facts about Wilde's London home—16 Tite Street.
The house was then still standing and very much as it had been forty
years earlier. Although re-numbered 34, the original brass plate was
there with " 16 " still faintly visible upon it. Whistler decorated the
interior. Incidentally, prior to settling down in his own house Wilde
lodged first at what had been Keats's house, also in Tite Street, and
later in Charles Street, Grosvenor Square. His mother and brother
afterwards went to live at 146 Oakley Street, not far away.

disastrous, with effects that coloured all the the rest of
his long life, in the case of the younger.

Douglas found himself confronting a bulkily built,
dandified man, with a sallow, clean-shaven face; a man
with a broad, intellectual brow and fine eyes, negatived
by the full sensual lips and heavy jaw. The Master,
gracious, infinitely magnetic.

And Wilde—Wilde smiled down at a fair, slim,
diffident youth, twenty years old, but looking still a
mere child, with almost extravagantly perfect features
and colouring. His future chief disciple.

They were, in the words of Frank Harris, an
extraordinary pair, and complementary in a hundred
ways, not only in mind, but in character.

Years later Oscar confessed that from the first he
dreaded Douglas's " aristocratic, insolent boldness."
To Douglas, Wilde was merely a quickening, inspiring
influence; Douglas, on the other hand, reinforced the
middle-class Wilde with precisely the qualities that to
an aristocrat are second nature. His own complete
recklessness in money matters also accentuated Wilde's
natural love of lavish spending.

That moment marked the beginning of the last
phase—act, volume, what you will—of Wilde's career.

The sublimated frenzies of sunflowers and blue china
and Japanese fans were by now things of a very definite,
very dead past. Wilde, it is safe to assume, was glad
enough to see the last of them, and of their intense and
silly devotees. Especially the devotees, who laid themselves open to such easy and unanswerable jibes. How
much he himself really believed in his own creeds, apart
from his incontestable sense of beauty and a fundamental faith in his right to annex at any cost any form
of pleasure that was available, is unguessable.

Yet the young man of the 1880's was a better man, in
every sense of the word, than the gross, arrogant, self-
assured, middle-ageing Wilde of ten years later. The

older Wilde's charm was more experienced, no doubt, his rapier-wit keener, his arguments more plausible, but. . . .

To Wilde, Douglas, confronting him on that sunny afternoon, must have represented the materialization of everything in the world worth having—a title, a family whose part in history gave it an almost regal status; in possession not only of youth, but of physical charm, with which went a vivid intelligence, and a sense of beauty as acute as his own. To this personification Wilde's reaction was as primitive, as pathetically and absurdly naïve, as that of a boy in the throes of calf-love, except that the " boy " was a blasé married man sixteen years older than Douglas.

After reading all that I can concerning the Douglas-Wilde friendship, much of it significant and a good deal that has no significance, I find myself ultimately agreeing with Edward Marjoribanks's summing-up in his *Life of Lord Carson*. I cannot accept the theory put forward by one member of the Douglas family that Wilde was " a mere boob," hypnotized by, and completely under the spell of, Douglas's radiance. Nor can I agree with Mr. Robert Sherard's theory that Wilde's descent was due to epileptic attacks after which his antisocial lapses faded completely from his memory.

There are, in any case, certain facts about which there can be no argument of any sort. Wilde was half a generation older than his disciple; if Douglas's personality stirred to violent life not only that sense of beauty which they both possessed and which every artist who has ever lived can comprehend, but all that was decadent in Wilde's nature, then an elementary sense of decency, to say nothing of elementary prudence, demanded a prompt ending of their friendship, or, as the only conceivable alternative, its equally prompt canalizing in formal and normal channels.

But from first to last during their association Wilde

never gave the smallest indication of realizing these obvious duties. He showed no sign of possessing moral fibre, or even of principles demanding the exercise of moral fibre.

If Douglas, for his part, was neither so untarnished nor so guiltless as his appearance suggested, Wilde's cautionary reactions should have been even more prompt and vigorous.

Whatever the facts, Wilde and Douglas were not— could not have been—equally experienced. On the shoulders of Wilde, to whom life had already taught much that a boy of twenty had had no chance of learning, the heavier responsibility must rest.

On that first afternoon, Wilde and Douglas had tea in Wilde's " den " downstairs, and afterwards Douglas went up to the drawing-room to meet Constance. According to Douglas, they " took to " one another from the first; she liked him better, he says, than any other friend of her husband, and she frequently came to stay at Lady Queensberry's house afterwards.

With Wilde himself, the friendship grew at extravagant and unhealthy speed. But Wilde was reaching the stage not merely of sneering at conventions, but of ignoring them entirely when they limited his own indulgences. And since conventions are in the main synonymous with the accepted decencies of ordinary civilized society, he became secretly, then less secretly, first a rebel, and finally an outcast.

There were other friendships, in which there could be no pretext of intellectual or social companionship, with underworld parasites.

When a man of talent has a major secret in his life, a primal necessity to conceal something, much of that talent, to say nothing of the drain on his physical energy, time and money, must be deflected to maintaining that secret. And in his case another person was involved as fellow-conspirator.

2. THE SUN IN SPLENDOUR

The four years that followed were extraordinary years—in the uprush of popularity, affluence and social success; in the fusion of the personalities, and in the deadly encroaching moral decadence which was ultimately to destroy the older man.

In the summer of 1891 Wilde had been inspired to write a play about Salome. The subject was obviously one which had immense, if horrific, potentialities.

His two previous attempts at drama had both been failures; he was denied even the consolation that either had been a *succès d'estime*. But this was to be something different from an ordinary play.

It was.

The story goes that one evening in Paris Wilde rushed into a café and ordered the small gipsy orchestra there to " play something in harmony with my thoughts. . . . A woman dancing with bare feet in the blood of a man she had craved for and slain," he added.

The orchestra obliged, so effectively and with such fervour that the audience are alleged to have listened " with blanched faces " while Wilde scribbled to the music like one possessed.

He wrote the final libretto in French. When the tragedy was finished, he insisted that it was more than a work of art; it was a mirror in which every man or woman could see his or her reflection. It may have been. But mirror or no mirror, so far as its performance in England was concerned in the following year, the Lord Chamberlain flatly refused to permit a licence to be issued. It dealt with a Biblical theme; Biblical themes were banned. The blow was all the more shattering because Sarah Bernhardt, to whom Wilde had offered the play, had accepted it enthusiastically for production in her forthcoming season in London. Wilde himself was so infuriated that he threatened to abandon his British nationality for French.

Five years later the play was produced, but in Paris. Its reception might be described as tepid. Later still, in 1902, Reinhardt produced it in Berlin. There its success was phenomenal enough to create for Wilde a posthumous fame and a posthumous fortune. Richard Strauss saw the play, and set it to music. After endless arguments, endless objections, its English production was sanctioned. With Sir Thomas Beecham conducting, it was produced in London on December 8th, 1910.

From *Salome,* Wilde, at the suggestion of George Alexander, allowed himself to be switched over to the writing of a modern comedy. After all, why not? Now he had Douglas as close friend, a perfect model for a succession of junior leads, an inspiration for and an authentic fount of information on every aspect of the aristocracy of which Wilde tried to convince himself he was a member, and to which he was admitted only because of his gaiety, his wit, his patient flattering. Medieval and scriptural dramas were all very well, but Douglas's world was the world he adored, the world in which his wit could flash like the tiaras on the brows of his countesses.

Furthermore, such a play would involve the use of material that demanded nothing in the way of study or of tiresome verification.

Alexander clinched the bargain by insisting on paying £100 in advance royalties. Wilde, following in the footsteps of the equally dilatory Samuel Johnson when his dictionary was commissioned, accepted the money, spent it, and did nothing.

But—again like Johnson—he did at last make a beginning. In the summer of 1891, at a cottage in the Lake District, he wrote *Lady Windermere's Fan.* Alexander read it, and shrewdly offered Wilde £1,000 for all rights in the play. But Wilde, perennially hard-up though he was, refused. The play, which had been

written in two months, eventually brought him in
£7,000.

Lady Windermere's Fan was produced. The critics
were divided into enthusiastic pros and supercilious
cons*; cons were in the majority, but William Archer
of *The World* labelled the play a classic. Frank Harris
compared it to the best of Congreve. What was considerably more important, the public, whom Wilde
congratulated from the stage as estimating its merits
almost as highly as he did himself, crowded night after
night to listen and to quote.

Wilde had at last arrived—by express!

Wilde followed up his encouraging start with *A
Woman of No Importance*, this time a play for Herbert
Beerbohm Tree, then in management at the Haymarket. The play was written in a house near
Babbacombe, lent by Lady Mount Temple. Wilde's
wife and two boys were with him; also Douglas. It was
produced in the spring of the following year, 1893,
with Tree† in the part filled by Lewis Waller when
the play went on tour in the provinces.

It proved another delight to Wilde's friends, another
exasperation to his enemies.

The tempo of his life was quickening; it was
throbbing dangerously under the intoxication of
popularity. He was acquiring money, fame and
adulation on a scale undreamed of in the days of
Woman's World. He had been notorious since his
youth as a brilliant talker, as a *poseur*, as one impossible
to ignore; now he was something more.

The plots and the situations of his plays involved no

---

* There was also one critic who referred to the play as "full of
saucy repartee and overdone with epigram peculiar to the author,
namely, the inverted proverb. But it made a hit."

† According to Sherard, Tree had a "great liking for Wilde, and a
huge admiration for his genius." Incidentally, *An Ideal Husband* was
withdrawn only because Tree had leased the theatre to Lewis Waller and
H. Morell, and it was needed for a revival. The "last nights" had been
announced some days before Wilde's arrest.

difficulties—all his life Wilde had been a generous employer of other people's ideas. In the spoken word lay his greatest asset. All plays develop in a succession of conversational exchanges, and conversation, particularly of the type spoken by the most scintillating members of the society in which the incomparable Douglas had his origin, was the one form of art of which Wilde was supreme master.

Remains that mysterious " sense of the theatre," which Arnold Bennett derides as pretentious nonsense, but which, nonsense or otherwise, is essential to any would-be playwright, particularly to one who has had no connection by birth or training with the stage. (And Wilde, it has been emphasized, had none whatever.)

I suggest that Wilde, though by choice a writer, was fundamentally an actor. In this double allegiance he was far from unique. Dickens was another, Stevenson another, Defoe another, of a band of writers whose outlook was literally dramatic. He saw himself always on an invisible but veritable stage, dominating, enchanting, intriguing, the most significant confirmation of which comes from the fact that the play on which his reputation rests, and which stands head and shoulders above the others, *The Importance of Being Earnest,* is *all* Wilde—Wilde releasing a succession of flashing phrases as Jack, as Algernon, as Lady Bracknell, as almost every member of the cast.

It is amusing to note that many of his characters took their names from the places in which Wilde happened to be staying when he created them.

Incidentally, he strongly objected to being considered a professional author; he preferred to be regarded as a man of fashion who wrote, as Walpole did, when time hung heavy on his hands. He hated talking of money in connection with his works.

Douglas's entry into the Wilde circle, and his

immediate promotion to the intimate friendship of
the Master, must have been an incredible experience
to a youngster just turned twenty. He had left Oxford
without taking his degree, and under a cloud so far as
his disreputable father was concerned. He was, indeed,
on hopelessly bad terms with him, in common with his
mother and brother Percy. But he was also financially
dependent upon Lord Queensberry.

There is one aspect of that four years' intimacy
which has, I think, been insufficiently realized—the
immense disparity, apart from the gap in their ages,
between the circumstances of Wilde and Douglas.

By 1891 Wilde, though his literary output had been
comparatively slight, was already the recognized leader
of the Aesthetic Movement both in England and in
America, in both of which countries he had achieved a
reputation as a lecturer. At the time that he first met
Douglas, he was a veteran, an elder statesman—if such
prosaic metaphors be allowable—among the aesthetes.
He was married and had two sons to support, and
although his income in those days was said to have
reached the comfortable total of two thousand a year, it
was insufficient to meet his own extravagant, fantastically ostentatious tastes and to keep his wife and
family as well.

Douglas, on the other hand, was extremely young,
and, while a highly eligible youth, was entirely
dependent upon his father for his income—an
allowance of £350 a year. (Which allowance was cut
off entirely two years later. Nor did he receive anything
from his father's estate until after Lord Queensberry's
death in December, 1899.)

He had, of course, no family responsibilties of any
sort.

He now found himself a member of an enchantingly
gifted, enchantingly broad-minded cosmopolitan circle
whose ideas were remoulding the world of ideas and

literature and everything connected with either, with his new companion an acknowledged leader among them. It may have been true, and probably was true, that he soon discovered that half of what Wilde said was said with his tongue in his cheek. But it was always worth listening to.

The list of Wilde's acquaintances at the height of his reputation, re-read today, is a staggering one. It includes Millais, Poynter, Ruskin, Rossetti; Aubrey Beardsley, the bank clerk who achieved astonishing purity of line in subjects which contrived to suggest anything but purity, whose work and personality Wilde detested, and who died of tuberculosis in his twenties; Ernest Dowson, the poet, another early victim of tuberculosis, living on a pittance from his publisher; Max Beerbohm; Latour and Legros, Latin Quarter geniuses whom Whistler brought to England. (Legros, once a provincial house-painter, ended by acquiring British nationality in order, he solemnly assured inquirers, that he might be able to say that he won the Battle of Waterloo.) There were Pissarro, too, and Edmund de Goncourt; Simeon Soloman, a Jewish artist of genius, who, after an appalling career, died from excessive drunkenness in St. Giles's Workhouse; Monet, Renoir, Cézanne, Degas, Holman Hunt and Watts-Dunton.

These, and innumerable others, Douglas met, the most charming recruit in that incongruous army of geniuses, and it was from the moment of his arrival that the descent quickened down that grimy and inglorious slope that ended in the final disaster.

Douglas himself shall have the first word here. In brief, he openly admits the worst side of their friendship. The " familiarities," he says, were rare, beginning nine months after that first meeting, and ceasing for ever six months before the final catastrophe. Wilde referred to the whole thing as " accidental," saying that in essence it reached up towards the ideal, and in the end became utterly ideal. Douglas, whatever the world —Oscar's world, his unfortunate wife's world—might think, insists that Wilde's love for him, at any rate before he went to prison, was the nearest he ever got to a pure and spiritual love.

It was not until Wilde had been dead at least eight years that it apparently first occurred to Douglas that Wilde really was " a very wicked man," quite apart from his sexual aberrations. Which is a little surprising in view of the fact that Wilde openly urged that it was the duty of every man to live his life to the utmost, and to have the courage to commit " what are called sins."

What was unknown by the general run of his acquaintances, friends and enemies alike, was that there had for some time previously been a considerable number of other young men concerned in a considerable number of incidents which had no connection whatever with either purity or spirituality.

However great his infatuation for Wilde, Douglas must have been doomed, as time went on, to realize the truth. And realizing it, he must also have known that unless the unbearable calamity of a complete and final separation was to be faced, nothing at all could be done about it. Wilde, in his turn, continued to face his world with the arrogance that for four years never faltered. He still talked brilliantly, if the brilliance was becoming a trifle suggestive of worn electro-plate on rather cheap metal. He still posed with no obvious effort—after all, he had been posing since his Oxford days, and before then. If the strain of writing, talking, posturing—and, above all, keeping his secret—was beginning to tell, a drink or a succession of drinks could be guaranteed to produce a prompt reaction. Other disciples, young, impressionable, uncritical, ready to hail him as the " Master," were always there to complete the restoration of his self-esteem.

Douglas and he went to Paris and thence to Algiers. From there Douglas travelled alone to Florence, where he had been persuaded to go by his mother, who apparently thought Wilde would not follow. She did not like Wilde, and, according to her son's statement, ended by regarding him as " a villain and a scoundrel," even before his conviction, and tried her utmost to end the friendship.

Wilde, however, did follow.

The next separatist step on the part of the Douglas family took the form of an invitation to stay at Cairo as the guest of Lord and Lady Cromer, the latter, Lord Cromer's first wife, being a close friend of Lady Queensberry.

At Luxor, Douglas met Robert Hichens, and E. F., otherwise " Dodo," Benson, and another friend, and the four of them went up the Nile together. In the course of that otherwise not particularly momentous holiday Douglas talked considerably about Wilde. Hichens, highly interested, asked Douglas to arrange a meeting with him. The meeting took place in London, and its sequel was *The Green Carnation,* in which Wilde's likeness was unmistakably drawn. Much of the dialogue was verbatim reporting of Douglas's conversational recklessness. The imputations conveyed did still further damage to Wilde's reputation.

Meanwhile, other strings were being pulled on Douglas's behalf. Partly through the influence of his maternal grandfather, General Montgomery, and partly through that of Lord Cromer himself, Douglas was appointed honorary attaché to Lord Currie, British Ambassador to Turkey.

Douglas, to quote his own words, did not get the impression that the appointment was to come into immediate effect. He told his host that he wanted to go back to London, " or at any rate as far as Paris," first. Lord Cromer raised no objections. Possibly the significance of the qualification " at any rate as far as Paris " did not strike him; possibly he assumed that purely business or family matters were involved. Actually, the prime motive was simply a longing to see Wilde again. Douglas told Wilde he was coming; Wilde wired back his delight. Douglas and Benson left Cairo together, and so travelled to Athens. For a week they stayed in rooms which Benson had there, a week in which the weather was perfect and the Acropolis enchanting. After that Douglas went on alone to Paris.

He lingered a week there alone with Wilde, and then went on to London, intending to spend a few days with his mother. Lord Currie, who appears to have received no notification of Douglas's plans, eventually heard of these wanderings, and was very angry indeed at what he regarded as a piece of gross impertinence. Douglas was informed that the appointment was cancelled, and that his chances of being employed in the Foreign Office might be regarded as at an end. The dismissal left Douglas—again I quote—" amazed but not particularly perturbed "; also, illogically, " quite unaffected." He adds that he was secretly delighted to escape from the necessity of going to Constantinople. That one can well believe. At the same time one cannot help feeling that his attitude towards the whole thing justified Frank Harris's label of " aristocratic insolence."

Douglas's prospects of a diplomatic career did indeed end with Lord Currie's irritation at his failing either to appear in person or to communicate directly with the Embassy. But it is difficult to justify the sneers contained in Douglas's *Autobiography* on the Ambassador's social position, to the effect that if Lord Currie—who, to quote Wilde, did not rise from the ranks of the aristocracy but was born in the purple of commerce—had been a little more *grand seigneur* than he was, he would not have made such a ridiculous fuss, and it would not have occurred to him (he was a newly created peer) that any assault on his dignity had been so much as dreamed of.

The attitude exhibits an unhappy blend of snobbishness and childish spite.

Wilde wrote *An Ideal Husband,* his third comedy of manners, during the summer of that year, in a farmhouse, near Cromer. It was produced at the Haymarket on January 3rd, 1895, with Waller as Sir Robert Chiltern, and, in spite of certain faults, was superior to his two previous plays. Transferred to the Criterion Theatre on April 13th, it ran there for another fortnight. As Shaw said, " his critics had to laugh at his wit, though it might be angrily ' like a child who is coaxed into being amused in the very act of getting up a yell of rage and agony.' "

In the meantime, keeping horribly in step with Wilde's rising reputation as a dramatist, there were rumours, at first faint and hesitant, then less faint and more definite. They echoed to the ears of the one man whose cunning and ferocity never slackened when it came to hunting down an enemy—Bosie's father, the eighth Marquess of Queensberry.

Lord Queensberry might have the mentality and culture of a third-rate racing tipster, but he moved in what the Victorians called the Highest Circles, and the Highest Circles discussed considerably the career and character and genius of Oscar Wilde. This raffish, reckless man-about-town, this vindictive little cock-sparrow, eternally at war with his own family, and whose private life was an embarrassment and a shame to his friends, vigorously disapproved of his son's association with the founder of the newest aestheticism. Even if his own life fell short of the Galahad standard, even if the children themselves were of age, and consequently beyond his legal jurisdiction, he was still a parent, as well as the titular head of the House of Douglas.

From the first he had distrusted Wilde. As time went on, and the friendship became intensified to a point not far short of idolatry, detestation was added to the paternal distrust.

Two more completely antipathetic flouters of morality than Wilde and Queensberry could scarcely have existed. But their flouting differed. Both justified the label of blackguard, but one was a blackguard who had thrown over every pretence of decent living; the other a cultured *poseur* for whom it was still necessary to sustain the moralities. In Queensberry's case, the truth was already known. He indulged in the conventional vices, but he had intangible assets in his rank and distinguished ancestry, and very tangible ones in his money. Wilde, possessor of neither, literally could not afford to exhibit even the conventional vices. The vice he did exhibit was unmentionable, criminal, and even more expensive.

Wilde, born of the upper middle class, never wholly of the upper class whose society he so passionately visualized and longed for, was insolently secure in the knowledge that he possessed brilliance enough to outdazzle any coronet in *Debrett*. He and Queensberry were alike in this—that they lacked principle, a definite standard of spirituality, as expressed in definite rules of discipline and service. Both were complete egoists, taking from life what pleased them and forgetting that there is no more ruthless creditor, and that the more reckless the debtor, the heavier the interest and the sooner the settling day.... But up to now Queensberry, though the things which were said about his way of life were not whispered, was still a rich man with a rich man's background, and Wilde, whatever ugly things were said about him, was still accepted in society, and in circles brilliant enough to despise it.

He was, too, becoming richer. No income would have made a man with his passion for spending really

LAD—D

wealthy; but he was sufficiently well-off to buy the clothes, the flowers, the jewellery he wanted; to travel in the late Victorian luxury of endless hansom cabs and invariable first-class railway carriages. The snobbery that went hand in hand with his arrogance, and flourished childishly in his passion for titled people and the visits and meals involved in being treated by them as an equal, increased. He both drank and ate too much, and over-eating and over-drinking made his heavy features still more flaccid and puffy, and gave his naturally sallow complexion an unwholesome pastiness.

The two men met for the first time in October, 1892. Lord Queensberry had come into the Café Royal while Bosie and Wilde were lunching there; Bosie, with considerable courage, went across and invited his father to join them. Queensberry did, though with a marked absence of enthusiasm, and shook hands with both. Oscar, deciding that in the double capacity of Bosie's father and a marquess the visitor was worth placating, exerted himself to please.

He succeeded so thoroughly that the lunch was prolonged an unconscionable time, and the hypnotized Lord Queensberry admitted that he found Wilde both charming and clever.

Exactly what Wilde thought of Lord Queensberry has not been recorded.

Meanwhile, the triumphal progress of " the wittiest playwright since Sheridan "* continued its short, desperately short journey towards its climax.

At Worthing, with Douglas as companion and, according to Douglas, collaborator as well, *The Importance of Being Earnest* was written. There were other visits to Oxford, and to Bracknell, where Bosie's mother had a house. The latter visit could scarcely have been at her invitation.

*It has been said that the great difference between Wilde and Sheridan was that Wilde was a poet and Sheridan was not.

Wilde's new comedy—his fourth and, in the opinion
of the world, incomparably his best—was produced on
February 14th, 1895, at the St. James's Theatre by
George Alexander. It was a play which no one else
could have written, or would have thought of writing,
a mocking, glittering challenge flung in the teeth of his
enemies, completely non-ethical, utterly disarming in
its will-o'-the-wisp disregard of any sort of theatrical
tradition. No moral lesson of any kind was inculcated;
every character literally lived by his or her wits—and
wit. Or, if they had none, acted as perfectly constructed
foils to someone else's wit.

With the final fall of the curtain at the end of the first
performance came the greatest moment of Wilde's life.

James Agate, surveying Wilde in that harsh,
neon-like clarity which was peculiarly Agate's own, had
no high opinion of either the man or his work.

" His plays," he wrote, " are, apart from their wit,
the purest fudge, put together without any kind of
artistic conscience and using all the stalest devices of
the theatre. They are plays in which the situation is
essentially false. None of the women whom Wilde
pretended to take seriously ever begin to come to life;
his Lady Windermere is not only a puppet, but a
puppet manifestly imbecile. But," admits Agate,
" there remains *The Importance of Being Earnest,*
probably the best light comedy in the language. Its
theme would have made a farce, but farce is far too
gross and commonplace a word to apply to such an
iridescent filament of fancy. Behind all Mr. Wilde's
whim and even perversity there lurks a very genuine
instinct of the theatre.

" Wilde's fame is sure in regard to this masterpiece
as long as theatre audiences enjoy wit."

To this may be added the comment of Mr. Vincent
O'Sullivan:

" The plays, with the exception of *The Importance*

of Being Earnest, derive very definitely from a French school long out of fashion. The substance is melo-dramatic. What saves them, what casts a glamour over them, is the style and the wit, which not only is Wilde's very own, but different from what anyone at any time in the history of literature has produced."

The statement concerning the plays' derivation is supported by the fact that Wilde's interest in foreign literature was practically confined to France. He did not care for Germany, denying that any art existed in that country—a sneer that Germany replied to with the softest of soft answers. Nowhere has Wilde been more appreciated or more popular.

He did not care for Ibsen. But it would have been surprising if he had cared. Osbert Burdett* pays a fitting and charming tribute when he says:

" In his first three plays, the utmost he achieved was to do more wittily than anyone else that which every West End dramatist was doing.

" His talent, at its best, is so gay, so playful, so genial, that it inspires an indulgence in its readers that survives the severe strictures that criticism must make upon his works."

3. ECLIPSE

Concurrently with Wilde's spectacular dramatic progress, Queensberry's vendetta against him pro-gressed too. His friendship with Wilde lasted only about two months. Then, according to Harris, Queensberry abruptly decided by some obscure mental process of his own that he had been completely hood-winked concerning Wilde's character; that the creature in sheep's clothing was a wolf after all, and an extremely vicious wolf at that.†

* *The Beardsley Period.*

† Harris's statement is, however, contradicted by Wilde, who says that the three met again on amiable terms as late as March, 1894. Wilde's memory must have been at fault: the 1894 meeting was far from " amiable."

On this occasion Douglas and Wilde were, as before, lunching at the Café Royal. The Marquess, confronting them, issued an ultimatum. Wilde and his son must part, and part permanently; otherwise Bosie would be disowned and his allowance entirely cut off.

It may be mentioned that there had been a parallel to this violent change of opinion in connection with Queensberry's eldest son, Lord Drumlanrig. When that young man was given a peerage of the United Kingdom by Lord Rosebery, and, as Lord Kelhead, had become the representative of the Douglas family in the Upper House, his father, in spite of the fact that he had been previously consulted about the new honour, and had given it his complete approval, lapsed into one of those half-insane rages which manifested themselves without warning or a shred of justification. He not only wrote violently abusive letters to the new peer, but other letters, presumably less abusive but equally violent, to the Queen and Mr. Gladstone. Lord Rosebery, whom he decided was the chief villain, he threatened to waylay and horsewhip.

In Bosie's case, the paternal *volte face* crossed the line that separated the impressive from the ridiculous. Wilde regarded the ultimatum with his usual air of languid amusement — amusement, nevertheless, possibly touched with the first sinister shadow of apprehension.

Not that he could have had any real fear of Bosie's defection. His own colossal vanity, as well as his knowledge of Bosie's temperament, in which there was all the Douglas defiant recklessness in meeting a challenge, ruled that out as inconceivable.

Douglas himself saw nothing amusing in the situation. He replied to his father promptly and vigorously. The letters exchanged between father and son at that time, and produced as evidence in court a few months later, form an oddly intimate sequence. The characters

of both men are revealed as nothing else could have
revealed them, especially that of the Marquess. It is a
character which, to Gilbert, who had already exploited
Wilde's personality, might well have suggested Wilfred
Shadbolt, the tragic comedian of *The Yeomen of
the Guard*; the character of a savage, ill-educated,
primitive, lacking most of a savage's elemental virtues;
possessing power, but tormented and goaded by an
inferiority complex. Lord Queensberry, writing in a
state of fury, became not merely incoherent, but
ungrammatical and incapable of spelling correctly.
Yet behind these preposterous letters, with their wild
and vicious insinuations, there is material for pity.
They reveal, unconsciously, the unhappiness of a father
in whom memories of a different past are not entirely
dead.

Wilde swore that it was not until he read these letters
that he learned that the Marquess objected to his
acquaintance with Douglas. The first, sent from
Carter's Hotel, Albemarle Street, and dated April 1st,
began:

Alfred,
    It is extremely painful for me to have to write to you in
the strain I must; but please understand that I decline to
receive any answer from you in writing in return. After
your recent hysterical impertinent ones I refuse to be
annoyed with such, and I decline to read any more letters.
If you have anything to say, do come here and say it in
person.
    Firstly, am I to understand that, having left Oxford as
you did, with discredit to yourself, the reasons of which were
fully explained to me by your tutor, you now intend to loaf
and loll about and do nothing? All the time you were
wasting at Oxford I was put off with an assurance that you
were going to the Bar. It appears to me that you intend
to do nothing. I utterly decline, however, to just supply
you with sufficient funds to enable you to loaf about. You
are preparing a wretched future for yourself, and it would
be most cruel and wrong for me to encourage you in this.

So far, the letter might have been written by any

angry and semi-literate Victorian father to any undergraduate son who was flinching at the prospect of
buckling down to the business of earning his living.

But its tone changed.

> Secondly, I come to the more painful part of this letter—
> your intimacy with this man Wilde. It must cease, or I
> will disown you and stop all money supplies. I am not
> going to try and analyse this intimacy, and make no charge;
> but to my mind to pose as a thing is as bad as to be it. With
> my own eyes I saw you with the most loathsome and dis-
> gusting relationship as expressed by your manner and ex-
> pression. Never in all my experience have I ever seen such
> a sight as that in your horrible features. No wonder people
> are talking as they are. Now I hear on good authority, but
> this may be false, that his wife is going to divorce him. Is
> this true, or do you not know of it? If I thought the actual
> thing was true, and it became public property, I should be
> quite justified in shooting him at sight.
> These christian English cowards and men, as they call
> themselves, want waking up.
>
> Your disgusted, so-called father,
>
> QUEENSBERRY.

Bosie's reply was prompt and brief. It was also
callous. He at once wired to

> Lord Queensberry, Carter's Hotel, Albemarle Street.
> What a funny little man you are.   ALFRED DOUGLAS.

One can almost hear Oscar's laughter, mocking and
encouraging, in the background.

His father answered, on April 3rd:

> You impertinent young jackanapes, I request that you
> will not send such messages to me by telegraph.
> If you send me any more such telegrams, or some with
> any impertinence, I will give you the thrashing you deserve.
> Your only excuse is that you must be crazy. I hear from
> a man at Oxford that you were thought crazy there, and
> that accounts for a good deal that has happened.
> If I catch you again with that man I will make a public

scandal in a way you little dream of; it is already a suppressed one. I prefer an open one, and at any rate I shall
not be blamed for allowing such a state of things to go on.

Unless this acquaintance ceases I shall carry out my threat
and stop all supplies, and if you are not going to make any
attempt to do something I shall certainly cut you down to
a mere pittance, so you know what to expect.

Lord Queensberry then for a space abandoned letter-
writing for more direct and, one imagines, more
congenial action.

He visited in turn all the cafés and restaurants
known to be frequented by his son and Wilde, telling
the proprietor of each that if he caught the pair there
together again he would thrash both and, in addition,
wreck the premises. The proprietors listened respect-
fully. Oddly enough, it does not seem to have occurred
to them to inform the police; perhaps because the
threats were too fiery to be believed; perhaps because,
after all, the threatener was a Marquess.

Wilde and Bosie continued their visits as usual.
Lord Queensberry, however, did not put in an
appearance.

On July 6th he wrote another letter—this time from
Skindle's, Maidenhead, and addressed to Alfred
Montgomery, the father of his first wife, who had
divorced him seven years earlier. He wrote:

Your daughter is the person who is supporting my son to
defy me. . . . Last night I received a very quibbling, pre-
varicating message saying the boy denied having been at the
Savoy for the past year; but why send the telegram unless
he had been there with Oscar Wilde at all? As a matter of
fact he did [sic] and there has been a stinking scandal. I
am told they were warned off, but the proprietor will not
admit this. This hideous scandal has been going on for
years. Your daughter must be mad by the way she is
behaving. She evidently wants to make out that I want to
make out a case against my son. It is nothing of the kind.
I have made out a case against Oscar Wilde and I have to
his face accused him of it. If I was quite certain of the
thing I should shoot the fellow on sight, but I can only
accuse him of posing. It now lies in the hands of the two

whether they will further defy me. Your daughter appears
now to be encouraging them, although she can hardly intend
this.

And then, halfway through, another lapse into
lunatic fury:

He [presumably Wilde] plainly showed the white feather
the other day when I tackled him—damned cur and coward
of the Rosebery type. As for this so-called son of mine, he
is no son of mine and I will have nothing to do with him.
He may starve as far as I am concerned after his behaviour
to me. His mother may support him, but she shan't do
that in London with this awful scandal going on. But your
daughter's conduct is outrageous and I am not fully convinced that the Rosebery-Gladstone-Royal insult that came
to me through my other son, that she worked that. It shall
be known some day by all that Rosebery not only insulted
me by lying to the Queen, which makes her as bad as him
and Gladstone but also made a lifelong quarrel between my
son and I.

Three other communications, a post card from Bosie
to his father, and two letters from the Marquess to
Bosie, close the distressing selection.

The post card breathed flat and unyielding defiance:

I am of age and my own master. You have disowned me
at least a dozen times, and very meanly deprived me of
money. . . . If O. W. was to prosecute you for libel, you
would get seven years' penal servitude for your outrageous
libels. . . . If you try to assault me, I shall defend myself
with a loaded revolver, which I always carry, and if I shoot
you or he shoots you, we shall be completely justified as we
shall be acting in self-defence against a dangerous rough,
and I think if you were dead many people would not miss
you.

To which the Marquess replied from Scotland on
August 21st:

I have received your postcard which I presume is from
you, but as the writing is utterly unreadable to me, have
been able to make out hardly one sentence. My object of
receiving no written communication from you is therefore
kept intact. All future cards will go into the fire unread.

I presume these are the hyerogliphics [sic] of the O. W.
posing-club of which you have the reputation of being such

a shining light. I congratulate you on your autography; it is beautiful, and should help you to get a living. I don't know what at, but say crossing-sweeping. My friend I am staying with has made out some of your letter, and wished to read it to me but I declined to hear a word. I shall keep it as a specimen, and also as a protection in case I ever feel tempted to give you the thrashing you deserve. You reptile.

You are no son of mine, and I never thought you were.

QUEENSBERRY.

And, finally, from Portland:

August 24th, 1894.

I received your telegram by post from Carters, and have requested them not to forward any more, but just to tear any up, as I did yours, without reading it, directly I was aware from whom it came. You must be flush of money to waste it on such rubbish. I have learned, thank goodness, to turn the keenest pangs to peacefulness. What could be keener pain than to have such a son as yourself fathered upon one? However, there is always a bright side to every cloud, and whatever is is light [*sic*].

If you are my son, it is only confirming proof to me, if I needed any, how right I was to face every horror and misery I have done rather than run the risk of bringing more creatures into the world like yourself, and that was the entire and only reason of my breaking with your mother as my wife, so intensely was I dissatisfied with her as the mother of you children, and particularly yourself, whom, when quite a baby, I cried over you the bitterest tears man ever shed, that I had brought such a creature into the world, and unwittingly committed such a crime.

If you are not my son, and in this christian country there are hypocrites, 'tis a wise father who knows his own child, and no wonder on the principles they intermarry on, but to be forewarned is to be forearmed. No wonder you have fallen a prey to this horrible brute. I am only sorry for you as a human creature. You must gang your ain gait. Well, it would be rather a satisfaction to me, because the crime then is not to me. As you see, I am philosophical and take comfort from anything; but really, I am sorry for you. You must be demented; there is a madness on your mother's side, and indeed few families in this christian country are without it, if you look into them.

But please cease annoying me, for I will not correspond with you, nor receive nor answer letters, and as for money, you sent me a lawyer's letter, to say you would take none from me, but anyhow until you change your life I should refuse any; it depends on yourself whether I will ever recognize you at all again after your behaviour. I will make allowance, I think you are demented, and I am very sorry for you.

QUEENSBERRY.

But Bosie's post card does seem to have had the effect of frightening his father so far as the restaurant excursions were concerned. There were no more of them.

After which came an abandonment of letter-writing, and instead a personal and unheralded visit of Lord Queensberry, accompanied by a bodyguard of one, to Wilde's house. The interview is oddly reminiscent of a scene in the best-known of all the adventures of Sherlock Holmes (and incidentally a contemporary sensation), *The Speckled Band.*

Beginning with threats, it petered out, as in the Holmes story, in a complete anti-climax. Oscar's opening gambit was a specimen of his unflagging effrontery. He supposed, he blandly told Queensberry, that he had called to apologize for the libellous letter he had written?

Queensberry dissented violently; the letter was in any case a privileged one. Then, abandoning defence for attack, he went on to accuse Wilde of having been locked out of the Savoy Hotel and, in addition, of having been blackmailed on account of a disgusting letter he had written to Bosie. The letter, added Lord Queensberry, had been found in the pocket of a suit Bosie had given to a valet.

Wilde said both stories were " untrue and quite ridiculous."

Queensberry, shifting his ground once more, swore that if he caught Wilde and Bosie together again he would thrash Wilde.

Wilde's retort to that threat was even more dramatic. " I don't know what the Queensberry rules are," he

said, " but the Wilde rule is to shoot at sight in case
of personal violence. Leave my house at once."

After which he rang the bell. And when the footman
appeared, Wilde said: " This is the Marquess of
Queensberry, the most infamous brute in London.
You are never to allow him to enter my house again. . . .
Now," he said to the two men, " get out."

Exeunt the discomfited and temporarily baffled
Marquess and escort.

Lord Queensberry seems to have realized, at long
last, that neither verbal nor written threats were likely
to make any breach in the walls of the friendship, and
that some entirely new method would be needed. It
was equally obvious that whatever form his next attack
took, it would be without the support of either family
or friends. His eldest son had died tragically after a
political career that might, had it been less brief, have
done something to restore the glory of the family
name; his second son, now his heir, sided with Bosie;
he had been long estranged from their mother.

And Bosie's own contempt for his father had
deepened into black hatred.

Wilde, for all his insouciance, seems to have grown
uneasy. He went to see Frank Harris to discuss the
vendetta in general: Harris, the friend whom he might
snub shatteringly; Harris, the irrepressible, the unblushing amorist, the leather-lunged blower of his own
trumpet; Harris, the shrewd, the credulous, the liar
whose lies were so dramatic and picturesque that his
acquaintances must have been disappointed on
the rare occasions when he substituted the literal
truth. But a friend, nevertheless, faithful after his
fashion.

" What is one to do with such a madman?" demanded
Wilde.

Harris for once had no answer ready. He was frankly
uneasy, his uneasiness complicated by a conviction that

a tougher personality was supporting and inspiring the morally flabby Wilde. He guessed—correctly—that the Douglas temperament was in command.

"Bosie," continued Wilde, "has written him a terrible letter, or rather a post card, since his father returns all letters unopened."

Harris might have been the biggest scoundrel in the Wilde circle. But the fact did not make him incapable of giving sound advice. He was aware that the rumours about Wilde were becoming more and more noisy and more specific, and that Wilde was treating them with increased arrogance and general defiance. Cesari, the head waiter at the Savoy, had only a few days earlier contributed, discreetly, a head waiter's point of view. "I do wish," he had said to Harris, "that Mr. Wilde and Lord Alfred wouldn't come here; it does us a lot of harm."

Harris asked to see the correspondence. He characterized Queensberry's letters as "appalling," and told Wilde definitely that he had better break off the friendship.

Wilde replied, "Bosie wouldn't let me."

"Then," said Harris, "keep out of the way of Queensberry."

Wilde, contending that Queensberry had quarrelled with everyone and ought to be in a madhouse, took no action at all in the end.

Lord Queensberry waited. His supreme object was to brand and humiliate his enemy before the largest possible audience. The first night of *The Importance of Being Earnest* was obviously a heaven-sent opportunity. But his malignant little mind could not go beyond a repetition of the insult that he had tried to inflict on the first night of Tennyson's play, *The Promise of May,* thirteen years before, when he turned up with a bouquet of carrots and cabbages ready to hurl on the stage. He booked seats in advance, but the very fact was his undoing. The management was ready for him, and he was refused admission.

That same month, on February 18th, he struck again. But this time the blow, which was as crude as might have been expected, was dealt with deadly cunning.

He called at the Albemarle Club, housed at Numbers 14 and 15 Albemarle Street, of which both Wilde and he were members, and handed the hall porter his card, on which he had written: " To Oscar Wilde, posing as a Somdomite," either rage or sheer ignorance being responsible for the spelling mistake. " Give that to Mr. Wilde," said the Marquess. The hall porter, realizing that it was no ordinary message, slipped the card in an envelope. And when Wilde called at the club ten days later handed it to him.

For the first time in his life Wilde had met something against which neither wit nor bluff was a weapon. He could threaten a bully with physical violence, but here was a deadly thrust from an enemy who was beyond the reach of physical chastisement or verbal annihilation. He could have ignored the card, as a man could " ignore " a public horsewhipping, and have left England and his world, a world consisting mainly of people who admired him to the point of fanaticism or who detested him.

Eventually, on the advice of another friend, Robert Ross, he went to a firm of solicitors (Douglas, as a matter of course, identified himself wholeheartedly and in advance with any line of action involving a head-on attack against his father), and instructed them to institute immediate proceedings for criminal libel.

On March 1st Wilde himself applied at the police court for a warrant for his enemy's arrest.

Taking all the circumstances into consideration, the act was one of supreme recklessness and folly. George Lewis, of Lewis & Lewis, the solicitors who normally dealt with his affairs, and who knew him personally and intimately, was not consulted. Wilde was like a patient who, fearing the worst, goes to a strange doctor. Lewis, who almost certainly must have been aware not only of the rumours that were casting shadows on his reputation, but—what was far more important—to what extent those rumours were justified, would have given different, if less palatable, advice.

As it turned out, ironically enough, the firm appeared on behalf of Lord Queensberry.*

It was Messrs. Humphreys, Son & Kershaw, solicitors of the highest standing, with a wide experience in criminal cases, to whom Wilde went. Unfortunately for him, Mr. Humphreys, its head, accepted without reservation his statement that there was nothing whatever to justify the libel.

Charles Russell, also of the highest eminence, undertook the defence of Queensberry.

Edward Carson, the advocate whose star was rising steadily in the legal world, was persuaded into acting as counsel for the defence. It required a very considerable amount of persuasion. He had been a fellow-undergraduate at Trinity College, Dublin, with Wilde. He had, at the time he was approached, very little except hearsay evidence to offer in favour of the defendant. Whatever the turn of events, unpredictable in any case, the reputation of Lord Alfred, the young son of the defendant, was likely to be dragged through the mud. And finally, the whole affair and the atmosphere enveloping it was utterly repugnant to the Puritan mentality of Carson.

But his scruples were eventually dissipated. One of the private detectives employed by the Marquess was rewarded by an extraordinary stroke of luck. He stumbled upon evidence damning enough to transform Carson the Puritan into Carson the Crusader, warring

*But returned their instructions at the end of the first day's hearing, in view of Lewis's previous friendship with Wilde.

against vice in the form referred to on the club card—except that there was no " posing." Carson's reluctance was swept away. From thence onwards it was his duty, detestable but inescapable, to fight the case with every weapon available.

His opposite number, Wilde's counsel, was Sir Edward Clarke, a great lawyer in the Victorian tradition, studiously courteous, occasionally pompous, but always the soul and essence of integrity.

He, too, had asked Wilde if there was any truth in the innuendo. And Wilde again answered " None."

Lord Queensberry was arrested on March 2nd, released on bail, and duly appeared at the second hearing at Marlborough Street Police Court a week later. He was committed for trial, and released again on the same bail.

The trial proper, the first of the three which in turn enthralled, shocked and stunned the listeners who daily packed the Central Criminal Court at the Old Bailey, began on Wednesday, April 3rd, 1895, before Mr. Justice Henn Collins.

The first trial was to prove the most dramatic, the most effective " theatre." It involved a double reversal. At the beginning of the case the horsey, insignificant little defendant *was* the defendant. And looked it. He entered the court hat in hand, speaking to no one, virtually ignored. He listened to the evidence " with subdued and angry mutterings." The plaintiff, on the other hand, entered with the air of a leading actor taking a call—magnificently assured, completely composed, sartorially splendid in tight frock-coat of dark material and a collar with side points, his hair banked on the top of his head and carefully parted. He answered his counsel's questions, " toying with a pair of gloves," his eyes fixed on the ceiling, in a carefully modulated voice, modulation which amounted to affectation, and which made him difficult to hear.

The examination lasted just over an hour.

Carson, cross-examining, was handicapped by the effects of a severe cold, superimposed upon an Irish accent which Wilde at one point had the bad taste to mimic. It was one of those cheap jeers which prove extremely expensive in the long run.

The duel between two fellow-Irishmen, each a genius in his own field, once fellow-undergraduates and acquaintances, extended from the first day to the third, although the issue was actually decided before the end of the second day. It was a duel which was to become a classic, and which is still held up to the forensic student as a model of legal attack, of brilliant defence by a layman, and ultimately of legal victory.

In the beginning, Wilde met every onslaught effortlessly and effectively. He treated Carson with airy and amused detachment. His attitude could hardly have been more contemptuous if he had been discussing art with some semi-literate tradesman.

" Do you think we are talking about finance?" demanded Carson caustically, in reply to Wilde's statement that " I have adored you extravagantly " in *The Picture of Dorian Gray* meant " financially."

" I don't know *what* you're talking about," said Wilde.

His letters to Douglas were also quoted.

" 'Your slim gilt soul walks between passion and poetry,' " read Carson. " Is that a beautiful phrase?"

" Not as you read it, Mr. Carson," retorted Wilde. " You read it very badly!"

A little later Wilde was invited to read a typical letter he had written to Lord Alfred.

" I decline," he said. " I don't see why I should."

" Then I will," said Carson. And when he had finished asked, " Is that an ordinary letter?"

" Everything I write is extraordinary. I do not pose as being ordinary," said Wilde airily.

The story of the notorious friendship was dealt with at considerable length. It became apparent that it had been an extravagant one in every sense of the word. Wilde, already in possession of the house in Tite Street in which his first meeting with Douglas took place, had not merely stayed with him at Oxford, Brighton, Worthing, Cromer and Torquay, as well as in various London hotels, but had taken rooms in St. James's Place, in which Douglas also stayed, from October, 1893, to March, 1894.

Yet, though these admissions may have had an ultimately damning effect on his case, the first day was a triumph for Wilde. In a succession of epigrammatic impromptus, he countered every attack of his dour and plodding enemy. Judge, jury and spectators alike felt that they were present at a drama as brilliant as *The Importance of Being Earnest,* a drama with the additional thrills of its belonging to real life, and being liable to pass from comedy to tragedy at any moment.

Carson waited. From past experience, both of his own powers and of the types of mentality that had opposed them, added to his knowledge, as yet uncommunicated, of Wilde's past, he was aware that he could afford to wait. Poise, self-confidence, drawling insolence—he had met all this before. Not all the wit, not all the butterfly flights of repartee flashing from the most brilliant Irishman of his generation, could obscure for ever the deadly truth. Carson was content to wait for the moment when the plaintiff should make the inevitable slip that would bring its inevitable and shattering sequel.

And at last Wilde made it.

Like some tragic game of question and answer the cross-examination went on. But the lost ground was never regained. Gradually a double reversal took place—the plaintiff became the defendant; the once-dazzled listeners to Wilde's repartee became his critics, shocked, contemptuous, hostile.

The second day came and passed. Wilde's position grew steadily worse.

On the third day Carson announced that he intended to produce in person a number of youths who, the plaintiff had admitted, had been his friends. But before they could be produced Sir Edward Clarke* was plucking at Carson's gown; there was a murmured consultation; the court made a brief adjournment.

When the two counsel reappeared, it was announced that the plaintiff withdrew his charges. The unfortunate Sir Edward, who, an English gentleman himself, had accepted his client's solemn assurance on the honour of an English gentleman (unfortunately an Irishman with another code), that he was entirely guiltless of Lord Queensberry's allegations, did his best to mitigate the abjectness of his client's surrender. But he and Carson knew from that moment how completely and shatteringly ruinous to that client's reputation the surrender was.

A verdict for the defendant was formally entered. To that verdict the jury added a rider. They found that Lord Queensberry's action had been " for the public benefit."

At which the spectators burst into cheers.

For the coarse-minded, raffish little Marquess, the ruin of his enemy, brought about through the evidence garnered so ruthlessly and with such patient cunning with the Queensberry fortune and influence behind it, that moment should have been enough. With a second trial imminent and Wilde in the dock, the links between him and the boy on whose account the vendetta had been launched and sustained for so long

---

*In the course of his re-examination of Wilde he had already fallen back on his last reserves, and reluctantly produced the letters from Queensberry to Douglas.

would almost certainly be snapped. Elementary
decency demanded that Queensberry should no longer
linger, gloating, at the later agonies and humiliations
of his victim.

But it was not enough. And elementary decency
never stood much chance where the eighth Marquess
was concerned. He continued to attend each phase of
the later trials, at Bow Street and at the Old Bailey.
His flushed, excited face registered every revelation
that damned Wilde still further.

Wilde himself, though he had gone to the Old Bailey
that morning, had not entered the court. After a consultation with his counsel, he had left before the final
statement was made.

"And so," asserted an editorial in the now-defunct
Echo, " a most miserable case ended. . . . The best
thing for everybody now is to forget all about Oscar
Wilde, his perpetual posings, his aesthetical teachings
and his theatrical productions. If not tried himself, let
him go into silence, and be heard no more."

The editorial hint was not acceptable to the
authorities. On April 5th the documents in the case,
that is to say, copies of all the witnesses' statements and
of the shorthand notes, were sent by Charles Russell
to the Public Prosecutor, " in order that there may be
no miscarriage of justice."

It was a course as obvious as it was inevitable.

The papers were delivered at the Treasury. A little
later Russell was asked to interview Mr. Hamilton
Cuffe, the Director of Public Prosecutions. There were
other consultations with Sir John Bridge, the chief
magistrate at Bow Street. And finally a warrant was
issued for Wilde's arrest.

On that same day, April 5th, Wilde had sent a letter,
written at the Holborn Viaduct Hotel, to *The Evening
News,* explaining why he authorized the withdrawal of
his action against Lord Queensberry. He said that it

would have been impossible for him to have proved his case without putting Lord Alfred in the box to give evidence against his father, and that although Lord Alfred was extremely anxious that this should be done, Wilde, rather than put him in so painful a position, determined to retire from the case and to bear on his own shoulders whatever ignominy and shame might result. It was an extraordinarily foolish letter, neither logical nor honest. All the facts stated must have been envisaged and discussed before the action was begun. *If* Wilde had known from the first that he would have to put Douglas in the box to substantiate his charges, why did he begin the action at all? (In point of fact, we know that Clarke never even contemplated his giving evidence.) On the other hand, once having begun it, he must have been perfectly aware what the failure of the action would mean to his reputation. And that knowledge, augmented by his own and Bosie's hatred of the Marquess, would have been more than enough to compensate for any embarrassment arising from the " painful position."

Finally, if he had realized too late that the colossal façade of bluff which he was putting up against Carson's long, slow, pitiless bombardment was doomed to collapse, why write the letter at all? It could deceive no one. Nothing that Douglas could have said against his father would in the long run have been likely to affect the charges against Wilde, charges wholly unconnected with the parental and personal delinquencies of Lord Queensberry.

The letter was, in short, the gesture of a man who, posturing to the last, was in process of losing not merely his reputation, but his nerve.

The tragedy extended in another direction.

From his spoilt boyhood onward, Douglas had always been " touchy," the result of the egoistic adolescence characteristic of his father and other members of his family. He was quick to assume that offence was intended, frequently where none at all was meant, and his natural and habitual veneer of charm and good breeding did not prevent swift and ruthless retaliation. He had a natural flair for conducting vendettas, and a naïve appreciation of his own skill in conducting them.

From this, presumably, sprang one of his most remarkable obsessions. It amounted to an utterly baseless belief that at the trial of Wilde he had been deliberately cheated out of going into the witness box by Sir Edward Clarke, and that by his exclusion not only had he missed the forensic opportunity of a lifetime, but his father, Lord Queensberry, had won a verdict which subsequently led to Wilde's ruin.

The obsession is the more inexplicable in view of the fact that immediately after the trial he not only wrote an intensely appreciative letter to Sir Edward, but sounded the same note in the book, *Oscar Wilde and Myself*.

Yet, in spite of this, thirty years after the trial Douglas wrote a long letter to Frank Harris for inclusion in the preface to Harris's *Life and Confessions of Oscar Wilde*. In that letter he gave an elaborate account of a conversation which he alleged took place between him and Sir Edward Clarke during the consultation that followed Lord Queensberry's amended plea of justification.

The whole thing is so detailed and convincing, as well as so intrinsically untrue, that one might have imagined it originating in Frank Harris himself if Douglas had not repeated and amplified the story still further in his *Autobiography*, published in 1929. Douglas had by then hypnotized himself into believing that not only had he told Clarke that if he were not put in the witness box they might as well throw up the

case at once, but that the case would have been won if
he had been put in the box.

It was Robert Sherard who, reading the *Auto-
biography*, exploded the story. From his home in
Corsica he wrote to Clarke on September 9th, 1929.
After apologizing for troubling him, Sherard says:

I am obliged in self-defence to answer certain aspersions
made upon me in his *Autobiography* by Lord Alfred
Douglas. In this book, which I trust you have not read,
there is a very foolish comment on the way in which you
conducted Oscar Wilde's case against Lord Queensberry for
criminal libel at the Old Bailey in April, 1895. Douglas
declared that you had agreed to put him in the box immediately after your opening speech on the prosecutor's behalf.
He was to give evidence to show the character of his father,
the Marquess, and a full account of Lord Queensberry's
alleged brutalities to his family, etc. He adds that you
promised to do so, and that you did not keep this promise.
He says that if he had been called and had been allowed to
destroy his father's character, Wilde would certainly have
won his case.

May I be allowed to point out to my readers the utter
absurdity of this statement, and shall I not be right in saying
that the judge would not have allowed such evidence to be
given as being entirely irrelevant to the point at issue?

Douglas's statements might be treated with contempt were
it not for the support that is being given to them by a
certain Frank Harris, who joins in this attack on your conduct of the case, in his widely circulated book.

Sir Edward's reply, dated a week later from Staines,
was as follows:

I have not seen the *Autobiography* of Lord Alfred
Douglas, and shall certainly not trouble to read it. But I
am glad of the opportunity of contradicting the statements
about me which you quote.

It is, you say, alleged that I agreed with Oscar Wilde that
he should " give evidence to show the character of his (Lord
Alfred's) father, the Marquess, and a full account of Lord
Queensberry's alleged brutalities to his family, etc." That
I " promised to do this and did not keep the promise." It
is added that " if he (Lord Alfred) had been called and had
been allowed to destroy his father's character, Wilde would

certainly have won his case." There is not a fragment of truth in any of these statements. I made no such agreement or promise. The question of Lord Queensberry's character was quite irrelevant to the case, and was never mentioned in my instructions or in consultation, and if an attempt had been made to give such evidence the judge would of course have peremptorily stopped it. You are at liberty to make any use you please of this letter.

Douglas carried his grievance against Clarke still further. He said that owing to Clarke's failure to cross-examine the Crown witnesses at Bow Street, both Wilde and Taylor* were committed for trial, and if he (Douglas) had known then as much about the law as he knew when the *Autobiography* was written, he would have urged Wilde to tell Clarke that if he did not cross-examine in the police court he must retire from the case and let someone else do it instead.

Clarke's personal explanation completely nullifies what in effect amounts to a charge of incompetent bungling.

Wilde appeared at Bow Street where, the day after his arrest, evidence against him was given by seven persons. When their successive examinations by Gill, for the Crown, were over, Travers Humphreys (*not* Clarke), who appeared for Wilde, announced that the charge had taken his client by surprise, and that he was not prepared to cross-examine the first witness (Parker).

The magistrate accordingly allowed the cross-examination of all the Crown witnesses to be postponed.

The hearing was resumed on April 11th. It was not until then that Sir Edward Clarke, whose offer to defend Wilde free of any cost had in the meantime been formally accepted, came into court and stated:

I have had the opportunity of reading the depositions which were taken last Saturday, and I am much obliged for the permission to postpone the cross-examination of those witnesses. But upon consideration I have decided not to ask

*Co-defendant with Wilde. See page 123.

for those witnesses to be recalled for cross-examination, as
probably no cross-examination could affect the result as far
as this court is concerned, and so far as your action in the
matter is concerned. And of course it is desirable on all
grounds that the investigation shall be taken in as short a
time as possible in this court. And, saying that with regard
to the witnesses who have been called, I shall probably take
the same course with regard to other witnesses, with a view
to shortening the proceedings before you.

The magistrate agreed. As Mr. Montgomery Hyde
points out in his book on the Wilde trial (to which I
am indebted for these details), Clarke could not
advantageously have taken any other course.

Douglas's statements to the contrary, and his
depreciation of Clarke's methods, have no justification
whatever. He knew it, but persisted in his grievance.
As late as 1931 he repeated, in conversation with Mr.
Hyde, that Clarke had broken his promise and entirely
let down his client, that at the time of the trial Wilde
and himself were so inexperienced in legal matters that
it never occurred to either of them that Clarke was not
performing prodigies of skill in his conduct of the case.
He added that he had even recollections of writing him
a long and pathetic letter of thanks for what he had
done. . . . It did not bear thinking of.

It does not bear thinking of now. But not for the
reason Douglas meant.

After the dénouement Wilde drove away from the
court with Douglas and Robert Ross. Wilde cashed a
cheque for £200, and from the bank went on to the
Cadogan Hotel in Sloane Street, where for the past four
or five weeks Douglas had been staying. On the way
there Ross noticed that they were being followed.

At about six o'clock in the evening, an inspector,
with the usual escort of a sergeant, arrived at the hotel.
They found Wilde and two friends smoking, and noted
that the floor was strewn with copies of the evening

papers they had been reading. Douglas was not there.
He had gone to the House of Commons, in an attempt
to find out from his cousin, George Wyndham, M.P.,
whether Wilde was or was not likely to be arrested.
The detectives asked Wilde to go with them in the cab
that was waiting outside to Scotland Yard. From there
they drove to Bow Street, where he was formally
charged under the Criminal Law Amendment Act.

In the meantime, Douglas, having failed to contact
Wyndham, had returned to the hotel to find a note
from Oscar, saying that he had been arrested, and
asking Douglas to go and see George Alexander and
Lewis Waller, both of whom had had a good deal to do
with the production of Wilde's plays, and ask them to
go bail for him.

Douglas, in a state of acute distress, carried out these
instructions. But he went to Bow Street first in an
attempt to bail out Wilde. He failed; he was not a
householder, and so could not be accepted as surety.

He left, to appeal to Alexander and Waller. Neither
would help. So for the time being Wilde remained in
custody.

According to Frank Harris, who saw Wilde when he
had been remanded, Wilde's failure to obtain bail led
to a complete cessation of his income. This, however,
must be an exaggeration, since the royalties on *The
Importance of Being Earnest,* which ran without his
name on the playbills for some weeks longer, were still
payable. He was nevertheless adjudged bankrupt and
sold up.

On April 6th Wilde was charged, Mr. Gill appearing
for the Public Prosecutor; Mr. Travers Humphreys
for the prisoner. For half an hour before the doors of
the public galleries at Bow Street opened crowds had
been gathering outside, but only friends and those
professionally connected with the case were first
admitted. Later, it was announced that the hearing

would be held in the Extradition Court, where there
was more space.

Wilde, wearing a black frock-coat and dark trousers,
appeared entirely unmoved. He was allowed to sit
down in the dock.

The case began. It was interrupted by an announcement by Mr. Gill that Alfred Taylor, a friend of
Wilde's, had been arrested and would appear with
him. The witnesses about to be called for the prosecution could thus give evidence against the two men
simultaneously.

Taylor, under a veneer of cultured affability, was a
blackguard, though not an unmitigated one. Educated
at Marlborough and Oxford, he had held a commission
in the Militia, inherited a fortune of £45,000,
squandered it, and then gone bankrupt. His subsequent profession, carried on behind heavily curtained
windows in his rooms in the upper part of 13 Little
College Street, at the back of Westminster Abbey, was
that of an organizer on an extensive scale of what was
in those days termed "unnatural vice."

In his elaborately decorated apartments, hung with
heavy draperies and lit only by shaded lamps, he
received his clients, miscellaneous riff-raff of every
social grade from public-school men to out-of-work
ostlers. At some time Wilde had drifted into this lair,
Ouida-ish in its impressive bad taste, poisonous in its
atmosphere. Unfortunately he had not drifted out
again—and stayed out. He became a constant visitor.
The raffish young degenerates who were Taylor's
clients became Wilde's friends.

The two men were remanded until April 11th, bail
being again refused. Wilde, it is stated, sighed heavily
when he heard the decision. He and Taylor were
driven off in the Black Maria to Holloway.

To revert to Douglas.

From this time onward his position had the three

nightmare qualities of helplessness, intense anxiety and friendlessness. His own father, who had launched this culminating—and the first successful—attack nominally for Douglas's sake, was his implacable enemy. And although the stories told by Frank Harris and others of the mass panic-stricken migration of Wilde's and Douglas's one-time friends to the Continent and safety has been dramatically exaggerated, it is certain that Douglas did find himself wretchedly alone, and, for the time being, entirely without funds.

Oscar, remanded, was taken to Holloway. Thereafter, for a quarter of an hour each day, his friend was allowed to see him. Douglas says that he looked at him with tears running down his cheeks. It must have been a time that both often recalled.

Starkly tragic though the whole thing was, it was shot with occasional gleams of humour.

As a supporter of a widespread idea that Wilde was " not quite right in the head," a rich woman wrote to the Home Secretary offering to instal the sufferer in her park lodge, " where he would be carefully guarded by two nurses from the nearest asylum." A well-known Frenchman, a boy at that time, was visiting London with his father. He was allowed to walk in the park. " But," said his father, " if any man with a sunflower in his coat, carrying a lily speaks to you, run back to the hotel as fast as you can."

The Central News issued, by authority, the following: " Lord Queensberry states that as soon as the trial ended he sent this message to Mr. Oscar Wilde: ' If your country allows you to leave, all the better for the country. But if you take my son with you, I will follow you wherever you go, and shoot you.' "

But the next day there was a second and corrected edition of the challenge. " The message," explained Lord Queensberry, " was sent before, not after, the trial was over." And what his Lordship had actually said was that if his misjudged son were persuaded to go with Wilde, he would feel quite justified in following him (Wilde) and shooting him, did he feel inclined to do so, and were he worth the trouble.

The day before the second trial began Douglas left London for Paris, where he stayed at the Gare Maritime. He had not wanted to go, but Wilde, backed by Clarke, had asked him to, as his presence was doing more harm than good. Douglas had refused to leave until the request was formally written. He then left for Calais. From Clarke's point of view the only danger was that he might dash back to London again.

It was noticed when the case was resumed that Wilde looked paler and thinner, and moved with a weariness altogether different from his normal pose of languor.

Sir Edward Clarke was in court. He announced that, with Travers Humphreys as his junior, he was appearing for Wilde. Arthur Newton, later to be associated with more than one case on Douglas's behalf, appeared for Taylor.

The case lumbered on its slow and sordid course. It ended on April 19th, so far as Bow Street and its aged and prejudiced magistrate was affected. (" I think there is no worse crime than that with which the prisoners are charged. . . . I shall refuse bail.")

Wilde and Taylor were committed for trial.

On Tuesday, April 23rd, the Grand Jury found true bills against both of them. The next day they appeared at the Central Criminal Court. An appeal by Clarke that the case should be postponed until the next Sessions was dismissed. And on April 26th, before Mr. Justice Charles, the trial proper began.

The same ground was traversed, or most of it. Clarke's speech for the defence at the end, which lasted nearly two hours, was followed by an outburst of applause. Wilde himself seemed " visibly affected."

On April 30th the judge summed up. The jury were

asked to answer four specific questions. They agreed concerning two; concerning the other two their foreman could only record hopeless disagreement. There was nothing for it but a fresh trial. Wilde himself was released on bail, the sum fixed as surety being £5,000. Of this sum, half was accepted from Wilde himself, Queensberry's elder son, Lord Douglas of Hawick, and the Rev. Stewart Headlam each standing surety for £1,250.

On May 20th Wilde surrendered to his bail. The last of the "three trials" began at the Old Bailey. (Taylor had taken no steps to obtain bail and had remained in custody.)

For Wilde, that period of nearly three weeks must have been one of unmitigated purgatory.

It has been pointed out that both before the original warrant for his arrest was issued, and again after the second trial, he had ample opportunities of escaping to the Continent, or even farther from British law. It has, however, been stated that those who represented British law not merely expected, but hoped, that this would happen.

Wilde declined to take advantage of both opportunities and hopes.

From his personal standpoint, there were several fairly obvious reasons for remaining to face the music. To have bolted would have involved far more than an ignominious anti-climax, entirely alien to the Wilde temperament and tradition; it would have converted a situation which had a sporting chance of ending in his acquittal into one involving final and complete social degradation. His status would be worse than that of a cashiered officer. He would be an exile, an outcast— with his account with Society still to be settled. And he would have betrayed the trust of the two friends who had stood bail for him, while he himself would have sacrificed £2,500.

Again, if the jury disagreed the first time, why should they not disagree a second time? And *if* that happened, if two juries *did* disagree, the law had a habit of deciding that to play the game any longer simply wasn't worth the candle. Justice grew bored with the weary and inescapable repetition of evidence, and of the expense involved. He would probably be set free without further argument.

Finally, the Wilde temperament must be taken into account, the temperament of the flamboyant egoist, of the *poseur* who was still prepared to challenge the fates, and who still retained faith in his ability to impress and dominate his surroundings, even the unsympathetic surroundings of the Old Bailey. If at the worst he failed, there remained only the final exit. But it would be the splendidly dramatic exit of a martyr.

I agree with Osbert Burdett in regarding Wilde's character as fundamentally theatrical and spectacular, and think it true that he viewed the world as a stage to be valued for the effects it afforded an actor, and that his test was the amount of attention, whether of applause or opprobrium, that one excited. He possessed, above all, an unerring instinct for the centre of the stage, and at the decisive moment of his fortunes the centre of the stage was not the boat-train to Dover, but the dock of the Old Bailey.

Frank Harris, it may be added, had a different theory. It was that Wilde stayed in England because it was easier than coming to an immediate decision. He had, says Harris, very little will-power to begin with, and his mode of life had weakened his original endowment.*

---

*Harris goes on to state that as soon as the bail was accepted he began to think of preparations for Wilde's escape. He says he actually met the owner of a steam yacht who, on hearing his object, was willing to lend the boat at the mere cost of running it. Harris afterwards went to the house of Willie Wilde, the journalist brother of Oscar, where Oscar was staying, and took him out to lunch, in the course of which he heard a first-hand confession that he was guilty.

That night, dining at the house of a friend, Harris proposed driving

The second trial of Wilde—he always spoke of it as the third, treating his fatal action against Queensberry as the first—opened on May 21st.

The case had the unusual distinction of beginning on the first day of the sessions, which were formally opened in state by the Lord Mayor, sheriffs, aldermen and Recorder. By special arrangement Mr. Justice Wills was on the Bench.

Sir Frank Lockwood appeared for the Crown. Sir Edward Clarke, with C. W. ("Willie") Matthews and Travers Humphreys, appeared for Wilde; Mr. J. P. Grain and Mr. W. Clarke Hall for Taylor.

In spite of a number of objections that were raised, it was decided that the two prisoners should be tried separately, and that Taylor's case should be dealt with first. Wilde, who had entered the dock with him, was again released on bail. Taylor's trial occupied two days, at the end of which, after a discussion with the judge on the wording of the counts, the jury returned a verdict of guilty on two of those counts.

It was an ecstatic moment for Lord Queensberry, who had been present at every stage of the trials. True, it was only Wilde's companion. But the mere significance of the verdict was a matter justifying a telegram, revoltingly triumphant, to Lady Queensberry: "Must congratulate on verdict. Cannot on Percy's* appearance—looks like a dug-up corpse. . . . Wilde's turn tomorrow."

It was in the course of the same afternoon that the Marquess and Percy, Lord Douglas of Hawick, meeting by chance at the corner of Bond Street and Piccadilly, came to blows. A policeman, after separating them

in a brougham, already waiting with a pair of fast horses, to Erith, where the yacht was lying with steam up. But Wilde refused.

It is a highly dramatic story of devotion on Harris's part, and coming from such a devotee doubly suspect. Robert Sherard dismisses the whole thing as sheer invention from beginning to end.

*Wilde's two sureties had been in court with him.

three times, arrested Lord Queensberry, another policeman arrested his son, and on the following morning,
the day on which the last trial of Wilde began, they
were charged at Vine Street with what Mr. Polly would
call a " fracass."

Each defendant accused the other. Queensberry
said his son struck him first; Douglas said he was merely
protesting against the succession of disgusting letters
that his father had sent Lady Douglas.

Both defendants were bound over to keep the peace
for six months.

The curtain rose on the last scene of Wilde's inglorious purgatory, so far as the public was concerned,
on the morning of May 22nd.

He arrived early in court with his sureties, and took
his seat below the jury and opposite Sir Edward Clarke,
his counsel. It was noted that he looked haggard,
and that his hair, usually immaculately parted, was
untidy.

Mr. Justice Wills arrived. He was followed by the
Solicitor-General, Sir Frank Lockwood, and Gill and
Avory. Clarke, Matthews and Travers Humphreys,
for the defence, took their seats.

The case was opened; Wilde was called just after
eleven o'clock to give evidence on his own behalf. He
was told that he might be seated.

Sir Edward Clarke concluded his examination by
asking if there was any truth whatever in the accusations
made against him?

" None whatever," said Wilde emphatically.

He was cross-examined. Letters from Wilde to
Douglas were quoted. Wilde said that they represented
an attempt to write a prose poem in beautiful phraseo-
logy. One particularly impassioned specimen ended:
" Shall I come to Salisbury. . . . My bill here is £49."

" That, I suppose," commented Lockwood, " is true
if not poetic?"

LAD—E

" Oh, no, no," said Wilde. " That was prose of the most sordid kind."

Referring to Taylor's career as revealed at the trial, Lockwood asked Wilde if he approved of it.

" I don't think I'm called upon to express approval or disapproval of any person's conduct," said Wilde.

Sir Edward rose to object to the examination of the witness as to his opinion of other people.

The judge supported the contention, but grimly pointed out that it came too late. It is possible that he realized that at that stage no minor technical issue could matter one way or the other.

The monotonous succession of questions and answers continued, here and there enlivened by flashes of the old Wilde.

" I admit that I am enormously fond of praise and admiration," he said, " and that I like to be made much of by my inferiors socially. . . . I like to be lionized."

" You, a successful literary man, wished to obtain praise from these boys!"

" Praise from literary people is usually tainted with criticism."

During the cross-examination Lord Queensberry, indefatigably vindictive, entered the court. As he could not find a vacant seat he stood, sucking the brim of his hat and staring at the prisoner.

Clarke re-examined Wilde, and then addressed the jury. It was a speech worthy of his reputation, and there was applause in court at its conclusion.

Sir Frank Lockwood who, according to an authority quoted in Christopher Millard's account of Wilde's trials, had been a personal friend of Wilde, and who had visited him even after the trials had begun, rose to address the court for the prosecution.

He was still speaking when the court adjourned.

The proceedings on the following day, mercifully the last one to be occupied by the case, were dramatic in the

extreme. Sir Frank Lockwood had hardly resumed the
thread of his argument when Clarke, to whose speech
for the Defence he referred, rose to protest against what
he described as " Mr. Solicitor-General's rhetorical
description of what has never been proved in evidence "
—the reference being to any intimate friendship
between Alfred Taylor, who had already been found
guilty and who was awaiting sentence, and the prisoner
in the dock.

Lockwood retorted that it was not rhetoric, but a
plain statement of fact. " My friend," he added scathingly, " hopes to preserve Wilde by a false glamour of
art."

" I protest strongly," said Sir Edward.

" Oh, you may protest," said Sir Frank . . . and, to
the judge, a moment later: " Oh, my lord, these interruptions should avail my friend nothing."

Nor did they, the judge holding that " Mr. Solicitor-
General " was perfectly within his rights. But a little
later, when Lockwood's sarcastic reference to Clarke's
" candour " raised a laugh, his Lordship was scathing.
" These interruptions," he said, " are offensive to me
beyond anything that can be described. . . . To be
pestered with the applause or expressions of people who
have no business to be here at all, except for the justification of morbid curiosity, is too much." He threatened that if there was a repetition he would clear the
court.

There were further references to Taylor. But with
regard to Wilde's co-partner in the wretched business,
while his career is the quintessence of degradation, and
while the excuses which may be made for Wilde have
no parallel justification in Taylor's case, it should be
put to his eternal credit that he did not, at the end,
forget the ethics of his public-school training.

He and Wilde had, of course, become intimate
friends, foul though the roads that led to that friendship

might have been. And when it was suggested—as it was undoubtedly suggested—that he might have given evidence against Wilde, and in so doing have mitigated his own punishment, he refused. What befell him after his prison days were over is uncertain. It has, however, been stated that he went to America.

Among the most odious of the creatures who furnished evidence for the prosecution was a youth named Alfred Wood, who described himself as a clerk out of employment. The absence of clerical work did not, however, prevent him from being profitably employed in other directions. He gave his evidence on May 2nd " in a very low voice," and was hand in glove with another youth named Charlie Parker in the practice of blackmail. He had gone to Oxford, stayed with Douglas, and by him had been presented with a suit of clothes in the pockets of which were letters from Wilde. These were stolen from Wood by Allen, yet a third professional blackmailer, and after being read by Allen were eventually returned, with the exception of one.*

Alfred Wood had been introduced by Douglas to Wilde. At precisely what point he first entered the younger man's life is uncertain, but there is a reference to him in *De Profundis* which suggests undergraduate days. According to his own evidence the meeting was at Taylor's rooms in Little College Street.

Wood had gone to America in 1893, returned, and " earnt a little by working for his brother, a turf-commission agent in Upper Islington."

Lockwood made his final speech for the Crown. The judge began his summing-up immediately afterwards. He was extremely outspoken. He said he would rather have tried the most shocking murder case than one of this description; that it called for " the cool, calm, resolute administration of justice." He dealt fully, and

---

* Produced at the trial of Queensberry.

on the whole with admirable impartiality, on the details of the case.*

The foreman of the jury interposed in connection with a matter which had been troubling him and his colleagues. He asked if, in view of the intimate friendships between Lord Alfred Douglas and Wilde, a warrant had ever been issued for Lord Alfred's arrest?

The judge said: " I should think not. We have not heard of it."

" Was it ever contemplated?" persisted the foreman.

" Not to my knowledge," said the judge. He continued: " We need not discuss that, because Lord Alfred may yet have to answer a charge. He was not called. There may a thousand considerations of which we know nothing that might prevent his appearance in the witness-box. I think you should deal with the matter upon the evidence before you."

The foreman remained unsatisfied.

" But it seems to me that if we are to consider these letters as evidence of guilt, and if we adduce any guilt from these letters, it applies as much to Lord Alfred Douglas as to the defendant."

" Quite so," said the judge. " But how does that relieve the defendant? Our present inquiry is whether guilt is brought home to the man in the dock. We have got the testimony of his guilt to deal with now. I believe," he concluded significantly, " that to be the recipient of such letters and to continue the intimacy is as fatal to the recipient as to the sender. But you have really nothing to do with that at present."

He dealt again with the subject after the luncheon recess.

---

* In *Three Times Tried*, the author asserts that while placing the issues before the jury in fair enough language, the judge imparted to his delivery, his tones and his manner a significance which deprived his statements of the impartiality expected of the Bench. But the writer himself was hardly impartial.

" There is a natural disposition to ask," he said,
" why should this man stand in the dock and not Lord
Alfred Douglas? But the supposition that Lord Alfred
Douglas will be spared because he *is* Lord Alfred
Douglas is one of the wildest injustice—the thing is
utterly and hopelessly impossible. I must remind you
that anything that can be said for or against Lord Alfred
Douglas must not be allowed to prejudice the prisoner,
and you must remember that no prosecution would be
possible on the mere production of Wilde's letters to
Lord Alfred Douglas. Lord Alfred Douglas, as you all
know, went to Paris at the request of the defendant,
and there he stayed, and I know absolutely nothing
more about him. I am as ignorant in that respect as
you are. It may be that there is no evidence against
Lord Alfred Douglas—but even about that I know
nothing. It is a thing we cannot discuss, and to enter-
tain any such consideration as I have mentioned would
be a prejudice of the worst possible kind."

The jury retired at half-past three. They were away
for rather more than two hours. Lockwood, according
to one narrator, thought Wilde would be acquitted,
and said to Clarke: " You'll dine with your man in
Paris tomorrow." But Clarke took a gloomier view, and
answered: " No, no, no!"

The judge, in response to a note sent from the jury,
returned. The jury themselves returned. Wilde took
his place again in the dock.

The jury found him guilty on all but one of the
remaining counts of the indictment.

Clarke rose to ask that sentence might be postponed
until the next session. His arguments were overruled.

Taylor joined Wilde. The judge addressed them in
a few scathing words, and sentenced each man to
undergo two years' hard labour.

Taylor took the blow with calm indifference, but
Wilde appeared to feel his position acutely. He made

a movement of appeal towards the judge, but the
warders hurried him away.

So, in a storm of contemptuous, self-righteous
execration, the Master, that dominating figure, with
the deep laugh, exquisitely modulated voice, and over-
florid yet entirely appropriate clothes, vanished from
London with its meetings at Romano's, and from Paris
with its salons, reputable and disreputable, into the
chilling, killing atmosphere of H.M. Prison, Wandsworth. The stone walls and iron bars not only a prison
made; the very isolation they inflicted, ghastly as it was,
formed a refuge from the hatred in which the world
outside held the prisoner. His friends could do little
—less than little—to mitigate that.

4. AFTERMATH

A great deal of ink has been spilled in connection
with the scenes which took place after Wilde's conviction. One excited spectator stated that when the
sentence was known " harlots lifted their skirts and
danced to the vociferous cheers of the ever-virtuous
British public."

Mass demonstrations of hatred are always shocking,
in the literal sense of the word, in that they openly defy
the conventional reticences of civilized society. Wilde
himself would certainly have regarded any violent
display of emotion on the part of the *hoi polloi* as
inartistic to the point of being disgusting. His attitude
must have been the same towards the insane jubilations
that took place six years later, when London heard that
the siege of an obscure South African town had been
raised. But the English, as Shaw has pointed out, are a
sentimental race when their traditional reserve has
been shattered.

The point which should be remembered in Wilde's
case is that a London crowd, even the far less educated,

far less reserved London crowd of fifty-odd years ago, would not have abandoned itself to such an orgy of exultation unless it had hated its victim—and it wouldn't have hated him for nothing. Wilde was, in effect, being repaid with horrible interest *not* merely for his pose, maintained to the last, as a " superior person " and his insufferably insolent attitude towards those less superior, less cultured: Londoners have never had a reputation for jeering at an idol who through sheer bad luck or his own folly has crashed in ruin. Their lapse on this occasion from their usual tolerant, Gawd-'elp-the-poor-blighter,-it-might-'ave-bin-me attitude was due to the fact that, concurrently with his pose of aesthetic superiority, Wilde had systematically indulged in what by Victorian standards was the vilest, most degraded sensuality in the vilest, most degrading company and surroundings. For twenty-five years he had preached the Gospel of Beauty, beauty abstract and concrete, and that, the average citizen had assumed, included self-discipline, clean-living and the social decencies—in short, the virtues inherent in the code of an English gentleman.

Now, at long last, he had been found out. Before a nauseated, incredulous world, the fact had emerged that the Master was proved to be a humbug, a hypocrite, a shameless liar, a degenerate steeped in vice.

That, I suggest, is the real explanation of the behaviour of the mob outside the Old Bailey on that spring afternoon.

To say that a convicted murderer could not and would not have received such a brutal reception is to miss the point entirely; a murderer commits—usually —a single act, and in making that wild, amateurish gesture achieves sudden release from some unendurable frustration.

Wilde's crime extended from months to years.

The verdict was a climax more tragically dramatic

than any its victim could have written or contrived. Wilde's personal friends were first stunned, then moved to bitter and passionate protest; his personal enemies were fiercely jubilant. Possibly for the first time in his life Wilde realized how many enemies he had made, how expensive the gentle art of making them may be. Almost to the end of his abortive action against Queensberry, he had treated the world outside his own especial circle with contempt that was no less insufferable because so languid, as much a part of his personality as his astrakhan-trimmed overcoat and his magnificent silk hat.

It has been urged in Wilde's defence that his crime was common among certain circles in every great city; that in France it was—and is—regarded as no crime at all, and in England should more fittingly have been regarded as a matter for the psychiatrist rather than the magistrate. It was further stated that it was, even then, so common in this country that the news of his arrest struck panic in what the social columnists refer to as "highly placed" quarters. Frank Harris, with his unquenchable passion for overemphasizing a situation, describes the flight to the Continent of guilty homosexuals as though half aristocratic England were likely to be involved in Wilde's debacle.

The judge, Sir Alfred Wills, was accused by one reporter of showing bias. A judge invariably *is* biased; the adjective is implicit in the phrase "summing up in favour of" or, alternatively, "against" the defendant. Furthermore, the prosecuting counsel was described as "vindictive." But a prosecuting counsel is there to prosecute, and any person fulfilling that function obviously lays himself open to the charge of vindictiveness.

But it is the sentence itself which has been most fiercely, most hysterically, condemned.

In dealing with the attitude of the law towards any

crime, that crime must be placed in its proper setting and period. In Wilde's case, the place was London and the period late-Victorian; a period when the mere word "sex" and everything connected therewith was regarded as having, at any rate, the possibility of an indecent implication, when a pregnant woman was invariably referred to as "in an interesting (or 'certain') condition," and the birth of her baby either as an "accouchement" or "the arrival of a little stranger"; a period when "nice" parents shrank agonizingly from the embarrassments of discussing, however vaguely, the "facts of life" with their children. (I know personally of one father who invariably retreated under a hurried smoke-screen of "Not very edifying, my boy, not very edifying.")

Apart from public opinion concerning this particular case, sentences in general in those days were far heavier, far more deserving of the word "savage" than now. To quote a single example, a few years earlier a wretched little servant girl who had stolen a few pence from her master, tried, driven half-witted by panic, to hide the theft by setting fire to the house. The flames were soon extinguished; the girl, who made no defence, was arrested. Today, she would probably have received a lecture, and have then been handed over to the court missionary and placed on probation. What she actually received was a terrific tongue-lashing from the judge, followed by a sentence of fifteen years' penal servitude.

Wilde, unlike this unfortunate child, knew exactly what risks he was running. He also knew that if he was found out and convicted the penalty would be a heavy sentence and social extinction.

He deliberately took the risk.

Finally, it is of importance to remember that the particular section of the law under which Wilde was indicted was not that which made a conviction liable to result in imprisonment for life, but the Criminal

Law Amendment of 1885. This Act originally dealt
with the procuring of young people for immoral
purposes; Henry Labouchere, M.P., and editor of
Truth, succeeded in widening the scope of the Act and
in increasing the term of imprisonment from one year
to two. The Act, so modified, had come into force on
January 1st, 1886.

After the gates of Wandsworth Gaol had closed on
Wilde, Douglas remained for a time in France. He
had left Calais for Rouen; he was there when he
received a copy of the June number of W. T. Stead's
paper, *The Review of Reviews.* It contained a leading
article on the Wilde trial.

Stead and Douglas were complete antitheses. Stead
was an honest and highly competent journalist, but hot-
headed and not always sound in his methods of
attacking the innumerable abuses against which he
unsheathed his nonconformist sword. Where social
evils were concerned, Douglas himself could not hate
more fiercely.

In this case, an outstandingly prominent member of
society had been found guilty of a peculiarly nauseating
type of crime, a crime involving the procuration and
corruption of youth. And as it happened, it was against
similar forms of corruption that Stead had lately conducted the bitterest campaign of his career.

The shocking and systematic recruiting of young
girls for the oldest profession in the world had led, two
years previously, to the presentation to Parliament of
the Criminal Law Amendment Bill. But while the Bill
was still before the Commons, Stead, then editor of *The
Pall Mall Gazette,* began to investigate—" probe "
would be the modern word—the situation on his own
account. Assisted by a prominent member of the
Salvation Army, he set to work with characteristic
thoroughness and personal enthusiasm. He described

the evils he discovered in a series of horrific articles headed " The Maiden Tribute of Modern Babylon," articles which had the unrewarding sequel of landing Stead himself in gaol on a three months' sentence for procuring, although the girl featuring as an example had been immediately handed over to the care of the Salvation Army.

There is little doubt, however, that the exposure played its part in converting the Bill, with its subsequent modifications, into the Act.

Stead was by then no longer on the staff of *The Pall Mall Gazette,* having started a new paper of his own, *The Review of Reviews.* With such recent memories of his own imprisonment, and of the searing comments of the judge who sentenced him, he might be forgiven a certain amount of triumph when the personification of the worst type of evil he had been fighting was brought to judgment. In a long editorial comment (I quote only the concluding portion), he wrote:

THE CONVICTION OF OSCAR WILDE

The trial and the sentence bring into very clear relief the ridiculous disparity there is between the punishment meted out to those who corrupt girls and those who corrupt boys. If Oscar Wilde, instead of indulging in dirty tricks of indecent familiarity with boys and men, had ruined the lives of half a dozen innocent simpletons of girls, or had broken up the home of his friend by corrupting his friend's wife, no one would have laid a finger upon him. The male is sacrosanct; the female is fair game. . . .

Another contrast, almost as remarkable as that which sends Oscar Wilde to hard labour and places Sir Charles Dilke in the House of Commons, is that between the universal execration heaped upon Oscar Wilde and the tacit and universal acquiescence of the public in the same kind of vice in our public schools. If all people guilty of Oscar Wilde's offence were to be clapped into gaol, there would be a very surprising exodus from Eton and Harrow, Rugby and Winchester, to Pentonville and Holloway. It is to be hoped that our headmasters will pluck up a little courage from the result of the Wilde trial, and endeavour

to rid our Protestant schools of a foul and unnatural vice
which is not found in Catholic establishments, at all events
in this country.   But meanwhile public-school boys are
allowed to indulge with impunity in practices which, when
they leave school, would consign them to hard labour.

The riposte was swift. It came, as might have been
anticipated, from the exiled Douglas, and it took the
form of a long repudiation of Stead's attitude,
extraordinary, considering the age of the writer, in its
shrewdness, its maturity, its broadness of outlook, to
say nothing of its inherent pathos. Indeed, had the
subject possessed greater anthological possibilities, it
might well have taken its place among the best-known
letters in English.

It was dated June 28th, 1895, and written from
Hôtel de la Poste, Rouen.

It began by saying that the writer believed Stead to
be a man with a conscience, and one who, if he thought
that a terrible wrong had been done, would not sit with
his hands folded and do nothing. It went on to refer
to Stead's admission that the common cant about
" unnatural " offences was worthless, while at the same
time he upheld the horrible and barbarous law which
condemned anyone guilty of these so-called " offences "
to a sentence Stead had calmly referred to as " probably
capital," giving the flimsiest and feeblest reason for
this. His argument apparently was that if these laws
did not exist, a taint or suspicion might be thrown on
friendships between people of the same sex. The letter
passed on to an elaborate and plausible defence of
homosexuality, and thence to ask whether Stead had
ever considered the relative deserts of Wilde and Lord
Queensberry.

The record of his father's faithlessness, his cruelty,
and his immorality is traced in shocking detail and with
heartbreaking detachment. Douglas concludes with the
bitter comment that this was the man who had been

made into a hero by the English people and the Press, who was cheered in the streets by the populace, and who crowned his career by driving out of England the son who was now writing.

Whether Stead, destined to end his life in the wreck of the *Titanic* seventeen years later, ever even acknowledged the letter is uncertain. It is quite certain that he did not publish it. A defence of homosexuality, however brilliant, was hardly a subject for the columns of a serious monthly edited and owned by an uncompromising, not to say fanatical, nonconformist.

Douglas left France for Italy. From Naples he went to Capri and, hiring a villa there, forgot, or at any rate edged from the forefront of his memory, the sordid nightmare of the immediate past. With Wilde he was still in touch; as a definite task he was making it his business to do what he could to mitigate the severity, not of the law's sentence—he was helpless there—but of that passed by Society on his friend. Two years' imprisonment represented definite and limited penance; ostracism for life left no possibility of rehabilitation.

Douglas loafed and explored, and swam in the pellucid Mediterranean, and turned for mental exercise to his first and truest love, poetry. Then Paris stretched out a long tentacle, and touched his arm. Less metaphorically stated, he received an intriguing letter from the editor of the world-famous *Mercure de France*.

He had already tried, and failed, to find an English publisher for some of his poems. France had proved more appreciative, several having already appeared in a periodical called *La Revue Blanche*. Hearing rumours of this, and of a prospect of others appearing, the *Mercure* not only offered to arrange for the publication of the entire collection, but asked Douglas to write an introduction, and at the same time to contribute his impressions of the Wilde debacle.

The offer was obviously irresistible. Here he was
actually being invited to air views which a narrow-
minded English magazine declined even to mention.
With it went an opportunity of doing something that
really mattered on behalf of his friend.

The second part of the scheme went agley. Douglas
had intended to include extracts from the letters Wilde
had written to him from Holloway. But two close
friends of Wilde, Robert Sherard and Robert Ross, took
it upon themselves to tell Wilde that Douglas intended
to publish all his (Wilde's) letters in a French newspaper. Wilde—a changed Wilde indeed!—became
panic-stricken. These letters, afterwards destroyed by
Douglas, who nevertheless clung to the belief that they
would have set Wilde's reputation on its feet again, at
any rate in France, were omitted from the article.

That was duly published. It appeared in French.
Douglas's knowledge of the language was, however,
unequal to the subtleties of translation, and another
hand, that of the editor, was responsible.

The article, which, incidentally, Sherard, then living
in Paris, made an unsuccessful effort to stop, even
though the letters were excluded, produced violent
repercussions in England as well as on the Continent.
Douglas came under such a concentrated fire of
criticism that he eventually stated that the article did
not represent his views. The article, as the original
English text, which survives, has proved, was an entirely
honest translation. In it, he described himself as the
child whom Oscar Wilde loved. He went on to reflect
on the curious fact that had he had the good fortune to
live in Athens at the time of Pericles, the very conduct
which had led to his disgrace would have resulted in his
glory. He blamed the Church for this change in public
opinion, and added the highly debatable statement that
there had always been, always will be, a thousand
Queensberrys to one Oscar Wilde.

Up to this point the violence of the article might be leniently attributed to the bitterness of a youth nursing a grudge against the social machinery which had caught his closest friend in its clumsy out-of-date cogs and destroyed him. But when Douglas went on to discuss the trial itself, his indignation ceased to be general and became recklessly personal. His attack on Lord Queensberry touched further depths of hatred; from his father he passed on to make an onslaught against Lord Rosebery and Mr. Asquith, with a final shot at the Liberal Party, which he sarcastically stigmatized as " the salt of the earth," and as " the maniacs of virtue," who had threatened a series of legal actions which would have created an unprecedented scandal in Europe. So, to placate them, Wilde had been found guilty, and a great poet sacrificed to save a degraded band of politicians.

All this, with its venom-inspired, inherently preposterous absurdities, from a boy in his twenties! No wonder — to quote Mr. Hyde — " opinion in France at this time as expressed in the literary journals was unanimous in condemning the senti-ments," stigmatized by one eminent writer as " clumsy and sensational."

The kindest thing one can say about the whole deplorable exhibition is that the writer lived to modify his views.

The poems had the unusual honour of being translated into prose, Eugene Tardieu, a journalist on the staff of *L'Echo de Paris,* being responsible for the French version. Though far from being his first appearance in print, they constituted Douglas's first book, an event which may have seemed to justify not merely a special edition at a higher price—the ordinary one being published at Fr.3.50—but a *de grand luxe* edition as well.

The book was, on the whole, a success, successful

enough at any rate to establish Douglas's reputation as a poet in France.

And Wilde?

He had been taken first to Wandsworth; then from there to Reading Gaol. In the course of this transfer he had been identified in his prison clothes, and with his head shorn, by spectators on the station platform. He accepted this and similar reminders of his degradation as part of the martyrdom which the inscrutable fates had designed for him.

The two years of his imprisonment passed. (Incidentally, had he been tried nowadays, good conduct would have reduced the sentence to eighteen months.) The time spent at Reading had not been wholly wasted on the futilities of oakum-picking and cell-cleaning. Prison saw the inception of perhaps his most exquisite prose work.

Wilde had travelled far and changed much since he wrote his last dragon-fly comedy. One critic compares the new Wilde to a querulous shadow moving about the earth, and adds—I am responsible for neither the simile nor the syntax—" that like a fox he, the darling of Society, had to find a hiding-place, to change his name, and to fly from England, the country that shelters every worthless alien and drives forth its artists."

Wilde's transmutation, however, was not complete; one doubts if any human transmutation ever is. There still remained much of the old impulsiveness, the old impatience and, above all, the old arrogance.

A decision to abandon Protestantism for the Catholic religion wavered when he discovered that it was not so simple as merely dropping one creed for another, and that, wisely enough, a preliminary period of instruction was demanded of the convert. For the Catholic Church, whatever its qualities, has never lacked worldly wisdom in dealing with world-weary minds and bodies.

Wilde faltered in his resolve, and for the time gave up toying with any idea of changing his faith.

He served his time and, on May 19th, 1897, was released. Friends met him, and the very considerable balance—to be exact £800—of the £1,000 that had been subscribed by a woman sympathizer on his conviction was handed to him.

He was offered further money by waiting journalists for a brief statement about his prison experiences, but haughtily refused.

On the same day he crossed to Dieppe, an exile for ever, so far as England was concerned. There he began that stumbling, contemptible, piteous descent which forms the ultimate, the completed tragedy of his life. When he had money he squandered it; when he was offered work, he accepted the offer—but did nothing further. The ability to talk brilliantly remained; his health, for some time after his release, was excellent. What had vanished for ever, as at last even his most devoted admirers and friends realized, was the capacity for any kind of sustained mental or moral effort.

He took the name of Sebastian Melmoth — "Sebastian" being suggested by the broad arrows on his prison clothing (today a vanished degradation of the convict), "Melmoth" after a novel called *Melmoth the Wanderer* written by his grand-uncle.

Douglas and he did not meet immediately. It had come to Douglas's knowledge that Wilde did not want to meet him. In a letter which is distinguished for its disarming and touching affection and simplicity, Douglas wrote saying that he had heard that Wilde hated him, but that he had not changed towards Wilde, and that he had remembered and kept to his solemn promise to stick to him through thick and thin, and that he longed to see him again.

Wilde replied that he loved him very much, but that "for the moment" they had better not meet.

Other letters followed. Wilde suggested that Douglas should come to Berneval, not far from Dieppe, where the exile had made a temporary home. Later he cancelled the invitation, owing to the renewed activities, or alleged activities, of Lord Queensberry. When ultimately the two came face to face again, it was at Rouen.

The meeting, Douglas recorded, was a great success. " Poor Oscar " had cried when they met at the station. They walked about all day arm in arm, and were perfectly happy.

Bosie wrote to his adored mother at the end of the year, saying that he still loved and admired Oscar, and thought that he had been infamously treated by ignorant and cruel brutes. He looked upon him as a martyr to progress, associated himself with him in everything, longed to hear of his success and rehabilitation, and gave up nothing and admitted no point against Oscar or himself, separately or jointly.

What master could demand more? What disciple could go further?

But " success and rehabilitation " were to be no more than the vainest dreams during Oscar's lifetime.

The two went to live at the villa Douglas rented at Polsilippo, near Naples. There " The Ballad of Reading Gaol " was written; there Douglas wrote "Triad of the Moon," and another sonnet to Mozart. . . . But, inevitably, arguments arose, and arguments tend to become quarrels. Money problems, also inevitably, obtruded themselves.

Between them, Wilde and Douglas possessed an income of about eleven pounds a week. It should have been sufficient, but was not. Wilde's sojourn in prison was hardly likely to have taught him anything of the art of co-relating income to expenditure. Otherwise life at Naples, with Robert Ross occasionally appearing as a critical third party, seems to have been, on the whole, a leisurely, healing interlude.

No more than an interlude. Lady Queensberry intervened. Wilde's personality had never magnetized her; his influence over Bosie she regarded not with the fanatical fury of her husband, but with the judicious disapproval of a mother who, throughout her long life, was her wayward son's shrewd and tireless guardian angel. She could be firm to the point of ruthlessness on occasion, and she was ruthless now. She came in person to Rome, and from there issued an ultimatum. Bosie was to end the partnership at once, and to join her. The alternative was the age-old threat of cutting off all supplies.

She received unflattering support from Wilde's wife and his wife's friends, who at the same time were urging him to leave Douglas and threatening a similar alternative.

Douglas recognized the inevitable and accepted it. Towards Wilde he behaved with his usual loyalty and generosity. Leaving him in occupation of the Neapolitan villa, he went to Rome, and with the help of his mother raised £200 which he sent to Wilde.

The extent of Wilde's gratitude was epitomized in a letter which he immediately sent to Ross. "As soon as there was no money," he wrote, with a distortion of the truth beyond defence, " Bosie left me."

It is said that one night at Naples he thought of committing suicide, but, believing that the souls of those who did were condemned to haunt the spot for ever, did not.

Wilde drifted back to Paris. Douglas went there, too, settling down in a flat in the fashionable Avenue Kléber. He and Wilde met at intervals.

When, in the autumn of 1899, war in South Africa broke out, Douglas, who knew Colonel Paget, of the famous Paget's Horse, offered his services as a trooper.

The Colonel, however, advised him to join the Duke of Cambridge's Regiment, a "gentlemen's corps," the adjective being derived from the fact that every member was expected to go to the considerable expense of paying for his own equipment. It does not seem to have occurred to him (nor, apparently, did it occur to Colonel Paget) that it would be as well to make sure in advance that the corps would accept him.

He passed the necessary physical tests, and sent a cheque for £250 to cover the cost of his equipment.

The cheque was returned; he was informed that his services were not required. Douglas regarded this as "a deliberate and cowardly insult." He wrote to Lord Arthur Hill, who had raised the corps, telling him exactly what he thought of him; also to the commander-in-chief, the Duke of Cambridge, saying exactly what he thought of both of them. That he might enter some less exclusive corps or proceed to a commission via the ranks was not, of course, to be contemplated.

The reactions of Lord Arthur and the Duke to his letters are unknown. Douglas himself went back to France and spent the £250 on buying a horse.

Douglas's passion for horseracing, either as an owner, or as, in his later years, a backer of other people's horses, ran, like an incongruous thread, throughout the pattern of his life. His luck in earlier days at the gaming table had encouraged his conviction that the gods of Chance were his friends. An occasional visitor at Monte Carlo, he was unfortunate enough to win £80 on the first occasion, with Wilde as his companion, and £200 afterwards when Harris was with him. This, however, was merely the first instalment of his beginner's luck. By the end of four days, when he had to leave for Paris, his winnings had climbed to nearly £1,700.

The luck continued. Within three months his newly purchased horse, a chestnut gelding named Hardi, which had never been placed in a race during the six years of his existence, ran in the Selling Race at Chantilly, won at a canter by two lengths, and followed that up by being dead-heated in a five-furlong race, in spite of the fact that there were eighteen runners and the odds against him were fifty to one.

He bought other horses and ran them in other races; sometimes there were other winnings. Hardi, dear old Hardi, after several victories, ended his career tragically. After bolting five miles while being exercised by an unskilful stable-boy, he injured himself too severely to race again. Fit only for drawing a cab, his inevitable fate if he were sold, his master decided that it would be kinder to have him shot.

The story of the rest of Douglas's career as a race-horse owner is one which consists chiefly of missed opportunities—of horses neglected by men he trusted or who disobeyed instructions; of horses he should have bought and failed to buy, or should have backed and failed to back; of big things missed by bad luck, bad judgment, or sheer stupidity. His racing career in France covered altogether rather less than two years. There were occasional wins, but they did not balance his losses. And though these were far in excess of what his capital justified, he always referred to those years as the happiest in his life.

It was happiness unshared by Wilde, who had a congenital dislike of any form of amusement involving physical exertion. To an acquaintance who asked if he ever played outdoor games Wilde said, " No," and then conscientiously amended the negative: " Why, yes, I did once play a game of dominoes outside a French café." Which is paralleled by Brummel's reply to the friend who asked him if he liked vegetables—" I once ate a pea." Wilde had an additional objection to Douglas's racing. By some distorted logic of his own, he reached the conclusion that any money spent by

Douglas on horses was so much deflected from his own allowance.

An impressive amount has been written concerning the last three years of Wilde's life. Many of the anecdotes current belong to the shadiest type of journalism. His general appearance has been compared with that of a tramp; a down-and-out. Actually, he was always well-dressed and shaved. His immense vitality and an innate sense of his superiority supported him, though at times his face would be swept by anguish and regret when some subject brought back the past, and he would stretch out his arm as though to ward off the phantoms of his destiny.

A pathetic though possibly fictitious story of Wilde appeared in an anonymous series of biographical anecdotes.*

The writer states that in the later nineties he was driving with the Prince of Wales through the streets of Cannes. Suddenly the Prince leant across and spoke to one of his friends, a French Count.

" Tell me," he asked, " who is that stout fellow dawdling by the kiosk over there?"

" That is an Englishman, or rather Irishman, your Royal Highness."

" I thought so. And his name?"

" Oscar Wilde."

" Good God!"

The others in the carriage looked with curiosity at the man who a few years before had lorded it over society, and was now an outcast. The Prince noticed their interest, and begged them not to cut the outcast. He himself leant right out of his carriage, caught Wilde's eye, and removed his hat.

Wilde was either too absorbed or too amazed to return the salute. It may have seemed to him too much

* *The Whispering Gallery; Leaves from a Diplomatist's Diary.* The authorship is now known.

like a dream of the past to be true. Whatever the cause, he stood stock still, staring apathetically after the retreating vehicle.

" Poor devil!" sighed the Prince. " What can one do?" Later, he asked the Count whether it would be possible to get in touch with Wilde without giving the tongue of scandal a chance to wag.

With the most elementary regard for money matters, he should have had no difficulty in living within his means, even if he did no work at all. He received a regular monthly amount from one friend—a Miss Schuster—and other sums from other friends from time to time. " Robbie " Ross undertook to supervise his financial affairs, and faithfully did so.

But Wilde was hopelessly, preposterously extravagant.

The progress downhill became faster and faster.

He planned to write two plays, both Biblical. One was the story of Pharaoh and the captive Jews; the other about Jezebel, the title of which was *Isobel.**

But, without embittering him against society, his tragedy had resulted in the dissolution of that willpower which enabled him to overcome his indolence and turn his thoughts into words.

A fortune-teller had once told him: " I see a very brilliant life for you up to a certain point. Then I see a wall, and beyond that—nothing." Wilde saw nothing either. What really killed him, says Ross, is that he saw no future worth living for.

In his last illness a friend called. Wilde awoke from

---

* After the first trial, when his property was put up to auction to pay his debts, and the house had no one in charge of it, extensive looting took place by invading gangs of hooligans. Among the property stolen was the manuscript of a poetical drama called *A Florentine Tragedy* (produced by the Literary Theatre six years after Wilde's death) and of *The History of Mr. W. H.*, an expanded form of an article, which under the title "A Portrait of Mr. W. H.," had been contributed by Wilde to *Blackwood's Magazine* in July, 1889. Thieves also stole the writing-table of Carlyle, for whom Wilde had a great admiration.

a doze. " I've had an appalling dream," he said. " I thought I was banqueting with the dead."

"And," said the friend, " I am sure you were the life and soul of the party."

The retort might have come from Wilde himself, the Wilde who had once insisted that there ought to be a special form of prayer for baronets.

Wilde died, after an operation for ear trouble, said to have originated in prison, combined with syphilitic conditions which were the direct result of his reckless living, and which the doctors could do no more than mitigate. There was a succession of recoveries and relapses; the end came agonizingly and suddenly on November 30th, 1900, after he had received the last rites of the Roman Catholic Church. He was forty-six, still by present-day standards a young man. The Fates would have been kinder if they had ended it all when he was forty.

Of him has been written :

His immense reputation rests upon the legend of his life, culminating in an immortal scandal, on the fringe of which his wit, his technical skill as a talker and writer, his plays, his novel and his verses form an appropriate embroidery.

The man's life is so theatrical in its development and so sordid in its close that curiosity, still unsatisfied, doubles back upon his writings to excuse a tantalized but half-reluctant interest.

He grossly exaggerated his position among his contemporaries. It is difficult to exaggerate his posthumous fame.

In all his work he was more interested in form than in substance. He wrote no poem that is of any value, though many a verse to indicate the effects to be admired.

An accident derailed him. He came into conflict with the law and was wrecked. But all that was exterior to him, as a beam laid across the rails is exterior to the express it wrecks. That the beam is there says nothing against the perfect adjustment of the express train, its power to make seventy miles an hour.

What about the final judgment on Wilde? The material upon which to assay not his intellectual brilliance, which is indisputable, but his justification for being included among the great is extremely limited. One uniquely dazzling comedy, several other comedies clothed in aged stage inventions, and in which dialogue alternately flashes and sentimentalizes; one poem which posterity is tending to regard with increasing doubt; a handful of fairy-tales; a handful of essays. Upon those collectively he must be judged.

Their paucity, however, or the fact of only one of them reaching the highest standards, need not have mattered. Horace and James Smith wrote *Rejected Addresses* and are secure; Wolfe is remembered for a single poem, Gray for another. On that ground Wilde is secure; *The Importance of Being Earnest* gives him his niche.

But of the rest of his work much is infected with the deadly blight of preciousness. Also much of it dates, as damningly as late Victorian furniture or a late Victorian musical comedy or a late Victorian drawing-room song. His highest honours of all are not literary but verbal. As a conversationalist he was, at his best, superb. The late Lord Grimthorpe, after attending a party which Wilde irradiated by his brilliance until the small hours, said that although he could remember nothing that Oscar said, he exhibited " a play of genial humour over every topic that came up, like sunshine dancing on waves."

At the time of Wilde's death, Douglas was not in France. He had taken rooms in London, and from there had gone to Scotland. A letter from Ross reached him saying that Wilde was ill, but not seriously. A telegram followed, announcing his death. Douglas reached Paris in time to attend the funeral.

The friendship, that friendship that had begun in Tite Street nine years before, and flowered like some exotic orchid whose roots are lost in strange and poisonous soil, was ended. Its withering had, I think, begun when the two parted at Naples. Or perhaps a little sooner. The Oscar that Douglas knew and worshipped changed. There were quarrels, too many of them, too many entirely concerned with money; accusations, recriminations, jealousies. They could be happy together for only a little while.

The *Autobiography* deals very fully, and with the candour which is one of its most intriguing qualities, with the financial relationship existing after the trial and exile of Wilde between him and Douglas, with Frank Harris as a third party. Douglas pays full tribute to the generosity of Harris, who was at that period more than comfortably off and could afford to be generous. On the other hand, Wilde showed an increasing tendency to conduct his affairs with the calculated unscrupulousness of a professional begging-letter writer.

Among the most consistent defenders of Wilde, so far as his life during the brief post-prison years is concerned, was his old friend Robert Harborough Sherard, a journalist of international reputation.

In a fourteen-page brochure, one of a series published in Calvi, Corsica, where he lived in his later years, Sherard destroys by painstaking and entirely convincing evidence the story propagated by Frank Harris of Wilde's systematic swindling of a succession of friends by selling the scenario of Harris's comedy, *Mr. and Mrs. Daventry,* to each in turn. If the statement had been merely made by Harris, and had remained unsupported, the harm done might have been inconsiderable; Harris's own reputation as a consistent liar would have given the libel its proper value. Unfortunately, however, Bernard Shaw accepted it as the truth, and in spite of the efforts of another friend of Sherard's, Mr. Hugh Kingsmill, during a prolonged personal interview, Shaw refused to take any part in nailing Harris's statement as a lie.*

A second brochure deals with the defilement of Wilde's character by statements originally circulated by André Gide and reprinted as factual by Dr. G. J. Renier, a Dutch author, who translated them from the original French into English and embodied them in his life of Wilde.

The statements are not worth repeating here.

After the funeral, Ross suggested that between them they should go through Wilde's manuscripts and letters with reference to their financial possibilities in assisting the two children, Cyril and Vyvyan, left otherwise unprovided for. Douglas refused, though if only out of loyalty to the memory of his dead friend he might well have accepted. He could have afforded to do so.

The death of Lord Queensberry in January, 1900, benefited Douglas to the extent of about £20,000, only £8,000 of which, however, was immediately available.† During the short time that Wilde lived after Queensberry's death, Douglas states that he gave him at least a thousand pounds. Wilde, however, considered that it should have been at least twice that amount.

---

*In a letter to Sherard (see page 304) Douglas, in turn, flatly contradicts this, and says he was actually present at a meeting between Harris and two of the defrauded purchasers.

†Douglas's capital was further reduced by £2,000 which Harris persuaded him to invest in a hotel de luxe. The proposition, as Harris outlined it, was no speculation; the profits were safe and immense. Had Douglas been a little more sceptical and a good deal more businesslike, he would have discovered that there was no hope whatever of immense profits, dependent, as they were, upon roulette and trente-et-quarante tables for which the French Government was alleged to have granted a concession. That concession was non-existent outside Harris's everfertile imagination. So Douglas lost another considerable share of his inheritance.

His refusal to co-operate with Ross was a major mistake in a life in which there were so many mistakes. If he had joined forces with him, he would almost inevitably, in the course of that partnership, have learnt about *De Profundis*.* But apart from his inherent dislike of Ross, the situation from a Douglas point of view would have been insufferable—with a mere picture-dealer not only senior partner, but legally and irremovably in complete command. Leaving Ross to carry on single-handed, he departed for Chantilly, and there, with great gusto and enjoyment, proceeded to dissipate what was left of his inheritance, and, possibly as a concession to his conscience, to write articles for the French papers, *La Mercure* and others. Later he returned to London. He had rooms in Duke Street; at intervals he went to Smedmore, his elder brother's home in Dorset.

That elder brother, Percy, was now ninth Marquess of Queensberry. The "funny little man," whose fun had largely consisted in making the lives of his wife and children a nightmare, and who, as he was dying, spat at his heir, had gone to a world where all sins are either forgiven or punished. Unless the statements made about him are gross exaggerations, there must have been much to forgive. His malevolence seems to have been limitless. To quote a single example. Even after his wife had acceded to his request for a divorce, he would harass her by systematically holding back, half-year by half-year, the money that the court awarded her to keep up her establishment and educate her children. Before his death he disposed of the family property, in order to carry out his oath that not an acre of it should descend to his sons. He had, however, been legally restrained from dissipating the proceeds. The new Marquess inherited over £300,000.

He was a contrast to his unlamented father in many

*See Chapter VII.

ways—recklessly generous, a sportsman, a kindly father, and a consistent friend to his brother. For the wreck he made of his inheritance, an over-sanguine temperament on the one hand, and on the other a congenital inability to take advantage of good luck when it did come his way, were chiefly responsible. Up to the time of his elder brother's tragic death in 1894 he had been a younger son, with no likelihood of succeeding to the Marquisate. The shooting accident at Quantock Lodge completely altered the situation. As direct heir, he found himself able to raise large sums of money on his expectations. The fact that when he did raise them it was at extortionate rates did not trouble the sanguine Douglas temperament.

He left the Navy before he was twenty, and went to America. From thence he migrated to Ceylon to manage a tea plantation; from there, with a son of Lord Southesk, he went to Western Australia, where the great gold rush had just begun. The two staked out claims; Percy, returning to London to dispose of them, found a gold boom in full swing, and netted £20,000 profit.

He was thirty-two. Even after the extortionate loans had been repaid, there remained enough to provide a respectable, if not a magnificent, income. But no fortune, however respectable, can survive the assaults of a born gambler with none of the born gambler's flair. Percy plunged, and continued to plunge. His capital dwindled . . . vanished. His wife and children, whom his father to the last refused to meet, had the bitterness of seeing the head of the House of Douglas reduced to bankruptcy.

He died in 1920, to be succeeded in the title by his eldest son, the present Marquess.

CHAPTER V

MARRIAGE

OLIVE CUSTANCE was the elder daughter of Colonel Frederick Hambledon Custance, C.B., of Weston, Norfolk, formerly of the Grenadier Guards, but during the war in South Africa, from which he had lately returned to England, in command of the Norfolk Regiment. He was a typical officer of the period, with rigid views on most subjects, and an unshakable conviction that those views were right. He was also a rich man, and devoted to his daughter.

She and Douglas had met at a wedding when they were both children, later in London, and later again in Paris. Olive intensified their friendship by Disraeli's tactics; she wrote " as one poet to another " to express her admiration of Bosie's work.*

The two fell in love. Her attitude towards Douglas is indicated by one or two quotations from a letter she wrote just before he left for America. Beginning " My own Boy," it continues: " Last night I dreamed of you and woke to find my pillow wet with tears. . . . Oh, how I miss you! But if I were to write for ever I should never be able to tell you how much I love you."

Nevertheless, up till then no suggestion whatever that they would marry had been raised. There were excellent reasons for this extremely un-Bosie-like

---

*She had developed into a romantic young woman with a penchant for writing verse, several volumes of which appeared. One of these entitled *Opals* had lately been published by John Lane. A passion for those particular stones lasted all her life. She collected them, wore them, and was known as " Opal " by her friends. But in her earliest letters to Douglas he was " Prince " and she " his Page."

prudence. For one thing he had no settled income, and very little of his capital left. He had no profession, and no training which would allow him to enter one within the near future. His sole possessions were, in short, youth and health and personal charm. His title, in England at any rate, was a liability as well as an asset.

But not in the United States. There the balance was very definitely on the credit side. America in those days was the land in which the daughters of millionaires were regarded as the obvious, almost inevitable, partners of impecunious British aristocrats. He set sail for that land of hope. His *Autobiography* deals with this matrimonial excursion possibly facetiously, certainly frankly. During the visit he met, he says, at least three girls who would have been glad of an opportunity of becoming Lady Alfred. One had an income of £20,000 a year.

His cousin, Percy Wyndham, was at the time— Autumn, 1901—serving as Second Secretary to the British Embassy at Washington, and formed a useful social link. Douglas had further assumed that his welcome would be that of any other well-born, well-bred young Englishman, and the American tradition of friendliness and hospitality might be taken for granted. In general, his assumption was correct. But he had overlooked one thing.

Wilde's trial and sentence were still recent; the tragedy of his post-prison days and of his death more recent still. America remembered him—he had taken every step when he visited the country to ensure that he should be remembered—very vividly indeed. It also remembered that this extraordinarily handsome young English lord had been his most intimate friend. Lord Pauncefote, the Ambassador, later to become himself the victim of a diplomatic *gaffe*, left his card at Douglas's hotel; Washington society was punctiliously courteous. But the committee of the exclusive

Yours very truly

Alfred Douglas

Photo   *Elliott & Fry*

AT THIRTY-SIX

Metropolitan Club, of which Wyndham was a member, felt impelled to ask him to justify his action in making Lord Alfred, associate of a notorious and convicted criminal, even a temporary member.

Percy Wyndham retorted that no explanation was called for on behalf of his cousin and guest, who, he added, would in any case hardly be likely to make use of the club's premises after the committee's action.

In the circumstances it was a safe guess. Douglas, who had already reported to Wyndham an additional and verbal insult received from a club member, left Washington and returned to New York.

Olive, meanwhile, continued to write at intervals. It dawned upon the fortune-hunter that, money or no money, she was the only girl who really mattered. The discovery, coupled with the Washington incident and the story as elaborated in the New York Press, suddenly made the American atmosphere intensely unattractive. New York and the Statue of Liberty were no substitute for London and Olive. He took an early boat home.

In London once more, he wrote to Olive asking her to meet him. The letter containing her reply staggered him. During his absence she had become engaged to Douglas's friend, George Montague, who later succeeded his uncle as Earl of Sandwich.

Montague, three or four years Douglas's junior, had been with him at Winchester. Their schooldays had begun a friendship that had continued up to and beyond the Wilde trial. Douglas, indeed, numbered him among " the lot of good fellows " whose attitude remained unaffected by the calamitous repercussions of the debacle.

But the totally unexpected, in the form of politics, intervened. Montague's family decided that it was his duty to stand for Parliament. And standing for Parliament created new values. A candidate must be prepared to be heckled about a good many things, including his friendships. That of a man whose name had been intimately associated with Wilde's was obviously a danger. . . . Douglas had been dropped.

Furiously, the victim had fallen back on the age-old and conventional course of " writing and telling him what he thought of him," and the less conventional course of recording the offence in a sonnet, " The Traitor," which concluded : " I shall know his soul lies in the bosom of Iscariot."*

Now Douglas returned to learn that this ex-friend had annexed the girl he wanted to marry. Events were shaping themselves more and more in line with the plot of a Surrey-side melodrama. He achieved an inter-view with Olive, and the plot proved even more faithful to tradition. During the hero's absence overseas, George, left in the sunshine of the heroine's smile, had made all the hay possible. Olive, very considerably in love with Bosie, though—like him—seeing no chance whatever of marriage, had naturally liked to talk about the absentee to one who had known him from his Winchester days onwards. The ex-friend had been only too willing to oblige. He even imitated Douglas's mannerisms—he was particularly good at imitations. Olive was amused. When, however, he went still further and exhibited Douglas's letters on the broken friendship, she was not amused at all. She despised George Montague's conduct, and had no hesitation in saying so.

George explained and excused. His chief excuse was that he himself loved her, and wanted to marry her. Her mother supported the idea. Finally Olive gave way, and they became engaged.

Douglas's reactions when he heard all this were romantic, prompt and practical. He discovered that

---

*By a superb touch of irony the sonnet, when published, was assumed to refer to Wilde, an error pointed out later in the complete edition of Douglas's poems.

Olive really cared for him; concerning his own feelings there had never been any real doubt. The absence of money seemed, as it has seemed to a million other lovers, a trivial impediment, to be laughed over and ignored. Still maintaining the best tradition, she finally agreed to meet him surreptitiously, marry him by special licence, and go off on a runaway honeymoon. The date on which all this was planned to happen was the following Tuesday, March 14th, 1902. It did happen. The eloping bride-to-be, taking only her personal maid into her confidence and—true Victorian touch!—telling the unsuspicious Mrs. Custance that she was visiting an old governess, slipped out of the Dover Street hotel in which they were staying, carrying nothing more than a small portmanteau by way of luggage.

The bridegroom had a more sympathetic send-off. He had told two members of the family of the plot. One, of course, was his adored mother. She gave him " £200, her fondest blessing, a diamond ring for Olive, and the promise of an allowance," a fairy-godmother combination of wedding gifts. The other confidante was his married sister, Lady Edith Fox-Pitt, who drove with him to the church, St. George's, Hanover Square, in her carriage and pair. His best man was a barrister friend, Cecil Hayes.

The bride arrived punctually; the ceremony was performed, and the couple left for France, after the bride had wired to her mother, breaking the news and telling her that their address for the immediate future would be the Hotel Rastadt, Paris.

There were, as they expected, considerable and violent reactions to the elopement. Colonel Custance, a pukka sahib caught in the double whirlpool of the unexpected and the unconventional, applied to Scotland Yard. The Yard was sympathetic, but with nothing on its records against bride or bridegroom,

could take no steps. Weeks passed. Reluctantly the
Colonel realized that the marriage could not be
annulled, even by the most infuriated parent. He and
Mrs. Custance "accepted" the young couple, and
invited them to visit them at Weston Old Hall. The
honeymoon stage was left behind. The young couple
travelled extensively, visiting Corsica and the Riviera,
returning to London, where their son, Raymond, was
born.

From London the family went to a Wiltshire
home, Lake Farm, between Amesbury and Salisbury.
Mrs. Tennant, née Pamela Wyndham,* Douglas's
cousin, was responsible for their settling here.

The newly-married Douglases were a well-matched
pair. Both were strikingly attractive young people,†
with similar tastes. Both were poets. Bosie, writing
many years after their wedding, gives it as his considered opinion that she had written better poetry than
any other woman of her time, "not excepting Mrs.
Meynell."

His own account of the gradual evolution of their
relationship is detailed, uncompromisingly frank, and
uncomfortably self-revealing. He analyses the whole
thing, beginning with his wife's first adoration of him
because of the feminine rather than masculine traits
he exhibited to the outside world. From the Oxford
days onwards, he adds, he had exercised a tremendous
attraction to people of both sexes, and quotes Wilde
as a case in point. It was precisely because he made no
effort at all to attract Wilde that he became infatuated.

---

*This lady had the unusual distinction of changing her name four
times, being in turn Miss Wyndham, Mrs. Tennant, Lady Tennant (when
her husband succeeded to the baronetcy), Lady Glenconner (when he
was raised to the peerage), and Viscountess Grey of Falloden (on her
second marriage when, six years before her death, she married Lord
Grey of Falloden).

† Olive at the time of her marriage was a slim and beautiful girl—and
Bosie worshipped beauty. But the passing years were unkind; she grew
stout and, with no instinctive understanding of how to compensate for
the ravages of time, lost her claims to Bosie's aesthetic devotion.

While at Oxford, he even suffered greatly from the jealousy of his friends. Each was anxious that Douglas should believe that he was *the* friend, to the exclusion of the others. It was a common experience for him (so common indeed that he used to enjoy ecstasies of secret laughter every time it occurred) for one friend to warn him against other friends. He adds that what kept him away from girls up to this period (1900-02), except in the lower forms of very infrequent casual liaisons, was just that he did not for a moment intend to put up with less love and admiration from a girl that he had been in the habit of getting from innumerable male friends. He was determined " to have nothing but the very *crème de la crème* in the way of marriageable love."

All of which is insufferable enough, though it might have been excused as coming from a vain, utterly spoilt youth. But middle-age should at least have taught Douglas to laugh at such flagrant coxcombry, even if the laugh were wistful and tinged with self-pity. Or at any rate to have omitted it from a biography given to the world a generation later.

The fact is, however, he never really grew up. All his life he remained psychologically and, in his own vision perhaps, physically too, the radiant and brilliant adolescent whom the gods loved. He never realized that such love, like the love of mortals, can grow cold. Perhaps it was as well.

Here, where so many references have been made to Douglas's personality, may be the best place to discuss what the *Autobiography* itself tells us.

All genuinely autobiographical writing is revelatory, often far more than a casual personal interview. One may talk to a man when he chances to be in a mood entirely foreign to his normal outlook on life, and leave with an impression that is not merely superficial, but unjust. But in the writing of a book whose mere execution must have occupied the best part of a year, and which has been subjected to a hundred moments of reconsideration and revision, the real and fundamental qualities of the author emerge.

And, to be honest—and no biography worth reading, let alone buying, is anything else—some of these, in Douglas's case, are qualities to make the hero-worshipper wince. Perhaps the most obvious, because the most fundamental, is an absence of any capacity to see the world, not merely his own, but other people's world, from an objective point of view. His instinctive courtesy, his kindliness, his willingness to interest himself in other people's affairs, only veneered his essential egotism. With that egotism went its frequent companion, an inferiority complex that drove him to self-analysis to reassure himself. He continually recounts his good looks, his astonishing youthfulness, his sensitivity to beauty. He stresses his capacity for writing exquisite poetry, and for criticizing poetry which fell short of his own standards. So much of what is labelled vanity by our enemies is nothing more than a defiant attempt at reassuring our sagging faith in our own values. Douglas, by these standards, was vain; he was also intolerant, not only of adverse criticism but of *any* criticism which assessed anything he wrote at a lower level than his own. Barry Pain, speaking of one of his characters, says: " It was not given to him to see himself as others saw him. He imagined in times of great abasement that there might be a difference in the way people spoke of him and the way they spoke to him, but he never had the slightest idea of how great that difference was." The words, one feels, would not be utterly inapplicable to Douglas.

It requires considerable assurance for any man to state that he suspected he was a great poet when he was twenty-three, and as the years went by, his suspicion became a conviction. At the age of sixty-six, he considered himself entitled to repeat this; not to say it, he insists, would be affectation and a concession to conventional modesty, fortified as he is by a very large and very powerful body of opinion among the best judges of poetry, the plain truth being that scarcely any qualified critic or judge for the last forty years has ever failed to praise him.

Finally he was, by today's standards, aggressively insistent on his social position; there are innumerable allusions to his rank, and his family's eminence, when no stress on either was needed, or even relevant. Great poets are not usually acutely class-conscious.

CHAPTER VI

" THE ACADEMY "

DOUGLAS, in those pleasant if not precisely carefree days of his marriage, records that his father-in-law, a first-class fisherman, taught him fly-fishing; that he came to love the sport as much as shooting, and that he ended by catching the second largest basket of trout ever taken from local waters.

But trout-fishing is no recognized form of income, nor a recognized career for a young and active poet with a wife and son to support. And in 1907 a new chapter in Douglas's life was begun. He became, for the third time, an editor.

The firm of George Newnes was one of the great three (its rivals being those founded by Alfred Harmsworth and C. Arthur Pearson), which fifty years ago began to specialize in magazines catering shrewdly, soundly and successfully for the taste of the middle-class, middle-brow mind. So successfully, indeed, that one of the founders achieved a viscountcy, both the others a baronetcy, and all three fortunes.

But among Newnes's unpretentious publications was an aloof, superior stranger, like a kingfisher among a colony of cheerful sparrows. It was *The Academy,* a " literary " journal catering for highbrows when the term was new and the gulf between them and humbler minds wider than it is today. It lived in Tavistock Street with *Country Life,** and the editor-in-chief of

* " Country Life, Limited," which included *The Academy,* was a separate publishing company under Newnes's control.

168

both journals was Mr. P. Anderson Graham. The acting editor of *The Academy* was Mr. Harold Child.

Mr. Child left to take up a position on *The Times*. Mr. Graham went down to Salisbury to spend a weekend with Sir Edward Tennant and his wife at Wilsford Manor. Lady Tennant (already mentioned), a charming and distinguished Victorian who had contributed charming if not particularly distinguished verse to *The Academy*, had an inspiration. Douglas, also a contributor, and a poet with a reputation, wanted a job. If Mr. Edward Hudson, managing director of *Country Life*, had no particular affection for *The Academy*, or objections to parting with it, why should not her husband buy it, and establish Douglas, with no official superior to cramp his individuality, as editor? Any professional defects there still were could soon be adjusted (oh, optimistic Lady Tennant!) and he would be governed lightly, if governed at all, by a sympathetic proprietor prepared to make every allowance.

Cousin Pamela's inspiration was carried a stage further. There were discussions between the Tennants, further discussions between Sir Edward and Mr. Hudson. *The Academy* changed hands; so did a cheque for £2,000. Douglas became the new editor at what the advertisements call " a commencing salary " of three hundred a year. He afterwards referred to it as a beggarly one, though actually it was more than the great C. A. Pearson was receiving, as an experienced editor, when he left Newnes to form a rival firm on his own account. Douglas, however, did not grumble at the time.

It was a gesture that was generous, well-meaning, everything a gesture should be. It ignored the fact that Douglas was—well, Douglas, with a poet's fine contempt for sordid, businesslike details. Experience apart, the editing of a weekly paper dependent for support upon critical readers who expect value for their money and concessions to their prejudices, as well as upon the advertisers who pay for the opportunities of selling their goods to such readers, is a business matter. For all his brilliance, Douglas was never at heart a journalist, even a journalist whose ambitions are to make a *succès d'estime* rather than a *succès fou* of his journal. He was impatient, intractable, and subject to violent prejudices. The mere breath of adverse criticism exasperated him.

The Academy moved from the premises in Tavistock Street to others in Lincoln's Inn Fields leased from William Robinson, a well-known gardening expert, who maintained a private office of his own on the same floor. The editorial staff was small, not to say microscopic. There was no need for it to be anything else; the work performed was purely editorial. Apart from Douglas himself, it consisted of two. One was Miss Alice Head, still an active and distinguished journalist, but then a girl of about twenty, who had been employed on the old *Academy,* and decided to follow it under its new editor to its new home. She found herself there installed as sub-editor and editor's secretary, in which double capacity she was paid fifty shillings a week, later on increased to three pounds. The other member of the staff was a minute office boy who invariably referred to Douglas as " The Lord." The printing, advertising and distribution side of the paper was entirely in the expert hands of Messrs. W. H. Smith, whose personal representative was Sir Herbert Morgan. The financial side, so far as it affected the proprietor, was looked after by Mr. Fillingham Williams. Douglas does not refer to him with enthusiasm.

The reorganized *Academy* appeared on the face of it to be an ideal field for Douglas's particular talents. He found himself at last with a position in which he both controlled and contributed to an established and dignified publication after his own heart. For a time he did both brilliantly. His own poems alone would have made its issues memorable. But he had, in addition, gathered round him a group of contributors that included Bernard Shaw,* Arthur Machen, James Elroy Flecker, whose tragically short literary life is memorable chiefly for *Hassan,* More Adey, Richard Middleton, a near-genius who died by his own hand, St. John Hankin, Hugh de Selincourt, and Robert Ross, later to be regarded, with others of Douglas's one-time friends, as an arch-enemy.

Douglas's conception of his duties can only be described as lordly. He would usually look in at about eleven, glance through his personal correspondence, go out to lunch, and be seen no more. Press days were an exception. Then he would stay to write a few notes or a poem. If there had been a large staff, such *dolce far niente* control would have been ruinous. But in *The Academy's* academic backwater, with only Miss Head and the minute office boy to sustain the burden of publication, life on the whole was very pleasant.

It is both significant and pathetic to discover how vividly that brief golden age of *The Academy* stands out in the memory of its sub-editor. To her Douglas was invariably charming, and the friendship, which included that of his wife, continued long after the magazine had run its course. There were, inevitably, excitements, disasters, violent upheavals in the office— it would be difficult to imagine any office with Douglas as editor being run like other offices. There were moments of acute financial stringency. There were complaints, which as time went on grew louder and more emphatic, on the part of advertisers, who, since it

---

* In 1908 Douglas, criticizing Shaw's play, *Getting Married,* said that the part that he heard simply teemed with indecencies. Shaw retorted that *The Academy's* critic must have been drunk, and that *The Academy* had risked a libel action with damages of £10,000. Douglas's answer was that he had seen the play himself, and that there had been nothing so unseemly as Shaw's talk about sacking *The Academy's* critic " since Herodias desired the head of John the Baptist " !

is their money that keeps any non-subsidized periodical
on its legs, have some right to a say in what direction
the legs shall wander. Problems of finance obtruded
themselves as ruthlessly as they did in the Micawber
ménage. Douglas's initial salary, as already stated, had
been fixed at three hundred a year. There is no doubt
whatever that it would have been very considerably and
generously increased if, from the normal editorship
point of view, he had justified the appointment by
learning such aspects of his new job as were unconnected with the writing of sonnets or violently
prejudiced articles. But from the beginning he was a
man with a suppressed grievance. He considered his
salary less than half what he should have received,
editorial experience or no editorial experience, and complained that it barely paid his out-of-pocket expenses.

Add to which, Douglas's political, and even religious,
opinions formed bases of future trouble.

Tennant was a Liberal, a brother-in-law of Mr.
Asquith, and M.P. for Salisbury. Douglas was a Conservative of the " diehard " variety (he credits himself
with having invented the word). To the end of his life
he regarded the Liberal Party, as typified in their day
in the persons of Asquith, Lloyd George and Winston
Churchill, as responsible for the destruction of nearly
everything that made life in England worth living.
His opinion of Labour went even further. He was
also a militant High Churchman.

To do Douglas justice, he did warn Tennant that
he intended to attack these enemies of England.
Tennant rashly gave him permission to go ahead,
adding good-naturedly: "A good deal of what you say
I entirely agree with."

This easy-going friendliness, however, was short-
lived. Douglas's attacks on the Prime Minister reached
a stage which goaded Tennant into stigmatizing them
as " in the worst possible taste," and although he after-

wards apologized for the statement, he must have realized that either he or Douglas would have to bring the partnership to an end.

The blow fell. Tennant informed Douglas, formally and finally, that he had decided to cut his losses and dispose of the paper.

Douglas was, of course, enormously indignant. He had held his editorship only about twenty months; the mere idea of dropping it was, in his own words, " utter misery." He writes with a bitterness that disastrously affects his syntax—never his strongest point—and has a Dickensian flavour, of " the casual want of consideration of very rich men in their treatment of the mere man of letters who happens to be his wife's cousin and, according to her own oft-repeated argument, one of the foremost poets of the age."

And the real reason for the change was, he suggests, Tennant's desire for a peerage, which Mr. Asquith was not going to give him so long as he (Tennant) was supplying his wife's cousin with the money to run a paper that was a very real menace to himself and all his most cherished schemes.

Douglas's antagonism to the proprietor and his views was stiffened by the arrival of reinforcements—a single personality, but with a dynamic, not to say demoniac, energy sufficient to justify the use of the plural word.

On the façade of a building at No. 76 Dewsbury Road, Leeds, there is a plaque bearing these words:

Thomas William Hodgson Crosland, Poet and Englishman, was born at King's View on this site, 21st July, 1868, and afterwards lived at Green Bank, Crosland Street. He died 23rd December, 1924, and is buried in St. Mary-le-bone Cemetery, London.

That is how his native city epitomizes the life of the man who perhaps, next to Wilde, most influenced the life of Wilde's most intimate friend.

He was the son of William Crosland, an insurance

agent—and incidentally the first in the city of the Prudential Company's staff—and, in his spare time, Methodist preacher; a genial soul who dressed the part in a round black hat and long black coat, and an umbrella that might have been borrowed straight from Gilbert's *Ruddigore*.

Crosland as a boy was gloomy and taciturn, a real problem-child to his mid-Victorian, conventional parents. Growing up, he became a schoolteacher who wrote verse in his spare time, circumstances highly favourable to the creation of still deeper gloom, even though some of his verses were accepted by local papers, *The Leeds Mercury* and *The Yorkshire Post* among them. He was, to quote his distressed father, " a doubter of religion and of little faith, one who wanted proof for everything." London was the obvious antidote to such comprehensive scepticism, and to London he came. There he obtained a job as a publisher's reader, contributed to a number of weekly magazines, became editor of *The Outlook* and, in 1902, published *The Unspeakable Scot,* a small, paper-covered volume, scarifyingly witty, which is alleged to have been written at a single sitting when Crosland happened to be more than usually hard up, and which most of its readers in the south of England and some in the north found extremely amusing. It ran rapidly through a number of editions, and put its author on the list of ironists to be labelled " dangerous." Later he wrote *Lovely Woman,* dedicated to Mrs. Crosland, to whom he referred as " an exception."

Crosland's career in London was to last for more than thirty years. He has been called " the last of the modern dwellers in Grub Street," and " the last of the Bohemians."* These and similar titles have been given

---

* He carried about with him a card on which was printed:
T. W. H. Crosland, JOBBING POET
Orders executed with the greatest despatch
Terms strictly cash

to a number of other eccentrics, who, deriving direct
from the Goldsmith, Savage and Johnson tradition,
exasperated hardworking editors and publishers by
combining outstanding literary ability with untidiness,
insobriety, unpunctuality, unreliability and a chronic
inability to keep themselves or their families on the
salaries that their brilliance commanded. Crosland, in
addition, was incurably pugnacious. There was, in the
words of a man who knew him, " a tortured spirit
within him that drove him sometimes to heights from
which he could discern real beauty, and sometimes to
depths of bitterness and malice. He exercised his gifts
irregularly. At times he refused to exercise them at all.
He lived precariously, towards the end, in a stupor of
Bohemianism, for which his persistent ill-health may
have been accountable."

One might suggest that " the stupor of Bohemianism " had a good deal to do with his persistent ill-health.

It was said, after his death, that he made three
separate fortunes. It may have been true, but if he did,
he lost them. What is certain is that he died bankrupt
and in comparative poverty, in a flat in Mitcham
Street, just off Edgware Road.† It is also certain that,
while he possessed devoted friends, he exercised to the
end his capacity for making enemies. A poet whose
poems had the quality common enough with near-
geniuses, of soaring at times to true greatness, he had,
says another writer, a keen eye for humbug and
pretentiousness, and was richly—perhaps too richly—
equipped with thoroughgoing prejudice.

Physically, he was an almost grotesque antithesis of
Douglas. Uncouth and untidy, with clothes that com-

---

†To Mr. Sorley Brown's invaluable biography I am indebted for the
correction of the prevalent idea that Crosland lived and died in squalor
and wretchedness. His home was in a working-class locality, but its
rent was £50 a year and it was one—to quote Mr. Brown—" such as
any journalist or literary man might be delighted to occupy." The rooms
were spacious and airy apartments, and he was, to the end, admirably
cared for.

mitted the double crime of being ill-fitting and shabby, and with his hair flapping ferociously over his forehead, he looked, as one critic acidly commented, like an inspired bus-conductor.

If ever there was a man of genius at war with the world, it was T. W. H. Crosland. With consummate literary ability and an original turn of philosophical bitterness, he achieved neither wealth nor happiness.

Beneath his violent prejudices, his turbulent hatreds, the crude and challenging Bohemianism in which he deliberately chose to exhibit himself to the world, Crosland was a poet. He could, when inspiration moved him, write verses that deserved to be included in any anthology. An epitaph upon himself is among them:

> If I should ever be in England's thoughts
>   After I die
> Say " There were many things he might have bought
>   But did not buy.
> Unhonoured by his fellows he grew old
>   And trod the path to Hell
> But there were many things he might have sold
>   And did not sell."

Douglas and he first met personally when a friend named Hannaford Bennett introduced them at a music hall. This was about 1904. Crosland told Douglas that he had been reader to Grant Richards and that it was on his recommendation that Douglas's volume, *The City of the Soul,* had been published by Richards. Some years later he came to see Douglas with a suggestion that he should be allowed to write an introduction to an edition of Douglas's *Sonnets* that was about to be published. His tributes to them were emphatic, and, coming from one who was himself a sonneteer of quality, especially flattering.

He came; he remained an assistant editor at a

salary nominally of seven pounds a week, though
Douglas asserts he never paid Crosland less than ten.
For the next seven or eight years he was Douglas's most
intimate friend.

From the beginning he backed Douglas against the
too-businesslike Tennant. Possibly from conviction,
but far more probably because it suited his pugnacious
temperament, he bolstered up the opposition by
suggesting to Douglas that, so far from being a mere
employee liable to be directed by a *nouveau riche,* he
was the editor of a powerful magazine from the control
of which it would be an extremely difficult job to shift
him, a view, of course, entirely in line with Douglas's
own opinion. That another man of letters—the phrase
that was an impressive, if slightly nebulous, alternative
to " journalist " or even " author "—should take such a
stand made their friendship even closer. It does not
appear to have occurred to Douglas that he was likely
to lose a good deal more than what he termed " his
miserable little salary " if he quarrelled with Tennant,
while Crosland had practically nothing to lose.

Crosland insisted that if Douglas himself conducted
negotiations, the result would inevitably be ignominious failure. In the end he had his way, and
went, though with misgivings on Douglas's part, as
ambassador. His bullying manner, indeed his whole
personality, was guaranteed to make his ambassadorship
a fiasco, and fiasco it was. In the *Autobiography*
Douglas laments his unwisdom in leaving the negotiations to Crosland.

Nevertheless, despite Crosland's defects of manner
and personality, Tennant maintained his reputation for
generosity.* He handed over to Douglas a property

---

* A letter from him, dated August 13th, 1908, is illuminative:
Dear Mr. Crosland,
    In spite of your desire that I should not reply to your letter, I
write to say that I regret that any action of mine or others should
lead you to give up work for *The Academy.* I shall be glad if you

which, according to its editor's own account, was rapidly being converted from one on which there was a deficit of three or four thousand a year to a profit-making concern. For this, it must be remembered, Tennant had paid, only a few months before, £2,000; now it was Douglas's, lock, stock and barrel, plus £500 in cash, Tennant's only stipulation being the not unreasonable one that any further sums required to keep the paper going should come from Douglas's pocket, or at any rate not from his own.

The former employee-editor, now owner-editor, was far from appreciative. For the £500 cash advance he did, admittedly, give a bill. But it was an empty gesture, since, according to his own statement, he had not the remotest intention of meeting it. The default was hardly likely to have come as a shock to Tennant.

Viewing the affair impartially, it is difficult to blame Tennant for ending the situation. He had made an expensive and unsatisfactory experiment; there was every prospect of its becoming more expensive and unsatisfactory still. He was a rich man, but rich men only remain rich by being businesslike, or entrusting their money to businesslike deputies. "Eddie Tennant's *homme d'affaires*" comes in for a blast of Douglas's scorn because he regarded *The Academy* as an unprofitable source of expense, which is what it was. Douglas's own statement is that the enterprise was abandoned just when he was involved in half-a-dozen controversies.

He and Crosland now found themselves in the undisputed possession of a paper of the highest literary

will reconsider your decision, and I have given instructions that payment shall be made weekly.

I admit that much of your criticism upon the management of *The Academy* is true and had I known as much as I know now of the difficulties before I acquired it, I should not have embarked on the venture.

Believe me, yours truly,

EDWARD P. TENNANT.

reputation, its possibilities limited only by their own inhibitions.

These inhibitions, unfortunately, were not limited to Unspeakable Scots and Lovely Women.

The financial history of *The Academy* thereafter is not particularly exhilarating. Douglas's method of dealing with contributors ought to have made it a paying proposition. It had a primitive simplicity which few editors of today would have the hardihood to apply. It was the same method he had used in running *The Spirit Lamp*.

Nothing whatever was paid for contributions. He just wrote to anyone, however distinguished, and asked for a contribution.

Concerning this new partnership, Miss Head comments: " I never could understand why two men of such wholly alien natures should become such close friends. He could not possibly have provided a greater contrast to Lord Alfred's exceptional beauty. Lord Alfred had blue eyes, perfect teeth, a schoolgirl complexion and a smile of infinite charm. . . . He (Crosland) angered me very much by the way he alienated most of Lord Alfred's friends and tried to run the business on dubious lines of his own, but I recognized at all times that he was a poet and writer of peculiar achievement.

" Crosland," Miss Head continues, " was invariably penniless: once when his landlady came to the office to try and get something on account, he presented her with his last book of poems, and shook her warmly by the hand. My sister declares that I once borrowed a pound of her housekeeping money, having lent the last available shilling of my own to Crosland. He influenced Lord Alfred most unwisely, and led him into all sorts of difficulties. Lord Alfred gave me a taste for good literature, and I am everlastingly grateful for his many kindnesses."

Miss Head, incidentally, remained at the offices of
The Academy for only a short time after Crosland's
installation. Life there rapidly became too exciting to
be bearable. Not only was there constant internal
friction; a terrifying succession of bills accumulated
which had to be met whenever there was any money to
meet them, and a still more terrifying succession of
writs which had to be met in any case. And on one
occasion office routine was enlivened by the arrival of
a belligerent bookie so inflamed by his sense of wrong
that it took five people to restrain him from attacking
the editor.

So she returned to the less exhausting atmosphere of
George Newnes Ltd.—and is there to this day, after a
twenty-year interval of working for William Randolph
Hearst.

There are endless stories of the "inspired bus
conductor." One is of the time when he had to take
a cab somewhere or other, and for his own inscrutable
reasons decided that one drawn by a white horse was
imperative. Unfortunately the only cab with a white
horse happened to be the last on the rank. The rank
insisted to a man that customers could not be allowed
to pick and choose, and that cabs must be hired in their
proper order. Crosland met the situation by hiring
every vehicle in the rank, and, preceded by a procession
of cabs, drawn by brown horses, ended it in the one
drawn by the white horse.

On another occasion, having by some fluke a
sovereign for which he had no immediate use, he
changed it into half-crowns and stood on the kerb in
Fleet Street feverishly studying the faces of the passers-
by. "Excuse me," he would inquire at intervals, "but
are you by any chance Doctor William Robertson
Nicoll?" And when the startled pedestrian protested
that he was not: "Thank God!" cried Crosland,
pressing a half-crown into the man's hand.

The most obvious explanation of their partnership, so incomprehensible to Miss Head, appears to be a treble one; their common passion for beauty as expressed in the English language, their inextinguishable sense of their right to say and write exactly what they chose, and a total dissimilarity in every other conceivable direction.

Not that they were always at loggerheads. And Douglas's elation at being completely his own master broke out in spite of his grievance against unappreciative cousins and their *hommes d'affaires*.

A letter to Miss Head, written from 26 Church Row, Hampstead, on December 1st, 1908, reflected this happy freedom. *The Academy,* he reported, was going strong now that he had got it in his own hands. There had been a profit on every number since he took it over. It had " increased enormously in circulation, going up steadily every week." And on the 30th of the same month he wrote to Crosland from his father-in-law's house that the last number of *The Academy* was a splendid one, and that all three of Crosland's articles were " corkers." He had had a lot of shooting, shot seven wild duck, and was very fit and well. A day later, still in Norfolk, he was delighted to hear that Crosland had got the better of Soames Edwards, and added that Tennant had had to climb down all along the line.

Another letter, dated March 5th, 1909, contains a pathetic apology for an exhibition of temper that afternoon. His nerves, explains Douglas, had been on edge; he had had three or four days' serious private trouble of which Crosland knew nothing, and which had nothing to do with Tennant and the rest of them. But " the troubles are all cleared up now." Would Crosland forgive him his ungrateful petulance? The paper was splendid; he thought it the best number they have ever had. The letter is signed, " Ever affectionately yours."

A letter from Percy Wyndham, written from East Knoyle, Salisbury, and dated March 28th, 1910, is of some interest:

" I am glad to see the line you are taking in *The Academy* about the House of Lords. In the rural districts the Lords and their House are popular with all classes. The same may be said of provincial towns if the political nonconformists are excepted, and in these days nearly all nonconformists are advanced radicals. The Lords are popular with the farmers and yeomen, large and small, and the labourers. We had an instance of this the other day at a village in this neighbourhood. A lady, a member of the Women's Imperial League, was addressing a meeting of villagers, agricultural labourers for the most part. In the course of her remarks she alluded to the Veto, but the Veto conveyed nothing to their minds. On its being explained that the Veto meant the destruction of the House of Lords there was a loudly expressed chorus of dissent. This being so, it is obvious that the Lords are popular with large sections of the community, and it would be a mistake for their defenders to adopt a too apologetic tone.

" No doubt the Lords have more than once adumbrated the real and final judgment of the country as expressed at the polls in a remarkable manner, but we want an upper chamber for those occasions when the Commons might persist in a wrong judgment. To countries with a written constitution no legislation is valid which is opposed to the constitution of the country, and the decision whether a proposed law is against the constitution rests not with legislature but with the judges of the Supreme Court, an independent body. The security which a written constitution gives, in countries which do not possess one, can alone be found in an upper chamber founded, if not entirely, on the hereditary principle. It is impossible to exaggerate the gravity of the situation."

Crosland as a sub-editor must have been something to remember, especially when he dictated with "a brandy bottle at which he took swigs in the intervals of flinging his clothes about." As a family man he can hardly have conformed to the Victorian model, but it is interesting to note that his small son, Philip, whom he occasionally brought to the office with him, was one of the most intelligent and well-behaved boys the much-enduring Miss Head had ever met. Philip Crosland lost his life in the 1914-18 war. It is a coincidental tragedy that Wilde's son Cyril and Douglas's nephew and namesake Bruce Douglas were also killed in that war.

After Douglas had edited *The Academy* for about three years there were further financial upheavals and complications. He himself had raised money on his reversionary interest in his mother's estate, and apparently reached the end of his tether, though not the end of his optimism. It was, he complained fiercely, "a scandalous and discreditable thing that not one solitary rich man in England" would back him. If he had been backed, he would easily have turned the corner and made the paper yield a good profit.

Poor Bosie—all his life a victim of the financial obtuseness of business people who persistently made fortunes in other directions!

Once again, the ever-faithful Cousin Pamela intervened. She persuaded Lord Fitzwilliam and Lord Howard de Walden to come to the rescue. When ownership of the paper formally changed hands, Lord Howard de Walden surrendered the two thousand pounds' worth of debentures he had been given in return for an earlier loan of that amount. His loss could not have distressed him greatly. Douglas assures us that they were quite worthless.

In a letter dated July 5th, 1910, Douglas wrote to Crosland, who had been unwell, that he considered the

current *Academy* " too appalling for words," a fact he
demonstrated on three more pages. A blunder about a
barrister's title had produced " howls of laughter in
the Town "; it was all very sickening. . . . When he and
Crosland sold the paper, they had hardly supposed
that it would be made the laughing stock of London.
They really would have done better to have sold it to
Harmsworth or Alfred Mond at once!

The paper, under the editorship of an inexperienced
Mr. Cowper, seems to have satisfied nobody. It
dwindled and drooped, and was eventually offered in a
moribund condition to the I-told-you-so-ing Douglas for
£25.

He refused to buy it and, after a distinguished and
variegated career lasting nearly half a century, *The
Academy* breathed its last.

Its brilliant group of contributors, and the kudos
resulting from that collective brilliance, became a mere
memory. Douglas himself evades any real diagnosis of
its financial failure during his command. It was
not jealousy or animosity on the part of his enemies;
according to his own account, they gave him a wide
berth throughout his three years of editorship and
ownership. The plain fact was that his worst enemy
was none of the people he " attacked with the utmost
frankness and outspokenness," but himself. He was
grossly unbusinesslike and, like nearly all grossly
unbusinesslike people, naïvely vain of his own capacity
for exhibiting business acumen in a crisis. He was
temperamentally unfitted for a job demanding the
unexciting but essential virtues that any successful
editor must cultivate. He abhorred regular hours,
regular duties, regimentation in any form; he saw little
reason to study, and still less to placate, the all-
important advertiser; he attacked and quarrelled with
his contributors; he was eager and prepared to attack
and quarrel with anybody on earth who denied him

entire freedom to do exactly what he chose exactly when and how he chose to do it. This incurable pugnacity was, paradoxically, reinforced by his own cleverness, and his consciousness of being clever. And he was never strong enough to resist the temptation to deflect time and energy from his real vocation to a succession of miserable, frequently petty conflicts, with the Law Courts as the scene of the final battle. While he was constantly leaping down into the dingy, unedifying arenas of Bow Street and Marylebone, he gave the world, his own natural and rightful world, no chance of placing him upon the pedestal for which he was fitted.

Enemy Number Two was, of course, Crosland. In battle, he and Douglas were a complementary couple. They fought with each other—but never with the venom and fury with which they attacked in unison some third opponent. Douglas wielded the rapier, Crosland the bludgeon, though occasionally they exchanged weapons. Guilty people, timid people, people with aversions from attacks that could only be countered with a writ, detested their activities; people with nothing more than a general preference for peace and quietness grew tired of them.

It is possible that Douglas may have grown tired of *The Academy*, that sedate, highly cultured literary spinster whom he embroiled in so many escapades and dragged into so many undignified prancings and gambollings. His partnership with her ended on a note which one feels must have made the old lady shudder. Wyndham had given Douglas £200 to tide him over the weeks that the negotiations occupied; Douglas records that, nevertheless, he could not have held out if he had not gone to Ascot and backed eleven winners in four days, one winner at fourteen to one.

POST-"ACADEMY"

The Academy might come to an end. But Douglas's

career as an editor did not, nor his exhilarating partnership with Crosland.

In 1920 he started *Plain English*. Its backer was a
friend of his brother's named James Conchie, who,
according to the *Autobiography*, had wanted to know
why so clever a fellow as Douglas did nothing, and had
been told that it was because all the papers boycotted
him, and that his only chance would be to get a paper
of his own. It does not appear to have occurred to
Mr. Conchie to ask why the boycotted genius did not
write under another name, or even attempt to make
a living at some other career. Instead he offered to start
a paper for him. Douglas attributes this generosity to
the fact that he had for two or three years been praying
to St. Anthony of Padua for a paper.

The proprietor, at Douglas's (or St. Anthony's)
request, paid £100 for the title of *The Academy* which,
by the issue of a succession of dummies, was still
technically in existence. The new venture, a sixpenny
weekly, was in consequence called *Plain English, with
which is incorporated The Academy*. Douglas found the
new editorship " a pleasing contrast " to his previous
one under Tennant's control, good-natured and easy-
going though the hands that held the reins had been.
Under Mr. Conchie he had, he says, an absolutely free
hand and a salary of £50 a month; to which were added
compliments and congratulations when a particularly
good number appeared. Starting with a circulation of
350, it rose eventually to 3,000.

The assistance of Crosland in this congenial venture
did not begin until a reconciliation on the grand scale
had been effected between them.

In *The Academy* days there had been frequent and
tempestuous quarrels in which both indulged to the
full in their passion for drama. The quarrels
commonly ended by Crosland collapsing with a heart
attack, or what looked like one, and Douglas, tearful

and repentant, restoring him with brandy. In 1914, when Douglas was arrested in connection with libelling Ross,* Crosland had refused to give evidence in his favour. Douglas wrote a letter which for once combined reproach with dignity. It concluded: " I can never feel the same about you again."

Just before the trial began Crosland changed his mind. He would give evidence. But he wanted £50 to give it.

Douglas wrote telling him to go to Hell.

The trial ended in Douglas's acquittal; the two renewed their friendship; Douglas advanced Crosland the money to pay for the printing of a little paper called *The Antidote,* and afterwards congratulated him on the result. " I have never seen anything so well done or so beautifully turned out," Douglas wrote.

His enthusiasm evaporated a few days later when he found out that Crosland had paid only part of the printing bill. He wrote to Crosland, who had added to his offence by attacking Douglas with an abusive letter, that he agreed that it was impossible they should ever be friends again.

To make this doubly sure, he added a typically Bosie-an summary of his ex-colleague's character. Crosland's idea of a friend was someone who would be the patient recipient of his vomited abuse and foul aspersions when he happened to be in one of his dog-like humours.

Crosland was " hereby invited " to go to his own place and find friends among his own class, which seemed to be a class that demanded everything and gave nothing in the way of loyalty. It was, said Douglas, switching irrelevantly to literature, now his sad duty to tell Crosland that he had never written a great sonnet in his life, that his articles were not half as good as he thought they were, and, added Douglas, with a waspish-

*See page 230.

ness in which one can detect a touch of hysteria, that he was a very ill-bred, ill-conditioned and low person, whose vanity was continually leading him into the most ridiculous mistakes, one of which was being idiot enough to suppose that when, last Wednesday, Douglas sent a wire to Crosland's house at Woking he was endeavouring to upset Crosland's wife, whereas (concludes Douglas) he had not even remembered that Crosland had a wife or thought anything about any such person.

The quarrel developed with the inexorable thoroughness of an attack of measles. Douglas, having had from Crosland half the issue— five hundred out of a thousand copies—of *The Antidote,* then proceeded to obtain further copies from the unpaid printers, Lakeman & Tasker, without Crosland's authority or consent. Crosland retaliated by issuing a writ against Douglas. It came to nothing, but the dismal squabble continued. Crosland, still on the warpath, issued another writ, this time a claim for more than he had been paid for his part in writing *Oscar Wilde and Myself.*

Douglas's counter-attack to this was to threaten to issue a writ demanding the return of £50 which Crosland had obtained from him in connection with work he had undertaken to do on a book called *The Wilde Myth* which Douglas was bringing out. That writ, too, was never served, and as the quarrel creaked and clattered towards its close the quarrellers fell back on weapons with which they were both more familiar and more happy. For, after all, if one sonneteer cannot attack another sonneteer with a poem, with what may he attack?

Douglas struck the first blow with a scathing parody of Crosland's " Epitaph," and followed up with a sonnet printed in January, 1918, in *The Irishman,* then edited by Mr. Herbert Moore Pim. It was headed

" The Unspeakable Englishman," and its first line,
" You were a brute and more than half a slave," is a
fair sample of the whole.

Crosland did not rise to such heights; what he did
was, in fact, oddly untypical. He wrote a poem which
he called " The Sonnet Alfred Douglas ought to have
Written," beginning:

" Oh, isn't it annoying Papa! First
Somebody in a rhyme betrayeth one
And then we are betrayed by our own son
Who's just fourteen!"

but did not send it.

The tumult and the shouting died down, and in
July, 1920, Douglas, now editor of *Plain English,* was
able to write to his old friend, Sorley Brown, that he
had got old Crosland as a contributor, and that he had
already contributed articles to the last two issues.

This complete reconciliation—as near complete, that
is, as any reconciliation between two such personalities
was ever likely to be, had followed a long letter from
Douglas to Crosland which was both an explanation
and an apology. It concluded with the disarming statement that Douglas was, and always had been, quite
devoted to Crosland, a fact apparent even in the sonnet
in which he attacked him.

So Crosland returned to the fold. But though the
falling out of faithful friends might mean the renewal
of love, it had also to mean a good deal more. The first
thing Crosland wanted settled was the amount he was
to be paid. Douglas had to make special arrangements
with the appreciative Mr. Conchie to ensure that
Crosland got four pounds per article, payable
immediately on delivery.

Crosland continued to write for *Plain English* for the
sixteen months of its existence. When that existence
under Douglas's editorship came to an end, he went off
and offered to write for the new editor, and did write

for him. It was in Douglas's eyes the last treachery, the culminating and unforgivable crime. And Douglas never saw or spoke to him again.

The complete freedom given him in running *Plain English,* with Crosland always in the blackground to stimulate, to suggest, to accentuate the dash and thrust of Douglas's eternal attacks upon whatever he considered worth attacking led, inevitably, to trouble and yet further trouble. He persuaded Herbert Moore Pim to leave his Irish paper and come over to act as assistant editor, and between them they produced what Douglas described without exaggeration as " a lively sheet." It fought tooth and nail against the compromise with the Sinn Fein Party. As " the only secular Catholic paper published in England since the Reformation " it fought Low Church ordinances. It also expended its energies in showing the public what the Jews in England were doing. . . . And it ended by teaching its editor at least one thing—that there was no place for him in English politics.

After sixteen months *Plain English* was taken out of his hands by what Douglas signalized as an ignoble intrigue. The people responsible were, he says, fatuous enough to imagine that it could be more successfully carried on by another editor. He retorted by starting another paper which he called *Plain Speech.* With the first number he took the ominous if heroic course of telling its purchasers that unless sufficient funds were contributed by them, that first number would be the last. Pim and his chief contributors (but not, of course, Crosland) remained to support the new venture. He also, he says, took with him nearly all the subscribers, so that at the end of a couple of months the new venture had a circulation of two thousand copies a week.

The financial crisis was also overcome " miraculously," to use the editor's word. To initial contributions amounting to £250, Mr. Ernest Brown, " a patriotic merchant in the City," added a regular

weekly donation of £50. The cost of each issue of
Plain Speech was about £75, but the balance he
obtained easily enough.

Ill-health put a premature end to the career of
Douglas's final experiment in journalism. He had
influenza severely, following the exhausting conflicts
involved in transferring his allegiance from *Plain
English* to *Plain Speech*, plus the further strain involved
in his libel action against *The Evening News* for its
defamatory obituary notice concerning a plaintiff who
was neither dead nor, in the opinion of the jury,
deserving of damnation.

He states, in referring to this period, that if he had
not proved that he would have been a valuable asset to
any paper on which he wrote, then nothing could
prove anything. Yet such was the astounding stupidity
of newspaper proprietors and editors that he had hardly
ever been able to get any of them to let him write for them.

He suggested, in 1937, to Lord Beaverbrook, who,
he said, had written to him more than once saying that
he considered him the greatest living English poet, that
he might be allowed to do a few articles for one of his
papers. Lord Beaverbrook replied that if Douglas
would send specimens he would see that they were
considered by *The Evening Standard*. They were sent,
considered, and turned down. Douglas was not at all
surprised, though *The Evening Standard* had always
been most kind and even flattering to him as a poet
and an author.*

---

* For one sonnet alone which the editor particularly liked Douglas had
received twenty-five guineas.

CHAPTER VII

" DE PROFUNDIS "

I HAD originally intended to include *De Profundis* and its implications and reactions under the section headed " The Litigant," since it was in the course of an action against Robert Ross that the significance and the mystery surrounding Wilde's posthumous publication first emerged. The story behind that action is so elaborately melodramatic that it is difficult to understand why it has not yet formed the basis of a stage play.

What personally I regard as Wilde's *tour de force* (apart from his best play) I found altogether too formidable to be treated merely as incidental to a trial for libel. For that reason it is dealt with here as a separate section. The bizarre story has been shrewdly and soundly summarized in a privately printed brochure written by Mr. Frederick Peters, to whom I am greatly indebted. The brochure has appeared since Douglas's death.

The inception of the actual writing of what Wilde himself called *Epistola, in Carcere et Vinculis,* for which the simpler, and far more effective, title of *De Profundis* was substituted by Robert Ross, took place while Wilde was serving his two years' sentence in Reading Gaol. The whole manuscript was contained in eighty closely written folio pages of about a thousand words each. In simple terms, it ran to the length of an average novel. When it was finished, Wilde apparently intended to dispatch it to Ross, who was living in Paris. At the same time, he wrote a separate letter of instructions, dated April 1st, 1897.

Those instructions were explicit and to the point. When he had read the manuscript, Ross was to have it typed, so that several copies—one assumes he meant carbon copies—could be made. " I assure you," said Wilde, Wilde-ishly, "that the typewriting machine, when played with expression, is not more annoying than the piano when played by a sister or near relation." In the same letter Ross was formally nominated as Wilde's literary executor, in full control of all his works for the benefit of the two children. In that capacity " you must be in possession of the only document that gives any explanation of my extraordinary behaviour. . . . When you have read the letter, you will see the psychological explanation of a course of conduct that from the outside seems a combination of absolute idiocy with vulgar bravado." Some day, Wilde concluded, the truth would have to be known, but not necessarily during his lifetime.

In point of fact, Wilde did not dispatch either manuscript or letter. He discussed them with Harris when he came to see him just before his release, and said, according to Harris, whose capacity for picturesque flights of imagination should always be borne in mind : " I am breaking with the past altogether. I am going to write the history of it. I am going to tell how I was tempted and fell, how I was pushed by the man I loved into that dreadful quarrel of his . . . and then left to suffer alone." And Harris continues : " He attributes his ruin solely to him, and did not hesitate to speak of him as Judas." (Douglas himself says in his " Summing Up " that he had been informed that at this time Wilde had turned against him, and did not wish to see him again.) Not even then, but at some time between the date of his release, May 19th,* and early in June did

* Ross says it was actually on that day.

De Profundis actually change hands. Before the latter date Wilde had left England, never to return. He arrived at Dieppe accompanied by Ross and another friend, Reggie Turner, and later settled for a time at Berneval, near that town. On June 15th he wrote from there to his executor. " Dear Robbie, You never told me anything about the typewriter or my letter; pray let there be no further conspiracies. I feel apprehensive." He added, with yet a further touch of the old epigrammatic Wilde: " It is only by people writing to me the worst that I can know the best."

What, if anything, *did* Ross tell him? There is no answer. What is certain is that the Machiavellian Douglas had already reappeared as a character in Wilde's continuous dramatization of life. The two had had no communication, or at any rate no direct communication, after the first eight months of Wilde's imprisonment. So far as he was concerned, Wilde had been left to spend the remainder of his sentence alone.

I have a feeling that in that isolation he found his way to heights and depths unexplored before. Apart from the isolation, prison life, with its absence of all the physical luxuries and social amenities that he had valued so highly, all the cultural contacts that had been the breath of life to him, contributed clarity of thought and a sense of perspective to the writer of *De Profundis*.

I have been privileged to see the *whole* of the suppressed portion. Let me say at once that I regard the unfortunate Bosie's statements on the extracts from that portion—and damning as they were, they represented no more than extracts—as the sheerest example of hysterical exasperation coupled with wishful thinking.

He refers to them as a dreadful piece of cold-blooded malice, lying and hypocrisy. . . . As the ravings of a lunatic, a man driven by impotent rage and malice and malevolent desire to injure a friend . . . with whom he resumed friendly relations when he got out of prison.

The portion read at the Ransome trial occupied nearly four hundred lines in *The Times*. But only about a hundred lines of those, or approximately a quarter, contained definite charges, provable or non-provable, against Douglas. The remaining three-quarters consist almost entirely of an analysis, a deadly dissection, of Douglas's character, the sort of analysis that a bitterly disillusioned father might apply to a son who had falsified every hope centred in his career. "Cold-blooded"? Yes. "Malignant"? Again, yes, if the object were to blacken for ever his friend's character. But, unfortunately, far from wholly untrue where that friend's personal character was concerned.

Perhaps, on re-reading those damningly direct accusations, those polished, plausible sentences, those charges against Douglas so convincingly paralleled by Wilde's charges against himself, one may feel that the old Wilde verbal hypnotism may be functioning, that he is holding up a distorting mirror. But it is quite certainly not "the ravings of a lunatic"; it is far too cogent and too calculated in its effect to have come from any madman's pen; it is a sustained, and in parts an extremely moving, narrative, told in prose which shows that Wilde's command of the English language had not deserted him.

He had no doubt that there would be much in the letter that would wound Douglas's vanity to the quick. If that proved so, let him read the letter over and over again till it killed his vanity. . . . Douglas's defeat was not that he knew so little about life, but that he knew so much, passing with swift and running feet from romance to realism. The gutter and the things that live in it had begun to fascinate him. . . . The real fool, such as the gods mock or mar, was he who did not know himself. Douglas had been such a one too long. Let him be so no more. The supreme vice was shallowness. . . .

This is the counsel of disillusion, not of illusion.

Wilde's flagellation of his friend has resulted in a chorus of condemnation from less frantically biased critics. Shaw, apparently referring to the complete book, describes it as "amazingly undignified." Mr. Peters, in his brochure, says that the suppressed passages "consist entirely of a bitter and quarrelsome string of accusations against Douglas." Mr. Hesketh Pearson calls the book "an extraordinary document, in which the tortured imagination of a man in duress exaggerated trifling incidents into momentous events."

Again I venture, with all humility, to differ.

My own contention is that Wilde was far saner and clearer-headed than he had ever been during the days of their intimacy. Apart from the logical balance of its composition, the sheer length of the book as a single essay—or, technically speaking, a letter, since it was actually begun "Dear Bosie," and concluded with the author's signature—is a tribute to the mental powers of the author. Eighty thousand words, even of the most rambling composition, demands both concentration and consistently sustained effort utterly beyond the powers of an unbalanced mind.

But I agree with Mr. Peters in one thing. The cutting out and joining up process which resulted in the book with which all the world is familiar was most expertly done by Ross.

When the whole of it is read as a consecutive narrative one realizes how its triple theme is woven into one. Firstly, the book sets out brilliantly to give a tabulated and logical record of Douglas's behaviour while he and Wilde were together. Pepys's confessions of his peccadilloes are not more convincing than Wilde's stories of Douglas's petulant and disastrous interferences and disruptions, while no modern accountant could be more detailed and exact concerning their money transactions. If his allegations, financial and

otherwise, against Douglas are false, Wilde stands as one
of the most superb liars of all time.

Secondly, supporting these details, there is Wilde's
analysis of Douglas's character. Again, one feels that,
if not the exact truth, it is damningly near to the truth.
It might not have been beyond the powers of Frank
Harris to invent those stories of discussions with Lady
Queensberry and others about Bosie's failings, but
coming from Wilde it is impossible to believe that they
are entirely fictitious. Thirdly, permeating the whole,
there is Wilde's personal philosophy with its imprisonment modifications, and including the purple patches
which moved the critics of a generation ago to so much
praise and pity.

The receipt by Ross of the manuscript and its
accompanying letter marked the beginning of what has
become known as the " De Profundis Mystery," and
one that may eventually achieve the dignity of being
bracketed with the unfinished portion of Edwin Drood
or the authorship of The Letters of Junius. For my
own part, I regard its problems as belonging to the
region of psychology rather than of plain fact.

Though Wilde's prison life may have had a definitely
disintegrating, though delayed, effect on his capacity to
work, it certainly had no obvious physical or mental
effects. In other words, he emerged from prison sane
and fit. And still sane and fit, he later went out to
France, and there joined up with Ross.

At the same time he began writing to Douglas again.
In June alone there were eight letters, breathing the
same pre-prison-days' affection. The last letter of the
series is typical. Now things were different; Douglas
really could create in him that energy and joyous power
on which art depends. . . . " Do remake my ruined life
for me," concludes Wilde. These letters the recipient,
hard-up as usual, subsequently sold for £350 to Bernard
Quaritch, a London book dealer with an international

reputation. Douglas stated that he was in complete ignorance of the manuscript, still unpublished and never even alluded to by Wilde when, soon after, the letters, with their perfervid appeal, had led to an ostensibly complete reconciliation.*

And this brings us to the real heart of the mystery. Had Wilde expunged entirely all memory of those pages in which he had blackened with such deadly effect the character of his closest friend? It seems beyond credulity. But if when they were once more together and the old Bosie magic was working its own spell, he *did* remember, what moral paralysis prevented his asking Ross to return the manuscript, or, alternatively, telling Douglas on the one hand that it had been written, and Ross on the other that Wilde's outlook, his feelings towards Douglas, were now so changed that it must be destroyed? . . . Or—a more subtle possibility —did he, remembering, put the whole thing away in his mind as an insurance heavy enough to neutralize any action against himself that Douglas, unpredictable, loved but not wholly trusted, might make at some future date?

Finally, did he succumb to the reluctance of the creator who is also the complete egotist to destroy any work which he regards as an artistic triumph?

It is all guesswork, and futile guesswork at that. What is beyond argument is that between the autumn of 1897 and Wilde's death in the spring of 1900 he and Douglas continued to meet, to part, to meet again, with the patient, watchful, prudent Robbie ever in the background, the Robbie whom Wilde liked and trusted so completely, and between whom and Douglas there was eternally smouldering jealousy and mistrust.

---

*Ross, on the contrary has stated categorically, in his own copy of *De Profundis*, that Douglas received a copy of the MS. on August 9th, 1897, and that Douglas's own letter to himself and George Newnes confirmed this.

Five years after Wilde's death, Ross, urged by Dr. Max Meyerfeld, translator of Wilde's works into German, published the linked-up extracts which the world knows as *De Profundis*. How did Meyerfeld become aware of its existence in any form? Ross's explanation seems the only one. In an introduction he states that the manuscript was known to be in his possession, " the author having mentioned its existence to many other friends."

Whether the friends did or did not include Douglas, it is indisputable that he actually reviewed it in *The Candid Friend*.

Soon afterwards Ross took a remarkable step. He formally presented the original manuscript, including the suppressed portion, to the British Museum, under the special condition that it was not to be available to the public before 1960, a date remote enough to make reasonably certain that none of those referred to in the book would be still living.

The Museum accepted both the manuscript and the condition.

Douglas's reactions when he heard what had happened were, as might have been expected, explosive. He contended that since the manuscript was actually a letter addressed to himself, it was his personal property. So it would have been—if it had been delivered to him by the postman or anyone else, though the *copyright* of the contents would have remained in the possession of the writer, or, if he were dead, his literary executor, in this case, of course, Ross. What Douglas conveniently ignored or forgot in the course of his ineffective attempts to recover it, was that no letter is owned by the addressee unless and until he actually receives it—and Douglas never heard of, still less received, *De Profundis*. Ross was absolutely within his rights in making the gift.

For the rest, it was stated years later by Bovis Brasol,

one of Wilde's many biographers, that " it would seem
that Wilde had given full instructions with regard to
those parts . . . he wished published, but that he allowed
his friend absolute discretion." " Would seem " is
scarcely evidence. But that Ross had legal right in his
capacity as literary executor there is no doubt at all.

Scene Two of the drama begins seven or eight years
later, when Arthur Ransome, a young journalist of
promise, who had once unsuccessfully visited the offices
of *The Academy* in search of a job, was inspired with
the idea of writing a life of Wilde. He mentioned this
to a friend, Christopher Millard, then secretary to
Ross; Millard referred him to Ross as an obviously
ideal source of information. Ross, in turn approached,
proved extremely helpful; he also showed an unfavourable bias where Douglas was concerned, which was
hardly surprising. So much bias, in fact, that Douglas,
following the book's publication, in complete ignorance
of Ross's reserve ammunition, brought an action for
libel.

Then, just before the case was heard, Ransome's
counsel produced, as he was legally bound to do, the
documents upon which the defendant's plea of justification was based. And among these was a copy of the
suppressed half of *De Profundis*. Therein Douglas
read again Wilde's terrifyingly lucid and plausible
account not merely of the progress and deterioration of
their friendship, but of Wilde's personal opinion of
Douglas's own character. And while Douglas might
have derived some consolation from statements,
financial and otherwise, which he knew and could
prove to be the sheerest invention, what the dead man
thought of him, and so piteously and logically set down
on paper, was beyond dismissal. Futile to pretend that
what Wilde had said about him had no more weight
than the ravings of a lunatic. Futile to stress Wilde's
wickedness and ingratitude. Those statements stood

for all time as a considered opinion, uttered in a voice from the grave, beyond effective contradiction; beyond legal, or even illegal, action, unchallengeable and final.

The shock to Douglas, always supersensitive to the faintest breath of adverse criticism, must have been terrific, shattering.

But if Wilde was beyond his reach, the others implicated were not. Ransome, nominally the defendant, young and inexperienced, was one; Ross was the other, the " Robbie " for whom there were literally insufficient words in Douglas's vocabulary of vituperation. Whatever the upshot of the libel action, Ross to the end of his life remained in Douglas's eyes the incarnation of villainy.

The remainder of the history of the Manuscript, in so far as it affects Douglas, belongs to the Ransome trial and is recorded under that section, as already stated. Some, though not all, of the suppressed portions were read in court as part of the plea of justification. That public humiliation, to which there was no anodyne, was a blow to his self-esteem mortal beyond recovery.

Yet he made an attempt to neutralize it. As a sequel to the action Douglas planned to include in his *Oscar Wilde and Myself,* written by him and Crosland in that same year (1913), certain passages from the suppressed portion. Ross, still entirely within his legal rights, was swift to check this infringement, and obtained an injunction against Douglas and his publishers, John Long Ltd. He went further. To ensure the copyright being secured also in the United States, he sent over a typewritten copy, and arranged for what was entitled *The Suppressed Portions of " De Profundis "* to be published there. But the entire edition was limited to fifteen copies. Two of these were deposited in the Library of Congress at Washington, a third was given to Sir Edmund Gosse, a fourth to Sir George Lewis. None of these were placed on sale to the public. Since the death of Ross in 1918, however, copies have occasionally come on the market, and it is upon the text of one of these, now in the hands of a private collector, that this chapter has been based.

CHAPTER VIII

THE LITIGANT

"WHAT songs the Syrens sang," observed Sir
Thomas Browne, "or what name Achilles
assumed when he hid himself among women, though
puzzling questions, are not beyond all conjecture."

Had he lived three centuries later, he might have
included in his list of problems the number of legal
actions in which Douglas was involved in the years 1910
to 1923. But here I have grouped some of the principal
cases.* Most of them are referred to in the *Autobiography*, but with a brevity which assumes considerable additional knowledge on the part of the
reader. They are also coloured with a bias which one
might expect in any case, and a vehemence which one
would certainly expect from a narrator of Douglas's
temperament.

The accounts given here are drawn from a number
of sources, but in the main from the reports in *The
Times*, a fact which has the double advantage of a
guarantee of dispassionate accuracy and of placing them
in their contemporary atmosphere.

One of the chief reasons for his constant preoccupa-
tion with the law is stated with complete, startling and
distressing candour by Douglas himself. The sums of
money he got in the way of compensation from people
who libelled him were for a long time in a small way

*The first two cases should, chronologically speaking, have been
included in the previous chapter. But it has seemed to me more fitting
for them to be among their legally comparable companions.

quite a source of income.* Legal actions were, as he was
certainly to discover, gambles. But the fact was an
incentive rather than the reverse. He and his most
formidable allies, Wilde first, Crosland later, were all
fundamentally gamblers. Douglas had a passion for
horse racing and for the breathless excitement of Monte
Carlo which neither of the others shared to the same
extent; Crosland, in any case, had never sufficient
capital to venture much. But the gambling for which
all three had a passion took the form of verbal
or written attack, delivered on every conceivable
occasion upon any enemy who stood a sporting
chance of being profitably defeated, using the
word " profit " in its widest, most comprehensive,
sense.

It was unfortunate for them that the enemy
triumphed so frequently. In Douglas's case, the fact
that he made a point of concentrating upon the big
people, although it might make him sure of obtaining
costs and damages if he won, was at the same time a
heavy handicap. The big people could afford to
employ, and did consistently employ, legal advisers of
the front rank, solicitors of the eminence of Lewis
& Lewis, and Charles Russell; counsel like Edward
Carson and F. E. Smith and James Campbell.
Douglas, perpetually short of money from the
Wilde trial onwards, was more restricted in his
choice.

It is pathetically significant that, despite their
fearlessness, their brilliant abilities, the help of the
devoted friends who were eternally coming to the
rescue, and, in the case of Wilde and Douglas, of
personal charm bordering upon the hypnotic, all three
died bankrupt, Crosland in health as well as finance,
Wilde in reputation as well.

Douglas was not a good loser where his libel actions

* Autobiography, page 238.

were concerned. He continued his feuds in books and pamphlets with unslackened vigour and virulence. It has been said that "A man with a grievance is a man damned." Douglas carried on his grievances with a persistence that may fairly be termed damnable.

1. *Versus* THE HON. FREDERICK WALPOLE MANNERS-SUTTON

From the seas of trouble in which *The Academy* spent much of its life two particularly high waves rose above the general level.

The first was known as the Manners-Sutton Libel Case.

The story, if one studies it in the columns of contemporary newspapers, forms a startling reminder of how far the Press of this country has travelled along the road of dignity and restraint in the course of the past generation.

On February 10th, 1910, Crosland was charged before the Common Serjeant, Sir F. A. Bosanquet, at the Central Criminal Court, with " having written and published a false, scandalous and defamatory libel of and concerning the Honourable Henry Frederick Walpole Manners-Sutton."

Mr. (later Sir) Edward Marshall Hall, Mr. George Elliott, K.C., and Mr. Storry Deans appeared for the prosecution; Mr. Valetta and Mr. Wing defended.

Marshall Hall's claim to real greatness has been frequently disputed, notably by Douglas himself. His enemies have suggested that he was little more than a combination of Sir Henry Irving at his worst and Serjeant Buzfuz at his best, and that his imposing presence and emotional rhetoric camouflaged intellectual mediocrity.

After an elaborate prologue he outlined the case

against Crosland, passing from a summary of the defendant's career to the possibilities open to him in fighting the immediate action.

" In the course of the case," hinted counsel sombrely, " it may be that the jury will be of the opinion that one, if not two other people ought to be standing side by side with Mr. Crosland in the position he now occupies "—a difficult feat to perform in any circumstances! Marshall Hall, thereafter abandoning his unfortunate mixture of metaphorical and literal English, came down to the plain facts.

His client, he explained, had made the acquaintance of Lord Alfred " by reason of the fact that the latter had married a lady with whom Mr. Manners-Sutton had been acquainted for many years "—in other words, Miss Olive Custance. He had been asked to be godfather to Lord Alfred's child. Two years previously, when Douglas had become editor and Crosland assistant editor of *The Academy,* and the two of them the only directors of the private limited company into which it had been formed, Manners-Sutton had mentioned that if ever they were short of money he might find someone to advance some.

In June, 1909, that fairly predictable state of affairs arose, and Crosland, as a delegate from Douglas, went down to Norwich to see Manners-Sutton and to ask for a loan of £500. The request was turned down. Crosland then tried to borrow £150. That, too, was turned down, Manners-Sutton contending that Bosie was drawing £15 a week as editor from the paper, that such a salary was excessive, and that he was not prepared to advance any money whatever unless and until the amount was reduced.

Crosland thereupon returned to London.

The editor's rejection of any suggestion of reducing his salary was immediate, his reaction typical. In a letter to Manners-Sutton, produced and read in

court, he began by referring to his temporary shortage
of funds and Crosland's futile attempt to raise them, and
proceeded, more in anger than in sorrow, from reproof
to abuse. The proposal, said Douglas, was a purely
business matter with ample security. Any Jew money-
lender would have regarded it as serious, and the only
reason Manners-Sutton had been appealed to was that
Douglas had believed " for the hundredth time " that
he had misjudged him, and that when it came to the
point he (Manners-Sutton) would be glad to have
an opportunity of proving that he was Douglas's
friend.

The letter passed swiftly from the plaintive to the
outraged, and thence to the haughty. Had Manners-
Sutton merely declined, with proper expressions of
regret, Douglas would have been surprised but not
annoyed. As it was, he not only absolutely declined to
stir a finger to assist him, but accompanied the refusal
" with gross impudence and brutal insolence."
(Manners-Sutton stated himself in court that he parted
from Crosland on perfectly friendly terms.) Douglas
had had no difficulty in arranging the matter in
another quarter, but was nevertheless glad that he had
applied to Manners-Sutton first, because he " thereby
acquired absolutely reliable evidence " as to the real
nature of Manners-Sutton's friendship. In the result,
says Douglas, indignation working havoc with his
syntax, " I find myself unable to muster up a sufficient
admiration for the latter to induce me to give you
further opportunities for continuing your manifesta-
tions of the former."

The letter descends from these heights to " Consequently I beg to inform you that neither I nor Olive
will ever speak to you again, and that I forbid you to
come to this house. Furthermore, I will tell you quite
plainly that I consider you to be a low, huckstering,
Jew-minded pimp."

And the letter began " Dear Manners-Sutton "—but the signature was merely "Alfred Douglas."

The recipient does not seem to have worried unduly, regarding the letter as merely a shot-across-the-bows affair.

Three days after it had been written, an article in *The Academy* appeared dealing with the affairs of four closely related firms of publishers, two of whom issued " fairly naughty or foolish books," and declared fat dividends, while the other two " hold up hands of pious horror at the bare idea of naughty books, and are entirely for religion and the world well lost." The article concluded: " We have a certain number of striking facts at our disposal with reference to this matter, but we will forbear for the time being."

Such forbearance did not last long; no longer, indeed, than until next week's issue of the paper. The attack, then renewed, became not only more vitriolic, but more personal.

"A certain scion of a noble house," it commented, " who in the intervals of exercising his feudal propensities is not above turning a humble penny, has apparently come to the conclusion that in Mr. Stead's exploded scheme there may possibly yet be money." (This referred to Stead's suggested " Union of the Churches.") Consequently it appears that we are threatened with the appearance of a newspaper entitled, if we mistake not, *The Reunion Magazine.*

" The bright young man is connected with two publishing firms which carry on two very different classes of business, for while one firm, of which he is the principal shareholder, is engaged in publishing various works and translations of various Christian liturgies, the other has gone in chiefly for dubious stories of a highly spiced character and anything else that will bring grist to the mill without actually compelling the intervention of the police."

The names of the firms were "withheld for the moment," but there were threats of reverting to the matter on a future occasion.

At this stage Mr. Manners-Sutton came to the fairly obvious conclusion that a Crosland-organized, Douglas-supported vendetta was under way. To anyone knowing anything about it, the paragraphs referred, and could only refer, to himself, he being a director of a publishing firm with religious proclivities, and in addition a shareholder in another firm that was making a good deal of money out of what was coyly referred to in those days as "naughty" stories.

He instructed his secretary to write to *The Academy*. The letter could hardly have been unexpected. Indeed, it was probably welcomed. Its tone was moderate enough. It merely asked that a notice should be inserted in the next issue of *The Academy*, stating that Manners-Sutton was not the gentleman referred to, and that further attacks should cease.

Crosland's reply was extraordinary.

He said: " I am in receipt of your letter of the 23rd instant in which you request us to state that Mr. A. E. Manning Foster is not the gentleman referred to. If you will be good enough to refer again to the paragraph, you will see that the only personal reference is to ' a certain scion of a noble house.' We have yet to learn that Mr. Manning Foster is the scion of a noble house. Consequently, when we give him the advertisement for which you ask it will be at our own time and without reference to your request. If your client desires to issue a writ upon us, we shall be pleased to receive it."

The reply continued: " I have also to acknowledge receipt of further letter of yours dated June 23. In this letter you say that a paragraph appeared in *The*

Academy of June 12 which is a libel upon the Hon.
Freddie Manners-Sutton. I am not concerned to give
the names of the persons to whom the paragraph in
question refers, and if your client chooses to apply what
we have said to himself, he is welcome. . . . We do not
propose to oblige you by stating that Mr. Manners-
Sutton is not the gentleman referred to. Rather, at our
own time and when we have completed our investi-
gations, we shall be disposed to say that he is the
gentleman. With regard to the action you threaten, we
have only to remark that in our view Mr. Manners-
Sutton is a person whom it would be difficult for
reasonable people to libel. At the same time, if he
wishes to make a fool of himself we shall be quite
pleased to receive his writ." The letter was signed by
Crosland as Director of the Welsford Press Limited.

Thus, in a blend of the first person singular and the
first person plural, pomposity, would-be cleverness and
bad composition, Crosland issued his challenge.

Manners-Sutton accepted it. No other course was
possible. A summons for criminal libel was issued. The
matter came before Sir Albert de Rutzen at Bow Street,
Crosland being represented by Arthur Newton, a
solicitor whose own career was to reach a spectacular
culmination. De Rutzen suggested an apology and a
withdrawal. As this was in effect precisely what
Manners-Sutton had already asked for, his own solicitors
agreed.

There the matter might have ended. But beside the
glowering " inspired bus conductor " there sat the slim,
youthful exquisite to whom any compromise, to say
nothing of public apology, was anathema.

Douglas, in a loud voice, cried : " Justify, justify up
to the hilt. Take him to the Old Bailey ! "

The result of that dramatic outburst was inevitable.
Any suggestion that an apology would meet the case
was abandoned on the spot.

The next step was Crosland's plea of justification. He supported that plea by dragging up from the past— a past in which Douglas and Newton had both appeared —what Marshall Hall referred to as " a certain incident."

It was an incident that had occurred five years earlier, and was unoriginal, sordid, and of the type charitably classified as " sowing one's wild oats." Manners-Sutton, who even then had known Douglas, had published one of Douglas's poems; the publication had led to litigation, and, at the author's suggestion, Newton had been consulted. That was in 1904. In the following year, according to the statement of counsel, Lord Alfred had introduced his friend Manners-Sutton to a foreigner who occupied a flat in the neighbourhood of Buckingham Gate, a flat which was, in plain English, a brothel. Two visits were paid there; on the first of these Douglas accompanied him; on the second he went alone, met a girl, and paid both her and the foreigner money.

The sequel was the appearance of a private detective, who said he had been set on Manners-Sutton's trail by the girl's father. Later the father, or alleged father, turned up in person with a claim for heavy damages on the girl's behalf, asserting that she was under twenty-one and that Manners-Sutton had ruined her character —the stalest of stale old plots. It was highly improbable that she was under age, equally improbable that he was her father, and practically certain that she had no character to ruin. But the callow victim was terrified, as terrified as the foreign gentleman, whose name was afterwards given as Baudemont, Boudemont or Beaudemont, nobody seemed very sure which, could in his most optimistic moments have expected. Manners-Sutton's first act was the very natural one of calling on Douglas, the friend responsible for the original visit. Ignoring his reproaches, Douglas pointed out that a claim was being made which, if not met, would inevitably lead to an action into which he, as well as Manners-Sutton, would inevitably be dragged. He added that he had already had sufficient scandal in his life, and that if Manners-Sutton wouldn't consider himself, he might at any rate consider his friends. Douglas advised a consultation with a solicitor, i.e. Arthur Newton. To Newton they went accordingly. He heard the story, and took an extremely gloomy view of the situation. If Manners-Sutton wanted to avoid hopelessly blasting his own reputation and the consequent reaction on his father, the ailing Lord Canterbury—and Mr. Manners-Sutton emphatically did—there was nothing for it but to pay up. This the victim of this grimy late-Victorian melodrama ultimately did, £1,000 damages to the father and daughter, with another £200 by way of costs.

Incidentally, the girl herself, " known as " Maggie Dupont, conveniently disappeared and, when *The Academy* case came into court, was alleged to be untraceable.

All this was told in the Old Bailey by Marshall Hall, Manners-Sutton's counsel.

Cross-examined by Mr. Valetta, the plaintiff stood by the accuracy of his evidence. Replying to counsel's " suggestion," he swore that he had never seen the girl since his second visit. . . . He and Lord Alfred Douglas had remained on terms of friendship up to the time when he had refused to advance the £500, subsequently reduced by Crosland to a mere hundred and fifty, to finance *The Academy*. References were made to two " naughty " books published by Greening & Co., the firm in which Manners-Sutton held shares, and to the other firm—Cope & Fenwick—of which he was a director.

There were further references to an even earlier scandal, the plot of which included a German baron, a game called "Fox and Geese," and the swindling of Manners-Sutton out of £500 and a pearl tie-pin. The money and the pin were later recovered, he stated, through the exertions of Mr. Newton.

Manners-Sutton incidentally had previously known Crosland at Monte Carlo.

Crosland in the witness box was magnificently defiant. He met Marshall Hall's cross-examination head-on. He admitted that he was bankrupt, but said that he could earn a great deal more money if he chose. He denied personally writing the article, but added that it would have appeared, so far as he was concerned, even if Manners-Sutton had lent *The Academy* the £500.

At one point Marshall Hall was unwise enough to comment: "Your solicitor tells me you're a difficult man to handle."

"I am," snapped Crosland. "And *you* can't handle me!"

The drama became more intense; the court more packed with spectators. The scene was in some ways reminiscent of the Wilde case. But with a difference. This was no dazzling exhibition of repartee on the part of a master of words battling against a deadly forensic onslaught that in the end broke through his guard and reduced him to ruin more complete than his bitterest enemies could have imagined. Here was something of a different character; verbal bludgeoning across the body of a scandal, five years buried, which had been dragged up from its grave. A case packed with crude thrills of the type to furnish such headlines as "Amazing Incidents of Smart-set Life," and "Peer's Son tells of Visit to West End Flat."

Later on came a further extraordinary passage of arms between Crosland and Marshall Hall.

Hall held up a poster on which was printed in large type: "Where's Maggie Dupont?" It was one

admittedly issued by *The Academy*—"A paper dealing
with intellectual and literary matters," quoted counsel
sarcastically, with Crosland's knowledge and con-
currence, and exhibited outside Newton's office.

" Your gang knows where she is!" shouted Crosland.
"And Manners-Sutton knows. And then you come here
and get a big fee to make me look like a liar!"

At which outburst the Common Serjeant told him
to confine himself to the answers.

The cross-examination shifted from morals to
finance. Names of a number of people who had had
monetary dealings with Crosland were mentioned.
There were denials and explanations, amplified by
outbursts of sheer bluff.

" Do you know Mr. Room?" asked Hall.

" Oh, yes," said Crosland. " He's just been called to
the Bar. He came down to examine me at my bankruptcy and make a show for himself. I may say he's
made no show since!" There was loud laughter in
court. Mr. Valetta, his counsel, however, was not
amused. On his objection, the learned judge stopped
this line of examination.

Douglas, inevitably, was called upon to give evidence.
He was examined and cross-examined. He dealt, detail
by detail, with the Manners-Sutton version of the
Buckingham Gate story, and denied practically everything the plaintiff had stated.

Later Marshall Hall referred to Wilde.

" Was there," he demanded, " ever anything to be
ashamed of in your relationship with him?"

Douglas answered without hesitation. " No, there
was not."

Did he, one wonders, recall that statement, made on
oath, when, years later, he recorded " the truth and
nothing but the truth " in his *Autobiography*?

The story is not worth prolonging further. The case
ended in the acquittal of Crosland.

Manners-Sutton and Bosie, after a seven years'
estrangement, became friends again. The reconciliation was brought about by Olive.

From Monte Carlo came a quaint little note of con-
gratulation on the verdict. A paper there, *Monte Carlo
Echoes,* said : "Frankly we are all very glad. Mr.
T. W. H. Crosland was much liked here. It was only
just before the trial that he was causing us rare fun.
He was an exceedingly able man, and we in Monte
Carlo will forgive much in your man of genius that we
cannot stand in your wooden nutmeg, your (more or
less) respectable nonentity."

2. *Versus* Dr. Horton and " The Daily News "

In June, 1910, Douglas, as proprietor of *The
Academy,* began civil proceedings for libel against Dr.
Horton, the well-known nonconformist leader, and
The Daily News. The grounds of the action lay in an
article which had appeared in the *News* on March 16th,
1909.

It ran :

" Some well-known organs, e.g. *The Academy,* have
passed into Roman hands. That once-famous literary
paper now passes its verdict on current literature with
a bias to Rome. Good books are those which favour
Rome. Books which criticize or oppose Rome are, *ipso
facto,* bad. This paper, therefore, is to be read, though
the public does not know it, with *The Tablet, The
Month* and *The Universe.*

" This is all quite legitimate, but the public should
know that the paper has become an organ of Catholic
propaganda."

Further extracts, though not referring explicitly to
The Academy, stated that there were " very few other
papers in which the apostolate of the Press has not,
apparently, secured an agent," papers which dealt with

news and books so as to favour the Church of Rome, "quietly, swiftly, and very effectively."

Mr. Justice Darling presided. Lord Robert Cecil, who appeared for Douglas and Crosland, said the paragraphs constituted a very serious charge against a paper like *The Academy*.

Douglas, examined by his counsel, denied that he or any member of his staff was a Roman Catholic. (It was not until the following year that he was formally received into the Church of Rome.)

Sir Edward Carson rose to begin his cross-examination. The moment must have recalled those three terrible days fifteen years before, during which the same deadly intellect had brought about the ruin of his greatest friend.

Sir Edward asked if the paper were not strongly anti-Protestant.

Douglas answered that it had been very strongly against nonconformity. "If you call that anti-Protestant?"

"More than that," insisted Carson. "Very strongly against Protestantism in the English Church?"

"Yes."

"Strongly against the Reformation?"

"I won't admit that," said Douglas. "But against the way that the Reformation has been distorted."

"Do you," continued Carson, "call yourself a Protestant?"

"No," said Douglas. "I strongly object to the word. I call myself a member of the Holy Catholic Church"; and added, with that fatal passion for a final jibe, "I presume *you* don't go to church?"

"Please don't presume anything about me at all," snapped Carson.

"I won't presume," said Douglas. "I will take it so."

Carson shifted his ground a little. "Protestant is a horrible word, isn't it?" he suggested. And when

Douglas agreed, continued: "And you don't hesitate to insult people who are Protestants?"

Darling intervened. "You object to calling yourself a Protestant?"

"I don't protest against anything," said Douglas. "Surely you can be a loyal member of the Church of England without hating and detesting the Church of Rome?"

"Nobody," said Carson, "asked you to do anything of the kind."

"You ought," said Darling, "to hate the Devil and all his works." Which legal witticism led to the third outburst of laughter in court that morning.

Sir Edward then referred to Mr. Arthur Machen, known to be a very High Churchman. An extract from an article by Machen was quoted. Referring to his youth, the author wrote: "I cursed the Protestant religion with all my heart and soul, and still do. I curse it and hate it and detest it with all its works and all its abominable operations, internal and external. I loathe it and abhor it as a most hideous blasphemy, the gravest woe, the most monstrous horror which has fallen upon the hopeless race of mortals since the foundation of the world."

"Those are the words," said Sir Edward, "of the man you employed to give an independent review."

"Yes," said Douglas.

"Aren't those disgraceful words?"

"Certainly not."

"Offensive words?"

"You may take them to be offensive. I don't see anything offensive in them."

Sir Edward quoted again from *The Academy*, apropos of Dr. Aked: "He provides weekly doses of heresies and imbecilities. . . . He deserves the same kind of notice that one cannot help giving to a peculiarly foetid drain as one passes by."

" Did Mr. Machen write that?" asked Darling.

Mr. Machen had written it.

Dr. Clifford had also come under fire. This time Dickens, not sewage, supplied the similes. *The Academy* compared him to the red-nosed man in *Pickwick,* to Stiggins, and to Chadband.

Sir Edward concluded the defence by reading a telegram sent by Douglas to Dr. Horton: "Your remarks regarding *Academy* in yesterday's *Daily News* are a combination of malicious falsehood, spiteful innuendo. Presume this is a method of retaliating for unfavourable review in *The Academy*. I call upon you to withdraw and apologize or send me the name of your solicitors."

Mr. Justice Darling summed up. He regretted that after four hundred years religious differences were still so acute—it is a judge's duty to exhibit the obvious. He quoted *Hudibras*—it is a judge's privilege to quote, even if the quotation has no particular bearing on the case. The jury were absent fifty minutes, and then returned to say they were unable to agree. They were told to try again, and did so.

After fifteen minutes' re-cogitation, they returned a verdict for the defendants, with a rider in the form of the personal opinion of their chairman that Dr. Horton should have taken more care in verifying his facts before writing the letter.

One can only assume that Douglas's memory once again failed to function when he stated in the *Autobiography* that he lost only one libel action, that against Arthur Ransome, among all those which he had to bring.

3. *Versus* ARTHUR RANSOME

This case, which came up before Mr. Justice Darling and a special jury on April 18th, 1913, and, including adjournments, lasted well into June, was the most remarkable, and at the same time the most tragic, of all Douglas's post-Wilde lawsuits.

The action was a double-barrelled affair, brought by Douglas against an author, Arthur Ransome, and a limited liability company, The Times Book Club. Two other defendants had originally been cited, a firm of printers and a firm of publishers; both these, however, had apologized and dropped out.

Mr. Ransome, who today has an impressive list of books to his credit, was even then an author with an established reputation.

The defence of The Times Book Club was that when they sold the book they were unaware that it contained any libel.

The libel concerned a book written by Ransome and published in the previous year called *Oscar Wilde: a Critical Study*. It contained passages which, while mentioning no individual by name, were alleged to refer unmistakably to Douglas. These passages, it was further alleged, were libellous and defamatory.

Douglas was represented by his old friend, Mr. Cecil Hayes, and Mr. Harold Benjamin. For Ransome there appeared Mr. J. H. Campbell (later Sir James Campbell) and Mr. McCardie (later Mr. Justice McCardie). For The Times Book Club were Mr. F. E. Smith (later Lord Birkenhead), Mr. Eustace Hills and Mr. W. G. H. Gritten.

Mr. Hayes opened the proceedings for the plaintiff. His case amounted to this—that it was made to appear that Lord Alfred was responsible for the public disgrace of the late Oscar Wilde and that after Wilde came out of prison he (Lord Alfred) went to live with him at Naples from purely mercenary motives, and abandoned him when Wilde's allowance was stopped, leaving the ex-prisoner penniless.

The story of Wilde's downfall, imprisonment and death was told with merciful brevity by Hayes.

Douglas, examined by him, gave an account of the notorious friendship, and particularly of his financial dealings with Wilde. He stressed Wilde's hopeless extravagance.

" If I gave him a hundred pounds on Monday he would have spent it all by Saturday," he declared.

" How did he spend it?" asked Darling.

Douglas could not enlighten him.

There was a cross-examination by Campbell concerning Wilde's past which moved Hayes to protest and —oddly enough, considering the extent to which the Wilde story was public property and the number of times it had already been told—the judge himself to old-maidenish alarm. He appealed to the Press to make their reports " as disguised as possible."

" These questions must be asked," said Darling, " but it would do incalculable harm to public morals if they were published." The cross-examination promptly switched over to less dangerous lines.

Mr. Campbell referred to an article which had appeared in *Truth*. In that Henry Labouchere, the editor, referred, in connection with a certain letter, to Douglas as " an exceptional young scoundrel." Douglas said he could not remember embarking on a correspondence. Then he did suddenly recall a letter that he had written soon after Wilde's trial, and said that he now considered the letter was abominable and that he was ashamed of it.

He referred to letters that he accused Lewis & Lewis, his father's solicitors, of using against him. Sir George Lewis, who was in court, was given permission to make a statement here. He said that there was not a word of truth in the accusation.*

---

*In the *Autobiography* Douglas says the letters written from Wilde to him were produced by Charles Russell & Co., his father's solicitors, at the request of Lewis & Lewis, also his father's solicitors, after having been stolen from Douglas by a servant and sold to the Marquess.

Later, Douglas mentioned that before the death of his father, Lord Queensberry, in 1900, he had had an absolute reconciliation with him.

"And did you," asked Campbell, "after his death write a letter in which you referred to him as ' Jack the Ripper '? "

" I do not think so," said Douglas.

Mr. Hayes asked for the production of the letter. Counsel said that he would produce it shortly.

Reference was made to the original publication of " The Ballad of Reading Gaol," which, originally published in England by Leonard Smithers, was later translated by Henri D. Davray, with Wilde's co-operation, and appeared in *La Mercure de France* in 1898. The same journal had agreed to publish a collection of his poems. Several of these had appeared in *La Revue Blanche,* which, despite its title, was referred to in court as " a dirty little rag." Its views were advanced, its circulation small, but it had asked Douglas to write an introduction to his poems, together with an exposition of his views on the Wilde case. And Douglas had accepted the offer all the more readily because the English market was closed to him. It was an article which had only youth and frustration as its excuse.

" Have you ever repudiated it?" asked counsel.

" I repudiate it now," said Douglas.

The case was obviously not going too well for the plaintiff.

Worse, infinitely worse, was to come. It concerned Wilde's last book, *De Profundis.*

Mr. Hayes said that in his opinion not merely extracts, but the whole, of the suppressed portion of *De Profundis* should be read. Darling assented, although with an unflattering absence of enthusiasm.

" I looked a little ahead," he said, " it seemed to me very dead water indeed."

Mr. McCardie, thus encouraged, began.

But presently he stopped. It had been observed that the plaintiff, who should have been in the witness box, ready to be cross-examined if necessary, was absent, in spite of the specific instructions of his own counsel. The judge ordered him to be sent for. Inquiries showed that he was not even in the court. Darling waited a short time, and then ordered the reading to be resumed.

It must have been an acutely uncomfortable period for Hayes. But ten minutes later Douglas reappeared. His explanation was simple. He had not wanted to hear the reading.

Darling told him that if he left the court again he would direct judgment to be entered against him.

His reluctance was not surprising. He had, necessarily, seen a copy of the suppressed portions before—it was the legal obligation of Ransome's counsel to ensure that he did see it. But though the shock had already been encountered, and although Hayes knew that the unpublished portion would be used by his adversary as a vital part of the defence, the shattering effects of the attack on Douglas's self-esteem, magnified in his case to supersensitive vanity, must have still remained. Familiarity would not breed contempt but intensified horror.

The incident of his absence from the court may seem a trivial one. But it had a significance that was far from trivial. It put Douglas, either as the plaintiff or as a witness, definitely in the bad books of a judge who had from the beginning had an inherent aversion from the case itself. And nothing happening thereafter, whatever attempts Darling may have made to achieve an honest and unprejudiced impartiality, was likely to alter his personal attitude towards the plaintiff.

Mr. McCardie resumed his reading. Douglas's attitude from the beginning remained that of a man numbed. He gave no hint that he knew anything of the disclosures looming immediately ahead. After a time he asked if he might sit down, and then if he might leave the box. Darling asked if he was feeling ill.

He said he was not, and was told to remain.

Darling himself read further passages; more still were read by Campbell.

The quotations ended with the judge's comment that it was plain that Wilde had written the letter for publication, because it gave him the *beau rôle* all the time—a singularly defective specimen of forensic logic.

Presently there came a protest from a different direction. The foreman of the jury intimated that they had had enough of *De Profundis*. The water was unbearably dead.

Campbell resumed his cross-examination. Under it, Douglas made a series of admissions which can best be described as unfortunate.

He stated that he had never lived on Wilde, and never admitted that he had. Counsel immediately produced a letter to a friend in which Douglas had written, apropos of expenses: " Oscar contributed everything, I contributed nothing! I had nothing to contribute."

Douglas's incurable, and, from the legal point of view, lamentable, habit of adding personal flippancies to his evidence brought a fresh warning from Darling.

He complained of being interrupted by Campbell, who was cross-examining him.

" You must allow me to finish my answer, if you want to get at the truth," said Douglas. Then he added scathingly: " But perhaps you don't wish it?"

" Don't be impertinent to learned counsel," snapped Darling.

" I accept your Lordship's rebuke," said Douglas.

" You will not only accept my rebuke, but act on it," retorted Darling.

The cross-examination continued.

Was it true, asked Campbell, that Douglas promised Wilde that he would use his influence with the Douglas family to put up the money for prosecuting Lord Queensberry, his own father?

It was.

Was it true that after Wilde's release from prison his friends undertook to pay him a pension of £150 a year, on condition that he did not further associate with Douglas.

It was.

Knowing that, did Douglas rejoin him?

Yes.

Did Douglas know that his leaving Wilde, when, as a consequence of that condition being broken, Wilde's allowance ceased, was, in his friend's own words, the most bitter thing in his life?

Yes, Douglas did.

Was not the plain text of *De Profundis* that Douglas was the ruin of Wilde's life?

Yes.

And finally, " Did you not admit it to be true?" Campbell demanded.

" Through a sense of quixotic generosity," said Douglas, " I let it pass."

After the position of The Times Book Club had been dealt with, Douglas's examination by counsel was resumed.

"All Wilde's best work was written in my company," said Douglas. But Wilde, he added, was far too conceited to recognize his assistance. " The Ballad of Reading Gaol " was written at Naples, not in prison.

" He owed its inspiration to Her Majesty's Government," commented Darling.

The evidence that followed is too long and too complicated to be worth reproduction. It occupied several days, and included the evidence of Mr. Didier, an expert called by the defence, who produced a guaranteed correct translation of " The Ballad of Reading Gaol " from the original number of *La Mercure de France*. A director of The Times Book Club also gave evidence.

Mr. F. E. Smith spoke at considerable length for the defence. He was astonished at the action. If there *had* been a technical defamation, he suggested no more than a farthing damages—firstly, because of the admission made by the plaintiff in connection with the letter to *Truth,* which had drawn Labouchere's retort that Douglas was " an exceptional young scoundrel," and secondly, the article in *La Revue Blanche.*

It should be borne in mind, said Smith, that it was no use for plaintiff to defy criticism by saying these events happened twenty years ago. However long it may be, it related to the very period of which he came to that court to complain. . . ." With regard to Oscar Wilde, years have passed since his fall, and men are beginning to think of the artist rather than the man's life. Now this legacy of infamy has been resurrected—unnecessarily resurrected—again."

There was a speech on behalf of the other defendant by Campbell.

There was another speech for the plaintiff by Hayes. He asked why Robert Ross had not been called.

" You may call him now if you wish," said Darling.

" But the onus of proving their justification lies on the defendants," Hayes objected.

" Mr. Ross," snapped Darling, " is not a party to the action, and the decision as to whether he should be called or not does not rest with him. He added : " I have listened in vain for any reason why he should be called. He was only Wilde's literary executor."*

There was a further clash when Hayes complained that Ransome's counsel had delivered sixty-three pages

---

* What he did not stress was that Ransome derived his facts from Ross, and that the statements forming the libel had been inserted at Ross's instigation.

LAD—H

of justification, but that the defendant had not gone into the box to substantiate any of them.

" Your object in trying to get Mr. Ransome into the box," said Darling, " is not to prove these particulars, but to enable you to put questions to him which you did not care to put to your own witnesses."

The first laughter in court came later. Hayes complained that the defendant's counsel had introduced matters which were intended " to throw mud in the eyes of the jury, so that they should not see the clear issue. The defence had throw nothing but brimstone and thunderbolts."

His Lordship summed up. He spoke of Wilde as " a very bad man of genius," and of Douglas as " if not a man of genius, a man of talent."

The jury were absent an hour and fifty minutes. They returned to announce that they found the words complained of by the plaintiff were a libel, but that they were true. With regard to The Times Book Club, there had been no negligence in circulating this book.

Judgment for both the defendants, with costs.

There were two sequels. They formed a double anticlimax to this unhappy case.

On the day after the verdict Darling sent for F. E. Smith and Cecil Hayes. He had, it appeared, received a personal letter from Lord Alfred in connection with the conduct of one of the witnesses for the defence. He, Darling, was handing over the letter, which was undoubtedly libellous, and would so hand over any other similar letters so received, to the defendants, who could instruct their solicitor to take proceedings if they chose to do so. He himself did not intend to answer it.

The second sequel was on June 26th, when Mr. Benjamin applied for leave to withdraw his client's appeal against the verdict.

Douglas had been served with a notice of motion to

furnish security for the costs of the appeal, assuming it to be granted. And he was unable to comply.

Mr. McCardie said the proper course would be the immediate dismissal of the appeal, with costs.

It was so dismissed.

4. *Versus* LIEUTENANT-COLONEL CUSTANCE

On February 26th, 1913, Douglas, still living in Church Row, Hampstead, was charged with criminally libelling Lieutenant-Colonel Custance, his father-in-law. The scene was Marylebone, the magistrate Mr. Denham. Mr. R. D. Muir appeared for the Colonel; for the defendant, Mr. Cecil Hayes.

Colonel Custance, examined by his counsel, told briefly the story of the marriage between his daughter Olive and Douglas in 1902. After eight years, in the course of which he must have wondered a good many times why the Fates, having made him the father of one poet, must needs make her fall in love with and marry another, certain settlements were executed.

Douglas had concurred in these. But a sense of injustice remained. He had begun to write abusive letters to his father-in-law. He had gone on writing them until September, 1911, by which time the long-suffering Colonel declined to suffer any longer. He wrote and told Douglas that he would open no more of them. It was a move for which Douglas was probably prepared. He retorted by sending post cards, with their inevitable publicity, instead. Also telegrams.

These culminated in a wire which was sent to the Colonel on February 12th, 1912, at his home, Weston Hall, Norfolk, where in happier days he had initiated the sender into the art of fly-fishing.

" There is no doubt that Olive was induced to sign settlement by fraudulent promise of consideration which is now being withheld from her. Am seeing lawyer this afternoon; the whole matter will have to be fought out in law courts."

There was another telegram the next day which announced the dispatch of three post cards and invited the colonel to proceed against him for libel.

One of the post cards dealt in detail with a settlement of £600 a year on Olive. Because, said Douglas, he insisted on his very natural right to have the custody of his own child, the Colonel revenged himself on his daughter by depriving her of the money he intended to give her; this, although he had £30,000 from the late Mrs. Custance. . . . There was no doubt whatever, concluded the post card, that he was a despicable scoundrel and a thoroughly dishonest and dishonourable man.

A second post card threatened to send similar statements to the Carlton Club, and the club at Norwich, to the Colonel's bank at Norwich, to his relations and friends, and to the tenants on the Weston Estate.

The boy, Raymond, had been staying with his grandfather, but Douglas had removed him. A further accusation was that Custance was deliberately breaking up the Douglas ménage in revenge.

It all sounds incredibly grotesque and childish and vindictive. Nevertheless, it was the Douglas method of attack.

At the end of the day's hearing the defendant was committed for trial and released on bail.

On March 6th the case was adjourned until the next session in order to give his counsel time to put in a plea of justification. There were further delays after that date. But at length, on April 24th, the case came before the Recorder at the Central Criminal Court. It was, mercifully, a brief affair. The defence, or rather plea for mitigation, given after the jury had returned a verdict of guilty without leaving the box, was, in effect, a double one—and neither part of it constituted a plea for justification. Firstly, that the defendant had been in a state of acute worry and strain, partly due, it was pointed out, to the fact that he had been made bankrupt on January 14th of the same year on a money-lender's petition. Secondly that the position held by Colonel Custance in society was so high that no one could possibly believe anything against him!

Finally, the defendant, through his counsel, tendered a complete and unequivocal apology, and a withdrawal of all accusations. He also agreed to the Recorder's stipulation that he should be bound over on his own recognizances of £500.

Douglas's reference to this inglorious fiasco is curious, and at the same time characteristic.

He says that he lost the case solely because, distressed and disheartened, he threw up the sponge, did not put in a plea of justification, and did not go into the witness box. By some mental process beyond any normal rules of logic, he is able to record in the *Autobiography* that he ultimately completely turned the tables upon his father-in-law.

5. CROSLAND *versus* " THE LONDON MAIL "*

On April 30th, 1914, Mr. Harold Benjamin, appearing for Crosland, asked for the attachment of the printer and publisher of *The London Mail,* who, in the current number, under " Things We Want to Know," had written : " If all decent people would not heave a sigh of relief if the Government decided to deport the unspeakable Crosland and the still more unspeakable Lord Alfred Douglas?" And a week later Randall Roberts, the editor, and Walbrook & Co., the printers, were summoned for contempt of court in commenting on a case in a way which was likely to prejudice a fair trial.

---

*This case, though one which did not involve Douglas, is included as being both relevant and interesting.

The case was held in the High Court on May 7th, before Mr. Justice Avory, Mr. Justice Rowlatt and Mr. Justice Shearman. There was an ingenious defence of the please-we-never-did-it-and-if-so-we-didn't-mean-to type, followed by apologies. There was an argument about the exact implication of " unspeakable " if the word were used in connection with the author of *The Unspeakable Scot*. It was finally decided that the respondents should promise not to do it again, and pay all the costs of the action.

6. CROSLAND *versus* ROBERT ROSS

Robert Baldwin Ross, born in 1869, was among the major characters in Douglas's life's drama, and, next to his father, the man whom Douglas most hated. Perhaps he was the only enemy whom he never even pretended to forgive.

He was a Canadian, though actually born in France; his grandfather had been the first Premier of Upper Canada, and his father Solicitor-General for the same part of the Dominion.

He went to King's College, Cambridge, but left at the end of a year without taking a degree. He is variously described as nervous, affectionate, sentimental and emotional, a pathetic-looking creature, rather like a kitten, a small, puckish, dapper little man, in the early days living on an allowance of two hundred a year from his mother. He contributed articles on art, literature and the drama to *The Saturday Review, The Academy,* and other important papers, and to *The Spirit Lamp,* the Oxford magazine edited by Douglas (" How We Lost the Book of Jasher "). For four years he was on the staff of *The Morning Post.* He also ran a little picture shop in Ryder Street, a shop which later on expanded into the Carfax Gallery in Bury Street.

Mr. Asquith appointed him Assessor of Picture Valuations to the Board of Trade.

Of Ross's private character, much that is uncomplimentary has been said, and some of it proved, but the fact remains that Wilde liked and trusted him sufficiently to appoint him his literary executor, an appointment confirmed by the English courts in 1906. Douglas began by accepting him as a friend, and passed through various stages of jealousy and dislike to sheer hatred. This change of emotion is registered in his description of the once-kittenish Ross in 1914, Ross having then become, in Douglas's view, sinister-looking, bloated and bald-headed, with snaky eyes, bulging face and body, with a nigger-like mouth and teeth.

Robert Ross's career ended suddenly in his rooms in Half Moon Street in October, 1918. He was then forty-nine. His valet, coming in to wake him, found him dead from heart failure.

On the evening of Easter Sunday, April 12th, 1914, Crosland returned to London from a short visit to Douglas at Boulogne that had been followed by a still shorter one to Monte Carlo.

As he was entering the flat in Mitcham Street, which he shared with a friend, he was greeted by Detective Inspector MacPherson, of Scotland Yard. MacPherson held a warrant for his arrest, issued three weeks earlier. The defendant, stated the warrant, had conspired with Lord Alfred Bruce Douglas on September 17th, 1913, and divers other dates between then and February 14th last, in a conspiracy together or with other persons unknown unlawfully, falsely and corruptly to charge Robert Ross with having committed certain acts "—in other words, with following all too faithfully in the steps of their common friend, Oscar Wilde.

The warrant was read. Crosland, confirmed supporter of the attack-is-the-best-defence theory, wanted to know why they had not arrested Ross. He and

Douglas, he said, had been to great expense; they had already done all the things which the police ought to have done, and supplied Scotland Yard with the information so acquired.

MacPherson, wisely leaving these questions unanswered, collected a number of documents that the defendant had brought back with him from France, other documents he found in the flat, and the defendant himself, and took them all to Marylebone Police Court, where on the following morning Crosland was brought up before Mr. Paul Taylor, the magistrate. There began the unfolding of a story which had all the grimy background of the underworld. But it was a more complicated story than usual, for with Ross the "unlawful, false and corrupt charges " had bracketed a second person, Christopher Millard, at that time his private secretary.

The career of Millard really justifies a section on its own account. At Oxford, where in 1906 he was a coach, he showed his mettle as a violent rebel, and never outgrew a state of immaturity which manifested itself in a general contempt for every convention and institution, from the Royal Family downwards, created by civilization. He was a Jacobite, a wearer of eccentric clothes, a connoisseur of exquisite food and rare books. At first a schoolmaster, he became assistant editor of *The Burlington Magazine* when it was edited by Robert Ross, then Ross's private secretary, and, finally, before he entangled himself in criminal proceedings which ended his official career, a clerk in the War Office. While working for Ross, who left him a pension of £100 a year, he wrote anonymously *Oscar Wilde: Three Times Tried* and, as " Stuart Mason," a bibliography of Wilde's writings. Further facts about his life are given in A. J. A. Symons's *The Quest for Corvo*, to which intriguing history I acknowledge my indebtedness, and in Osbert Burdett's *Memory and Imagination*.

There was a brief discussion, following which Crosland was remanded on bail, the necessary surety of £500 being provided by Mr. Sholto Douglas, the artist.

On the 21st, when Crosland appeared in court again, Sir George Lewis asked for a further week's adjournment, firstly because Mr. E. Wild, K.C., counsel for the prosecution, was engaged on another case; secondly, to give Lord Alfred, who was still in lodgings in Boulogne, an opportunity of coming over and facing the charge. Crosland made a vehement protest at the delay. The magistrate curtly told him to be quiet, and remanded him until the 28th.

On that date the case began its tortuous and prolonged hearing. Wild and Eustace Fulton, instructed by Lewis & Lewis, appeared for the prosecution; A. S. Comyns Carr, instructed by Messrs. Carter & Bell, was for the defence.

Practically the whole of that first day was occupied by the case for the prosecution, following a preliminary statement by the magistrate, who had, it appeared, read in the Press a letter addressed to himself by the absent defendant. No such letter had, however, been received by him prior to publication, which had taken place entirely without his knowledge or consent.

Mr. Wild mentioned that an apology had been issued, and the incident closed.

In opening, the prosecuting counsel said that he was going to ask that a separate charge of incitement to commit perjury be granted against Crosland.

The assembly of the court on May 1st provided another sensation, when the magistrate announced that he had received a communication from Lord Alfred Douglas, saying that if he was given an assurance that no steps would be taken against him in respect of his failure to appear before the Recorder in the matter of Colonel Custance until the Ross *versus* Crosland case was finished, and if Lord Alfred was also assured that no obstacle would be put in the way of his being granted bail, he would at once return to England and place himself at the disposal of the court.

It was obvious, commented the magistrate, that it would be quite impossible for him to give such an undertaking.

So obvious, indeed, that one imagines that even Douglas did not expect his gamble to come off.

On the following day " Charlie," an unpleasant young criminal serving his second sentence, gave evidence. He had barely embarked upon his story when Ross came forward, and " Charlie " at once testified that he had never spoken to or even seen him before in his life. " Charlie's " evidence was resumed. It was, to use a cliché of the courts, a long and rambling statement, dealing with a series of interviews with Millard, with Douglas, and with Crosland. The general impression he conveyed was of a sustained determination on their part to build up a case against Ross, a case which would compel Scotland Yard to take action and ruin the common enemy. Eventually, said the witness, Lord Alfred and Crosland drew up a statement about Ross which, so far as " Charlie " was concerned, was entirely untrue. There were visits to the Yard, which refused to take action; there was a dinner at the Grosvenor Restaurant; afterwards he and a man named Carew, who mysteriously became involved in the case after an ineffectual attempt to persuade Ross to write an article on Wilde for an American encyclopaedia, went to the Wilton Hotel, but Lord Alfred took him away in a cab. On the way to yet another hotel at Euston " they changed cabs three times for fear that Millard and another man might be following." It was all excessively melodramatic, and in the best Sherlock Holmes tradition. One feels that the young scallywag must have had the time of his misspent life.

On the following morning he and Douglas went to

Kensington, where, oddly enough, considering the day was Sunday, " Charlie " was to go before a lawyer and formally swear to the truth of the statement he had signed. But at this vital juncture he jibbed. He refused to go, he refused to sign. There was a first-class row, with " language," understandable enough in the circumstances, from his aristocratic patron. The next day Douglas and Carew tried again; " Charlie " still refused.

On May 12th—the day, incidentally, on which Crosland was adjudicated bankrupt for the second time, his first failure having been in 1906—Ross went into the witness box to give evidence. His story included some interesting information concerning Wilde's finances.

He had, he explained, been a close friend of Wilde, had looked after his affairs, and was with him when he died. As his literary executor, he had rescued Wilde's estate from bankruptcy, and between 1900 and 1906 had paid off every creditor in full, with four per cent interest.

Christopher Millard, said Ross, had returned to his post as private secretary after his three months' imprisonment, but on Millard's associating again with " Charlie," and being censured by the magistrate for so doing, Ross, apart from occasional literary commissions, had ceased to have anything to do with him.

Further facts emerged. Collectively they do not present a very edifying picture—Douglas's establishing himself in the flat adjoining Ross's, until requested by the landlord to leave; Douglas's contacting Millard, and, through Millard, Carew.

Millard's evidence followed. It included a long letter that he had written to Douglas. The letter accused him of irretrievably ruining a fellow Catholic who had done him no harm. Douglas, in a reply, had referred to Ross as the foulest and most filthy beast that ever drew the

breath of life. Later came a letter, this time signed
"Murray," saying that Lord Alfred felt that he might
have done Millard an injustice, and suggesting a
meeting. They did meet several times. According to
Millard there were further suggestions that he might
supply information, or even purloin letters of a com-
promising nature which could be used against his late
employer.

After all this evidence the case was adjourned. The
defendant himself had influenza, though not severely
enough to prevent a flying visit to Boulogne. There
was another adjournment owing to the illness of his
solicitor. When Crosland recovered and the case was
resumed, he gave evidence which flatly contradicted
much of what had previously been said.

" I have been ten years," he said, thumping the ledge
of the witness box, towards the end of his examination,
" trying to bring this thing about and I am here now,
very happy and comfortable."

In further evidence, two days later, he expressed his
disbelief in the statement that Ross had received no
payment for the work he did in connection with Wilde's
estate. He added that he always understood that
De Profundis was considered by Ross as his own.

Counsel for the prosecution pointed out that Ross
had already sworn that he had not received a farthing
for it.

Crosland adhered to his accusation against Ross.

" Were you," asked counsel, " in an impecunious
state at the time these alleged incidents occurred?"

Crosland said he was.

" Would the same have been true of Lord Alfred?"

" Oh dear, no," said Crosland. " I have never known
him to be hard up."

" Is that as true as the rest of your evidence?"
demanded Wild caustically.

" Lord Alfred," retorted Crosland, " would squeal if he hadn't got fifty pounds in his pocket."

" Did it occur to you," said Wild, " to take down the boy's statements before a solicitor, or make any independent inquiries as to the truth of those statements?" Apparently it hadn't occurred to him.

And when Wild referred to " Charlie " as a dinner companion, Crosland said : " I won't have you talk to me like that. I am as big a master of sneers and jeers as you are. Keep a civil tongue in your head." Later, after an argument, he called Wild a liar.

There was a final crossing of swords between Comyns Carr and the magistrate. After which, Mr. Taylor said that he saw no evidence that either of the defendants was actuated by a desire to obtain money. Nor was there a particle of evidence to justify the shadow of an allegation against Mr. Ross of any conceivable offence.

A clean sheet with a vengeance.

Crosland was committed for trial and released on bail.

The trial was begun before Mr. Justice Avory on June 28th. F. E. Smith and Ernest Wild were for the prosecution; Cecil Hayes for the defence.

F. E. Smith opened the case, his own description of which was " unusual, disagreeable, and of a somewhat protracted character." The previous hearings had certainly proved it all three. He summarized the story of Ross's friendship with Wilde, and the ten years' " conspiracy "—a word to which Hayes objected— between Douglas and Crosland in enmity to Ross. He quoted remarkable letters from Douglas to Ross, in which Douglas stated that he had known all along that Ross had the unpublished half of De Profundis in his possession, and threatened to thrash him " very severely with a horsewhip." He read a still more remarkable post card from Crosland, beginning " How's Fluffy?" and ending " How is the Wilde Movement?"

At the adjournment at the end of the first day Crosland was again admitted to bail.

The case dragged on. Generally speaking, the same people testified to the same things to which they had testified at the police court. Ross reiterated that he had never previously known, nor even heard of, the boy "Charlie," who in turn reiterated that he had never before met Ross. There were comments from the judge on the recklessness with which people identified voices on the telephone, and at one point an incoherent outburst from the defendant. Wilde's comment in the preface to *Dorian Gray,* to the effect that there could be no such thing as a moral or immoral book, was quoted—one might have hazarded a guess that it would be—and Ross was asked if he saw anything immoral in *Dorian Gray.* Ross said he did not, adding, after Avory had elaborated the point, that he did not see how any printed word could have an immoral effect on anybody.

The defendant gave evidence. It concluded a prolonged attack on Wilde and on Wilde's writings. Concerning Ransome's book, Crosland said that he should not like to express his opinion in the witness box. Upon which there was laughter in court. The listeners must have been glad to find something to laugh at.

For several more days the ding-dong of examination and cross-examination continued. There were a number of awkward questions for the defendant to answer—F. E. Smith saw to that. But Crosland did answer them, with a directness and vigour which by their very crudity produced an atmosphere in his favour. His finances, his relations with his wife, his other legal actions, his differences of opinion when he shared the direction of *The Academy,* were all dealt with.

Avory was elaborately and scrupulously fair, though one feels there must have been a strong inducement to exhibit bias. He pointed out, as the magistrate had

done, that no shadow of an implication against the
character of Ross existed; that the only question the
jury had to decide was whether the prosecution had
satisfied them that the defendant did not believe the
charges against Ross to be true.

The jury, after half an hour's deliberation, found
Crosland not guilty.

They were exempted from further service for five
years. They had, one feels, earned the exemption.

The comments of the absent Douglas on the case
were, as usual, extremely typical and illuminative.
They represented the attitude of the born litigant or
born punter or any other incarnation of the born
gambler all the world over. He had lost in the Custance
case because his nerve went as he was demoralized; in
the Ross case, Crosland's acquittal, involving necessarily
his own, was a triumph; he proved himself more than
a match for F. E. Smith, whom he succeeded in making
look rather foolish several times.

Incidentally, he states—and here there is no reason
for disbelief—that from the moment of Crosland's
arrest and while he was on bail Lady Queensberry kept
Crosland supplied with money, the total amounting to
about £250. The weekends spent at Boulogne were
nominally at Douglas's expense, though it was a fairly
safe assumption that the funds came from the same
source.

7. *Versus* ROBERT ROSS

Two months later, in October, 1914, Douglas
returned to England. But before leaving Boulogne he
had, with the ardent co-operation of Crosland, completed his reply to the unpublished portion of *De
Profundis*. It took the form of a book which he afterwards disavowed, a tremendous onslaught on the

literary reputation of Wilde. It appeared, he records
ruefully, on the very day war broke out.

Before leaving France he had written to Lord
Kitchener. There were, it is true, three separate
warrants out for Douglas's arrest, apart from the fact
that he was a man in the middle forties without
army or, indeed, administrative experience of any sort.
But he could at least speak French. And even if
Kitchener did not care to use his services as an
interpreter, was there not, with England's acute
shortage of officers, some job for him in the commissioned ranks?

Douglas probably argued that much was being forgiven and forgotten in those hectic days. Unfortunately,
Lord Kitchener was never one of those who forget and
forgive easily. He replied at once, politely but
discouragingly.

Douglas does not seem to have been much surprised
at this official rebuff. He decided, as an alternative to
the English Army, to try his luck with the Foreign
Legion, where, granted a sufficiently robust physique
on the part of the recruit, the past—practically any sort
of past—could be conveniently ignored. It was part of
the Ouida tradition. He obtained a letter of introduction to the commandant. But the friend who
furnished the introduction said frankly that he considered the idea a mad one, and the applicant himself
totally unfitted to stand the hardships inescapable under
the Legion. . . . Douglas, his war-fever ebbing, came
to the same conclusion. The letter was never presented.

By that time he was back in London. He says that
an impending sense of trouble hung over him all the
way from France, and that he spent the whole time
saying his rosary. His premonitions were justified. As
he was coming down the landing stairs at Folkestone
a smartly dressed, affable gentleman, otherwise a
detective, greeted him.

The detective, carrying his bag for him, told him that he was to go to the local police court to be formally charged. Douglas was astounded. He had realized that he was being arrested, but assumed it to be on the Recorder's " Bench " warrant in connection with the Custance case. The detective explained that Ross, not Custance, was concerned. Douglas then assumed—and again assumed wrongly—that it was a mere formality in connection with the recent case in which he had been jointly charged with Crosland, and that as Crosland had been acquitted, he would be acquitted, too. He soon discovered that the formality was anything but " mere." A new warrant had been issued on information sworn by Ross. Poor Douglas!

He was driven in a car to the police station, locked in a cell, and told that he would be charged as soon as the detective concerned in his case arrived from London. He luxuriated in a tea of bread and butter and cake and several hours' solitude; finally, the man from Scotland Yard arrived. Douglas heard the warrant read, with its charge—by now familiar—of falsely and maliciously publishing a defamatory libel, and replied that he would prove justification and prove it up to the hilt.

He records that he felt for the moment quite exhilarated, as he invariably did at the beginning of a fight.

Detective Number Two proved as friendly as Detective Number One—if anything more so. He and the exhilarated Douglas were driven in another cab to the railway station, where the Scotland Yard man bought first-class tickets to London, followed by whiskies and sodas for them both. He refused to allow Douglas to pay anything. Friendliness, nevertheless, did not make him lose sight of his job; on the journey to London he opened Douglas's despatch-box and extracted a number of letters. (According to the prisoner, none of these had any bearing whatever on the case. But it was several months before he was able to get them back.)

The next day Douglas, represented by Mr. Waples Canwarden, was brought up before his old acquaintance, Mr. Paul Taylor, and committed for trial at the next sessions of the Central Criminal Court. Owing to the fact that there was a warrant still out for his arrest at a superior court, that of the Recorder, in connection with the Custance case, he could not be released on bail. So yet another cab took him to Brixton prison.

He was put in a small, cold cell and left to his thoughts. And here for once the Douglas optimism seems to have failed him. The Catholic chaplain came to see him, but the visit brought no consolation. Douglas says he asked vulgar and impertinent questions about his family, told him that he would deserve any punishment he got, and refused to administer the Sacrament on the following morning.

Douglas, left alone at last, picked up a Testament, the only book in his cell, and read about Peter's angelic rescue from Herod's soldiers, and regained some of his old buoyancy of spirit.

He spent five days in Brixton, and was then, after a preliminary visit to the police court, taken to the Old Bailey. Here, to his delight and surprise, he encountered Olive. She went with him to a corridor outside the courts, where he had a further surprise; his father-in-law, accompanied by Colonel Custance's brother, Admiral Custance, suddenly appeared. At the sight of Douglas and Olive they were, according to Douglas's account, " livid with rage." It must have been a highly dramatic, highly unpleasant reunion. The court proceedings brought it to an end.

The Recorder lectured Douglas at considerable length; after which, two sureties for the defendant's

better behaviour in future, his cousin Sholto Douglas
and an Anglican priest named Mills came forward to
sign the necessary documents. His release, however,
was not immediate. Twenty-four hours' investigation
of Mr. Mills's financial status was demanded by the
police. According to Douglas, this was at the
Machiavellian instigation of Sir George Lewis. As a
result he was driven to Wormwood Scrubs, since the
alternative to finding satisfactory sureties—and technically he had not yet found them—was six months'
imprisonment. At " The Scrubs " he went through the
routine indignities of a medical examination and a
bath. He was then given a supper of bread and cocoa,
and shut in a cell with only a plank bed to sleep on.

His mind reverted to Oscar, who had had to endure
these conditions for two years; for the first time since
he had read the unpublished half of *De Profundis* he
thought kindly of him. Douglas gives a typical
description of the few brief hours between his waking
on the following morning and the arrival of his two
sureties, now accepted as responsible people, to take
him away. Apart from the kindness shown him by one
of the warders, which reduced him to tears, his comments are entirely condemnatory. He was sufficiently
broken by the ordeal, indeed, to resolve upon
abandoning his plea of justification; he would climb
down and apologize to Ross at the ensuing trial rather
than run the risk of being found guilty and committed
to prison again. He suspected, or rather was certain,
that this burnt-child attitude was precisely what Sir
George Lewis hoped would result from those few hours'
incarceration. It does not seem improbable.

It was unfortunate that the child had an ineradicable
passion for playing with fire. Under the combined
influences of sleep in a comfortable bed in his mother's
home in Cliveden Place, and a meal of eggs and bacon
and toast and marmalade, the lesson was rapidly

obliterated and all his former defiance and truculence returned. He would, he decided, spend the rest of his life in an underground dungeon rather than climb down an inch where his enemies were concerned! He consulted a solicitor who was not to his liking, and exchanged him for another, a Mr. Edward Bell, who was. Their partnership, in spite of occasional friction, was from the first to prove so satisfactory that, according to Douglas, they never lost a case.

Mr. A. Comyns Carr was briefed as his counsel.

Douglas deals in considerable detail, and with the gusto of one who is telling a story that is not only dramatic, but of the all-comes-well-in-the-end class, with his adventures in the apparently hopeless task of collecting the evidence that constituted his only hope of winning. After fruitlessly visiting Guernsey and a dozen other places, he received an anonymous communication that sent him off in search of a mysterious " Mr. E.," who lived in a street near Campden Hill. This gentleman was the respectable father of a son who was alleged to be one of Ross's victims. But no one was known at the number given—and the trial was only about a week ahead. He prayed to St. Anthony of Padua, and almost immediately after met a beautiful little boy of about ten who smiled and said: " What do you want? Can I help you?" Douglas told him that he was looking for someone, and added " Mr. E.'s " name and the number of the house. Whereupon the child explained that the numbers of the street had been changed, and redirected him so successfully that Douglas found the place without difficulty. He interviewed " Mr. E." and his wife, and obtained the address of the brother of the boy whose name had been linked with Ross's, the boy himself having gone to South Africa and there died.

The brother had joined the Army, was stationed at Goring; he could, said " Mr. E.," tell the whole story.

The grateful Douglas, now firmly convinced that the beautiful boy who had uttered the Boy Scout-like "What do you want? Can I help you?" speech was not a real child, but a supernatural visitant evoked by St. Anthony, went to Goring. He found that the regiment had moved to a town in Norfolk. He followed it there. There were further difficulties with the colonel, who refused to produce " Mr. E.'s " son. There was a scene, in the course of which Douglas, with or without the moral support of his favourite saint, threatened that unless the youth was produced he would publicly expose the colonel as a man who was trying to shield Ross and all that Ross stood for. Possibly owing to the fact that the threats were made in the presence of the adjutant and several other officers, the colonel ended the interview abruptly by going red in the face and stumping out of the room.

But he later allowed the interview to take place.

The young soldier told his story, signed it when it was written down ,and was subpoenaed to appear at Douglas's forthcoming trial. Further witnesses materialized, including a man at Yarmouth who gave the names of a number of useful people, all, as Douglas naïvely records, respectable, though the man himself eventually failed to put in an appearance. (He was found in a London hospital, " suffering from narcotic poisoning," administered, as a coroner's jury would certainly have recorded, by some person or persons unknown.)

The case came on before Mr. Justice Coleridge at the Old Bailey. Sir Ernest Wild, K.C., with Mr. Eustace Fulton, again for the prosecution; Mr. A. Comyns Carr, instructed by Edward Bell, for the defence. According to Douglas's account, the trial " went his way " from the first.

Wild put his client in the box. Comyns Carr's cross-examination of Ross was, says Douglas, " quite as sensational as that of Wilde by Carson, the trial itself being the most sensational ever held in the Old Bailey."

How like Douglas, running so pathetically true to form! For at the two Wilde trials proper, now nearly twenty years old, he had not even been present. And with every respect for the mental equipment of the two pairs of duellists, there is no question of comparison.

As for Douglas's further contention that he had won before the case was half over, one's kindest comment is " perhaps."

The trial began on November 19th, and lasted in all eight days. There were four separate libels, extending from November, 1912, to March, 1914.

Douglas complains that the daily papers, with totally inadequate brevity, reported it in no more than mere paragraphs or half-columns, and that although Mr. R. D. Blumenfeld, then editor of *The Daily Express*, to whom he complained, assured him that this " mere-ness " was not due to prejudice or unfair feeling, the treatment he received destroyed his last vestige of belief in British fair play. It does not seem to have occurred to Douglas that the coincidence of one of the most sensational phases of the most sensational war that had ever threatened civilization might have had something to do with reducing the space available to Press reports of libel actions, even in *The Times* and even when they involved a Douglas.

One or two illuminative remarks of his were, however, recorded.

Apropos of Wilde, Douglas said: " He seemed to have a kind of adoration of me. I was a kind of sacred object."

In writing to his father-in-law he had referred to the ancestors of Colonel Custance as grocers.

" That," commented Mr. Justice Coleridge, " shows that the witness is a snob."

Mr. H. G. Wells was among the witnesses for the

prosecution. He had known Ross for twelve or thirteen years, and both the plaintiff and his wife were on friendly terms with himself and Mrs. Wells. His cross-examination in connection with *Ann Veronica* makes old reading today. *The Academy* had attacked it as a glorification of a couple living together unmarried.

" It is a stupid rendering of the case," said Wells.

" Have you not constantly written advocating the view that the ordinary bonds of marriage are nonsensical?" asked Carr.

" I have done nothing of the sort," retorted Wells.

Mr. (later Sir) Edmund Gosse, who had known Ross since 1890, also gave evidence; so did Wilde's second son Cyril, a barrister holding a temporary commission in the Army, and later killed on active service. He said that Ross had been a second father to him.

The judge summed up. The jury retired.

At the end of an hour and twenty minutes the foreman announced that they were in two diametrically opposed camps, and could not agree. The judge suggested that they should retire again.

They did, but still failed to agree.

Douglas was remanded to come up for trial at the December sessions, and the jury were exempted for seven years. Nine of them, states Douglas, afterwards waited outside the court to shake hands with him.

On December 11th he appeared again, this time before Mr. Justice Avory.

But it was a very brief appearance. He was told that the prosecution had entered a *nolle prosequi,* duly signed by the Attorney-General—in plain English, that the prosecution was proceeding no further with the case, and that consequently he was free. This, claims Douglas, amounted to an even greater victory than a verdict for the defendant would have been, because it was in effect an acknowledgment of guilt on the prosecutor's part. He adds that he was also paid his costs and out-of-pocket expenses.

It may have been so. On the other hand, the fact remains that shortly after the case was dropped a public testimonial, accompanied by a gift of £700, was presented to Ross as "a faithful friend and a distinguished man of letters." The signatures on the testimonial included those of the Prime Minister (Mr. Asquith, later Lord Oxford and Asquith) and his wife, the Bishop of Birmingham, H. G. Wells, Edmund Gosse, and about three hundred and fifty others. Ross resigned his post at the time of the trial, but was later appointed Adviser for the Purchase of Works of Art under the Felton Bequest, Australia, as well as an additional trustee of the National Gallery. Ross, with a touch of irony, gave under the biographical information supplied to *Who's Who*: "*Recreation*—editing new editions of Oscar Wilde's works."

The Ross testimonial which followed the trial had, in turn, a sequel which, in one opinion at least, is heartbreaking evidence of ingenuity wasted on ignoble ends.

Douglas published an eight-page pamphlet, printed in Galashiels on hand-made paper, and priced at a shilling, headed "Striking Tribute to a Solicitor." It purported to be an account of a presentation made to Sir George Lewis, and was dedicated to the London papers which had printed accounts of the Ross testimonial. A number of his friends and clients, reported Douglas, had decided to present Sir George with an illuminated address and "a purse containing seven hundred sovereigns" [sic]. The pamphlet, elaborating this story, went on to say that the proposal was understood to have originated with Mr. Albert Stopford, a client of Lewis & Lewis, who, before having had time to complete his arrangements, had fallen a victim to the malice of his enemies and was now serving a sentence of twelve months' hard labour. The names of three other clients, also in prison, were added.

Mr. H. G. Wells and Mr. Edmund Gosse, the account continued, eagerly took up the idea, the latter being responsible for the testimonial. Followed a list of well-known people alleged to have signed this imaginary document, among whose names were jumbled a number of fictitious German and Jewish names—" Mr. Schnaden Freund," " Professor Kind-snatcher," and so on.

This childishly scurrilous invention ended with an account of a mob of misguided soldiers and citizens who had got wind of the presentation, and demon-strated outside Sir George's Rottingdean house, one of these drowning Mr. Asquith's attempt to reason with them by playing " Der Wacht am Rhein " on the cornet-à-piston.

8. *Versus* THE COURT OF CHANCERY

On June 30th, 1915, an application was made by Douglas in the Chancery Division before Mr. Justice Eve that his son Raymond, who had been made a ward in Chancery, should spend the whole of his school holidays and at all times remain in the custody of his father—a variation of an order made in May, 1913, by which the boy was to spend three-fifths of his school days with Colonel Custance, his grandfather, his father paying the school fees.

Mr. Comyns Carr, on behalf of the applicant, began by pointing out that originally Lady Alfred had been joined with the Colonel as respondent, but was now added as applicant. She had, said counsel, recently approached Lord Alfred and his mother, Lady Queensberry, with a view to a reconciliation. A letter she wrote to Lady Queensberry on May 31st was quoted. It may be quoted here.

After referring to her debts, and the fact that at any moment her father could stop her allowance, she said: " Bosie was cruel to me before I went to Weston, and I have often been very unhappy with him, but I love him above everything, and would never have left him if he had not taken away Raymond. The Ransome case has done him so much harm; you don't know what people say. Everybody I know takes my father's part, and, God help me, I don't know where to turn to for advice and comfort.

" My father is angry all the time because I love Bosie still—and I am utterly miserable. But would it do Bosie any good if I am turned out to starve? I am utterly helpless since I made those settlements. Perhaps it would be better for Bosie to divorce me for desertion? I only wish I had courage enough to kill myself ! "

Another letter followed a phone message from her mother-in-law.

" I have told Daddy that you spoke to me, and that I am so much happier. . . . He will be angry, perhaps, but he knows I shall always love Bosie, though I am afraid to live with him again at present. I don't think Bosie loves me any more. I trust you. I have done all this for Raymond's sake, though you know I love Bosie."

Finally, counsel quoted from a letter written by Lady Alfred to Bosie on December 11th, 1914, after the Ross libel case had ended.

" Darling Bosie, I am so glad and so thankful. . . . I have been very happy here this visit. . . ."

He submitted that these letters showed that Lady Alfred had a deep affection for her husband, whose attitude was that he was in as good a position to take care of his son as Colonel Custance, and that the atmosphere of contention between the parties must be bad for the boy.

In January of the current year, counsel continued,

Lord Alfred had wired to his father-in-law saying that
he would like to come to a friendly agreement with
him. He received a letter in reply from Messrs.
Lewis & Lewis, stating that after the way he had treated
Colonel Custance, the Colonel was not prepared to have
any direct communication with him. If any matter
arose concerning Raymond's future, it must be submitted to the court for decision.

Mr. P. O. Lawrence, K.C., replied for the
respondents. Three letters from Bosie to his wife were
read. The first, written at the Hotel Cecil on
February 2nd, 1915, began by saying that there was no
reason why he should take any notice of her ill-natured
and offensive exhortation to go and fight the Germans.
Douglas then took considerable notice of it by recalling
certain facts. The first was that he had already made
two applications to the Government for a commission.
Both had been unsuccessful. The second was that,
" owing to the horrible persecution " he had undergone
" at you and your father's hands, and of your allies and
assisters, Lewis and Robert Ross," it was only a few
weeks since he had been safe, and even free, to serve
his country. Douglas's third point was that everyone
had agreed that it would not be right or suitable for
him to *enlist* (his own italics) as a private at his age, and
in view of his position. There was no other man in the
whole Army in the ranks in a position corresponding to
his (" the younger son of a marquess and a very well-
known poet and man of letters "). . . . They didn't want
men in the ranks who were the sons of marquesses with
nephews of eighteen and nineteen who have commissions . . . though she and her precious father
thought anything good enough for him. He didn't
quite see, concluded Douglas loftily, why he should
put himself in the position of having to serve in the
ranks. To do so would be a tacit admission that he
considered himself *declassé* and that he had behaved in

such a way as to forfeit his standing as the son of a very ancient and noble house.

Mr. Comyns Carr had originally intended to put Lady Alfred in the box. He changed his mind, however, and she was not called.

In giving judgment, Mr. Justice Eve said that Lord Alfred was perfectly within his rights in making the application, but there must be good grounds for varying the order. The letters showed that Lady Alfred was deeply attached to her husband. But they also showed that she adhered to the view that it was better for the boy that the present arrangement should be continued.

He would not say one word in detriment to Lord Alfred, but he could not altogether shut his eyes to the fact that he had never learnt self-control. One unfortunate incident was the inclusion of the boy's portrait in a work dealing with Oscar Wilde.

He could not see his way to vary the order of the court. The application must be dismissed with costs.

On July 16th Mr. Justice Eve refused a second application to vary the terms of the order so far as it affected Raymond's school holidays.

In this case the application was made on behalf of Lady Queensberry, his grandmother.

9. *Versus* HENRY SAVAGE

On January 27th, 1920, Douglas appeared at the Mansion House on a charge of publishing a defamatory libel concerning Mr. Henry Savage, of Yeoman's Row, South Kensington, in a letter addressed to Mr. W. G. Partington, of 173 Fleet Street.

Mr. L. H. Cannot, prosecuting, said that both Mr. Savage and the defendant were connected with journalism. Mr. Savage had in the previous year contributed an article called "A Bookman's Lost Atlantis" to *The Bookman's Journal,* which was edited by Mr. Partington. A marked copy of that number of the paper was sent anonymously to Lord Alfred, who sent it on to Mr. Partington with a letter saying that he did not suppose him to be personally responsible for sending it so marked, but assumed that it had been sent by the author of the article out of what he called an "exhibition of pitiful, pointless spite." Lord Alfred remembered showing Mr. Savage some kindness when editing *The Academy;* this, and the fact that he was a votary of the Oscar Wilde cult, had, said Douglas, apparently moved him to demonstrate after the fashion of his kind. . . . "If you will take my advice," the letter went on, "you will cut out Henry Savage from your paper." While the letter was not intended for publication, Mr. Partington was at liberty to show it to Mr. Savage if he cared to do so.

Mr. Partington did care. And, as a result, Mr. Savage brought the action. There was an examination, followed by the inevitable cross-examination of Mr. Partington. There were complicated arguments concerning the moral significance of *Dorian Gray.* Mr. Comyns Carr, for Douglas, asked Mr. Partington if he knew that the publishers of the collected edition of Wilde's works refused to include it. Mr. Partington did not know. Mr. Carr quoted "A Wildeana book with a verbatim account of The Author's Trial, prefaced by articles by Lord Alfred Douglas and others," issued by Charles Carrington at a guinea.* "Would you," asked counsel, "regard a book containing an account of the trial of Oscar Wilde as an obscene book?" Mr. Partington did not know the book. Didn't he know enough to say whether a verbatim account would be an obscene book? Mr. Partington, it seemed, had never even read an account of the trial. On being further

---

*Carrington was also the publisher of *The Return of Dorian Gray,* both books appearing in Paris.

pressed, he admitted that he considered a book containing a verbatim report *would* be obscene, and that he would not like to have it stated that such a work had been written with a preface by him. . . . He did not know that the poem " The Sphinx," which the article referred to as " that curious product of perversity," was a peculiarly filthy production.

He had never found any of the articles contributed by Savage contained anything objectionable. And, finally, and fatally so far as the plaintiff's case was concerned, he did not think the letter conveyed the impression that Mr. Savage was addicted to certain practices.

At this point the Lord Mayor, Sir E. Cooper, said that he had made up his mind. No jury would convict if he referred the case to another court. By " belonging to the Oscar Wilde cult " the letter merely meant that Mr. Savage was one of those who " wrote up " Oscar Wilde.

The case was dismissed.

10. *Versus* " THE EVENING NEWS "

On February 4th, 1921, the following announcement appeared in what is known as the " Lunch Edition " of *The Evening News*:

SUDDEN DEATH OF LORD ALFRED DOUGLAS

FOUND DEAD IN BED BY A MAID

HEART FAILURE AFTER A CHILL

The story was then elaborated. It was followed by an obituary notice—one of those in which the writer has come, not to bury Caesar, but to blame him.

It began:

A GREAT LIFE SPOILT. . . . HOW THE EVIL GENIUS OF THE DOUGLASES DOGGED LORD ALFRED,

and continued:

A brilliant and most unhappy career is ended. Lord Alfred Douglas was born, in a sense, under the happiest auspices. He was a Douglas, the son of one of the most ancient families in Britain. He was connected with many of the " best people " in society, he had brilliant capacities, and showed that he was certainly to be numbered among the poets.

He might have done anything, and, his poetry excepted, he did nothing and worse than nothing.

The charity which is fitting at all times, but most fitting when we are speaking of the newly-dead, urges that much should be forgiven to this poor, bewildered man, who, with all his gifts, will perhaps only be remembered by the scandals and the quarrels in which he involved himself.

It is a great thing, in a sense, to be born a Douglas, but the family inheritance had gifts from evil fairies as well as from good ones.

It would not be true to say that all ancient races are degenerate, but there are very marked signs of degeneracy in the House of Douglas.

Many of them are violently eccentric, to put the case mildly.

But a little later the error was discovered. Douglas was still very much alive, and *The Evening News* inserted in its 6.30 edition a short notice admitting the fact.

LORD ALFRED DOUGLAS

AN UNFOUNDED REPORT OF HIS DEATH

The Evening News learns that the report that Lord Alfred Douglas died suddenly is without foundation.

We regret having given currency to the inaccurate statement.

" I am very glad to say I am in the best of health," Lord Alfred said this afternoon.

Two months later he emphasized the fact by bringing an action for libel against The Associated Newspapers, the company controlling *The Evening News*.

The case opened on November 25th before Mr. Justice Horridge, sitting in the King's Bench Division, and a special jury. Mr. A. S. Comyns Carr and Mr. Ignatius Keppy appeared for the plaintiff; Mr. Hogg,

K.C., Mr. J. B. Melville and Mr. Lawson Campbell
for the defendants. When the case was called, the judge
asked whether the action was one which might be tried
by a mixed jury, as matters might be discussed which
were not suitable for such—" matters of an indelicate
nature," amplified his Lordship, and explained to the
embarrassed jury the sort of thing that might arise.
When he had finished, several women members
requested permission not to serve. They were excused,
and their places taken by men.

Mr. Comyns Carr then opened the case. He pointed
out, what one would have imagined to be fairly obvious,
that to publish a statement to the effect that a person
is dead is not in itself libellous. The libel lay entirely
in the obituary notice.

The Evening News had stated that Lord Alfred " had
done nothing, and worse than nothing." Mr. Carr also
complained of the use of the word " degenerate," and,
to put the case tactfully, of the meaning which might
reasonably be attached to the phrase.

The Evening News, he contended, had not
apologized. It did not apologize now. On the contrary,
it pleaded justification, and supported it by giving
details of Douglas's past. Mr. Comyns Carr contended
that the facts which they quoted, Douglas's failure to
take a degree at Oxford, the old, old stories of his clashes
with his father and his friendship with Wilde, and the
friction between him and Colonel Custance, constituted no justification at all.

Mr. Hogg, K.C., counsel for the defendants, rose. He
said that in the circumstances *The Evening News*
obituary was " a very kindly one." He summarized once
more the plaintiff's clashes with authority. He quoted
letters from Wilde, letters already referred to *ad
nauseam* elsewhere. He quoted articles in *The
Academy*.

This last brought the plaintiff to his feet in indignant

protest. Counsel, he said, had made a mistake in one of the stanzas. He should read what was there.

Mr. Justice Horridge told the plaintiff that if he did not behave himself he would have him removed from the court.

" He is reading things that are not in the book," said Douglas.

" You have no right to interfere," retorted the judge. " You have your counsel behind you, and you must not interrupt."

No case was humdrum in which Douglas played any important rôle.

Mr. A. E. Olley, editor of *The Evening News,* explained in detail how information of Lord Alfred's death had been received by phone from a woman who described herself as a private secretary.

A doctor, a former Roman Catholic chaplain in the Army, and the Catholic Bishop of Clifton gave evidence of Douglas's physical and mental fitness. They were followed in the witness box by the plaintiff himself. He expressed his shame and horror and repugnance at the Wilde letters; and added that in condemning *Salome* he had described Wilde as the greatest force for evil that had appeared in the world for three hundred and fifty years.

The story of the quarrel with his father-in-law over the custody of the boy was told; so, under cross-examination, was that of certain verses in *The Chameleon* and of the story of " The Priest and the Acolyte," and of his translation of the play *Salome.*

The cross-examination trailed on. Once or twice the monotony was broken by " laughter in court," as when the plaintiff admitted he had written to the King complaining of the way in which he had been treated by Colonel Custance, and had received a reply thanking him for the letter, and saying that it would receive attention. There was further laughter when Douglas added: " I knew that the King was shooting in the same county as my father-in-law, and I wanted him to know the kind of person he was associating with." He then admitted that he had written to Lord Clonmell calling him a damned Irish pig-doctor " because Lord Clonmell had taken Lady Alfred to a boxing match." At this point a juryman, with whom one has every sympathy, inquired plaintively if it was necessary for them to hear all this? It had to be allowed, said his Lordship, lest either side should say that justice had not been done. So the revelations inexorably continued.

Douglas was questioned about his contempt of court. The questions involved " Eve and the Serpent," a general indictment of certain aspects of the Chancery Court, and a play upon Mr. Justice Eve's name. It was, said Douglas, " not violent abuse but a satire, and some people have called it brilliant." There was one place in which he referred to " Balmy Eve." He had also referred to the Lord Chancellor as a shameless Smith, " because of the most mischievous and abominable decisions ever given."

" So if a judge is against you," commented counsel for *The Evening News,* " he is a leering knave and a pitiable pup."

On Monday, November 28th, the case came to an end. Horridge, summing up, was definitely in Douglas's favour; and the jury were absent only a quarter of an hour before bringing in a verdict for the plaintiff.

They assessed the damages at £1,000, and added their collective opinion that the original letters of Wilde ought to be destroyed.

11. *Versus* THE RT. HON. WINSTON LEONARD SPENCER CHURCHILL

In 1923 the litigation pitcher, already considerably chipped, was taken to the legal well once too often.

This particular visit really dated from some three years earlier, when Douglas, as editor of *Plain English,* which had ended its career of tactless plain speaking in 1923, published a series of articles dealing with the official communiqués that had followed the Battle of Jutland.

Douglas had written the articles with his usual contempt for the law of libel. In effect, they charged a group of Jewish financiers with deliberately influencing the tone of the official communiqués for their own ends.

The politician directly responsible for the communiqués, and so influenced by the financiers, was stated to be Mr. Winston Churchill.

This charge had led to another. The editor of *The Jewish Guardian* wrote to *The Morning Post* in protest. *The Post* printed the letter, or at any rate part of it, upon which Douglas immediately launched an action for libel against the latter paper. In the course of the action he was cross-examined by Sir Patrick Hastings. Readers of the *Autobiography* will hardly be surprised to learn that Douglas could say without fear of contradiction that he wiped the floor with Sir Patrick almost as effectively as he did in the case of Marshall Hall. (Had Sir Patrick thought it worth while, he might have contradicted him. But he did not think it worth while.)

With which consolation, a grievance against his own counsel, and a farthing damages without costs against the *Post,* Douglas had had to be content.

All that belonged to the *Plain English* days. Mr. Churchill himself, as well as Mr. (later Earl) Balfour, had then specifically stated upon oath that Mr. Churchill had had nothing whatever to do with the issue of the statements about the Battle of Jutland, and that it was an inherent impossibility that any sinister Semitic influence could be laid at his charge.

Churchill could have brought an action on the strength of the *Plain English* articles alone. But for reasons which were afterwards stated he did not do so.

The truculent Douglas waited until the summer of 1923, then he returned to the attack. This time it was launched from a different angle. At a public meeting convened by what declared itself to be " The Lord Kitchener and Jutland Publicity Committee," held at the Memorial Hall, Farringdon Street, on August 3rd, he addressed a large audience of the general public.

He referred first to *The Jewish Guardian* letter that had appeared in *The Morning Post*. Also the fact that, while his action against the *Post* had been tried, that against *The Jewish Guardian* itself had not yet come before the court. In connection with the *Post* action, Douglas mentioned that he had confidently expected a verdict of £1,000, instead of the farthing he received. He also said that Comyns Carr, his counsel, " a poor frightened rabbit," appeared to have lost the wits with which nature had endowed him. After which, he passed on from the charges he had made against one eminent Jew, Sir Alfred Mond (later Lord Melchett), to those against another, Sir Ernest Cassel; also against Mr. Churchill.

The statements he made were, in effect, an amplification of the article he had written in *Plain English*. They were more specific and unequivocal. He charged Churchill with issuing a report (the first of three) on the Battle of Jutland which he knew to be false, and with afterwards receiving a large sum of money from Sir Ernest Cassel. He reminded his audience that he had stated at the time of *The Morning Post* trial that he did not believe a word of Balfour's evidence in connection with the production of a draft report in Balfour's own handwriting. Douglas had then been asked if he knew that Balfour had sworn that he wrote the report himself. Douglas had known, but had not believed that statement either. And when asked by Sir Patrick Hastings if he was suggesting that Balfour had forged the report, he had retorted that it was quite possible that Lewis & Lewis had forged it.

Douglas passed on to his second accusation. It was again specific, and even more dramatic—that Lord Kitchener had been deliberately murdered as the result of a plot by the Jews. He knew more now, he told the meeting, than when he had first made the charge in *Plain English*. He quoted the evidence of a man whose parents lived on a farm in the Orkneys, in sight of the spot where the *Hampshire* went down. Kitchener had embarked with a body of picked experts in finance, transport and commissariat, their object being to accompany him to Russia to replace the corrupt Bolshevik Jews who were holding all the key positions there. The *Hampshire* left, but without the destroyers who were to have accompanied and protected her. The Hidden Hand of Jewry had ordered them to put back. Between Birsay Bay and Brough Head the *Hampshire* struck a mine and blew up. The wreck floated for some considerable time after the explosion, but—the Hidden Hand again—the lifeboat did not even start until five hours after the news of the explosion had been received, and when it had traversed a mile or so of the ten which separated it from the wreck it was recalled. Of the seventy men who drifted ashore, only eleven survived the night. Those eleven were cared for by the hospitable farmers of that inhospitable coast. They remained there for several days but, as soon as they were sufficiently recovered, they were taken by the authorities to London, since when, added Douglas significantly, no trace of any of them had been seen. The Orkney farmers themselves were forbidden to talk. No divers had been sent down by the Admiralty to investigate the cause of the *Hampshire's* sinking.

To these appalling revelations Douglas added his own solution of the mystery. Where he had received his information he refused to say, lest his informant should suffer the mysterious fate of the *Hampshire* survivors, but the Duke of Northumberland, hand in glove with *The Morning Post*, had for two years had all the evidence in his possession. Incidentally, the Duke had collected £30,000 from the public after the murder of Sir Henry Wilson, and never accounted for the money.

Finally—or nearly finally—Douglas said that he knew a German naval officer personally acquainted with Captain Hermann, who had commanded every submarine in the North Sea during the war. Hermann had solemnly assured Douglas's informant that there was not a German submarine or mine within a hundred miles of the *Hampshire* when she sank.

The meeting ended with a resolution, passed unanimously, demanding that the Government should form a Committee of Inquiry into the circumstances which caused the death of Lord Kitchener.

Douglas's reasons for launching this particularly virulent and melodramatic campaign at this particular time are obscure. His enemies might have shrugged their shoulders and murmured the couplet concerning Satan's employment for idle hands. His friends, as always, rallied round him nobly. The committee included his sister, Lady Edith Fox-Pitt; Harry de Windt, the explorer; General Prescott-Decie, who was in the chair; Colonel Haines; the Hon. Mrs. Greville-Nugent and Mr. Cunningham.

The meeting was reported in *The Border Standard*. And that report was, in turn, published by Douglas as an eight-page pamphlet that was printed in Galashiels.

It was this pamphlet which formed the basis of the action for libel brought against Douglas in London in the following November.

On the 6th of that month he was charged—
inaccurately—as The Honourable Lord Alfred Bruce
Douglas, before Sir Chartres Biron, with having at the
Temple Station on October 30th published a
defamatory libel on the Right Hon. Winston Leonard
Spencer Churchill, in the form of a pamphlet entitled
" The Murder of Lord Kitchener and the Truth about
the Battle of Jutland and the Jews." Sir Richard Muir
and Mr. Vincent Evans conducted the case for the
Director of Public Prosecutions. The defendant was
not legally represented. Lord Queensberry and Lady
Edith Fox-Pitt, his brother and sister, were in court.
So, too, was Mr. Winston Churchill.

Sir Richard, opening the case, pointed out that the
issues were extremely simple. Did Lord Alfred publish
the pamphlet and, if he did, was it or was it not
libellous? The truth or the reverse of the statements
made in the pamphlet were entirely immaterial.

The story of the anti-Semitic attacks in *The Academy*
and *Plain English,* and the subsequent publication of
a letter from the editor of *The Jewish Guardian* in *The
Morning Post* and of the sequel in the libel action
brought by the defendant, was briefly told. From
that, Muir passed on to the Memorial Hall meeting,
and the publication of Douglas's speech in pamphlet
form.

It was stated that he had had about forty thousand*
copies of the pamphlet printed, and arranged for its
distribution in London. Two thousand copies had
actually been sold.

Defendant, who accepted full responsibility, was
asked if he had anything he wished to say before being
committed for trial.

Douglas had. But his statement was brief—merely
that he had intended to show that his action had been
in the public interest.

* This number was afterwards amended to thirty thousand.

He was then committed for trial, bail being allowed on two sureties of £100 each.

The trial began on December 10th, before Mr. Justice Avory at the Central Criminal Court, which was crowded. The Attorney-General, Sir Douglas Hogg, K.C. (later Lord Hailsham), Sir R. Muir and Mr. H. M. Green appeared for the prosecution. Mr. Cecil Hayes once again represented the defendant.

The case was opened by Hayes entering a plea of justification. Then the old story, originating in 1921, was once again unfolded.

The prosecution opened with the statements that, as Lord Alfred had been aware from the first, Mr. Churchill had not been responsible for the first Jutland communiqué; that the articles in *Plain English* were a mass of fantastic lying, and that no action had been taken then merely because it was the considered opinion of the Attorney-General that it would be better not to give the writer of such articles any further free advertisement, but to let the whole thing die down.

The actual facts regarding the published reports of the Battle of Jutland were then dealt with, detail by detail.

Lord Balfour, on receipt of an account of the losses of ourselves and the enemy from Lord Jellicoe, the naval commander-in-chief, had personally drawn up the first report. With that, and with a supplementary communiqué, Mr. Churchill—who had not been at the Admiralty for months, nor a member of the Cabinet since 1915—had had no connection whatever. It was not until Lord Balfour decided on his own initiative to ask his old friend to collaborate with him in drawing up a third statement, one which might act as an antidote to the generally depressing effect that the two earlier communiqués had had on public opinion, that Mr. Churchill came upon the scene at all.

The myth of his having received from his Jewish

friends suites of furniture, money or anything else in circumstances which, had it been true, would have amounted to bribery of the crudest and most infamous sort, was also dealt with.

Lord Balfour gave evidence. Cross-examined by Mr. Hayes, he denied that Mr. Churchill had continued to render assistance at the Admiralty. There were typically Balfourian touches in the course of the cross-examination.

" Did you see the leading article in *The Times* on the Battle of Jutland?" asked Mr. Hayes.

" Probably not," said Lord Balfour.

" Do you read *The Times*?"

" It is not the sort of journal I abstain from reading."

" Was there not a storm of indignation in the Press that an English victory was made to seem like a German one?"

" There was a strong attack made on me," said Lord Balfour.

" I am sorry——" began Mr. Hayes.

" It did me no harm," said Lord Balfour airily.

Then Churchill himself gave evidence. His memory of what happened, he said, was absolutely clear. In brief, it amounted to this. He had been called in unofficially, and asked to write an appreciation of the actual situation for the neutral Press, and with the second but perhaps even more important object of counteracting the depressing effect of the earlier reports upon the home population. He had said he would only do so at the direct request of Lord Balfour, whom he had not even seen since they had crossed swords on the Navy estimates. The direct request was made, and the " appreciation " written.

The rest of Mr. Churchill's evidence was, in the main, a flat and complete denial of the statements made in the articles printed in *Plain English,* in the speech at the Memorial Hall, and in the report in the pamphlet concerning his connection with Jewish financiers and his resultant highly profitable transactions on the Stock Exchange. His friendship with Sir Ernest Cassel actually dated from the parliamentary days of his father, Lord Randolph Churchill.

As already stated, he had deliberately ignored the original libels in *Plain English* on the advice of the Attorney-General.

After a long and singularly inept cross-examination, the case was adjourned.

The cross-examination was resumed on December 12th. Counsel asked why Mr. Churchill had taken no action against *The Morning Post,* which, in the course of an article headed "A Front of Brass," wrote: " It is only charitable to suppose that Mr. Churchill is in fact incapable of telling the truth or anything like it."

Mr. Churchill cheerfully retorted that he had had to put up with a good deal of abuse at election time.

Defendant's counsel, going off at a tangent, referred to the Quorn, and to the possibility of Sir Ernest Cassel's being appointed Master. " You remember how he used to speak," said Mr. Hayes. " A full-blown German naturalized in England! Do you remember what he looked like sitting on a horse?"

"What," inquired Mr. Justice Avory, tactfully ignoring any question of Sir Ernest's horsemanship, " was the matter with his voice?"

To which Mr. Hayes answered: " I suggest the German accent."

The cross-examination dragged on. Towards the end, Mr. Hayes said: " I suggest that throughout the war you were a wholly discredited person."

" I repudiate that suggestion," said Mr. Churchill. " I do not believe it true. If it were, it would be undeserved."

The Dardenelles campaign came under review. So did the amount paid for his book, *The World Crisis,*

and a leading article in *The Daily Mail*. Also whether
a man telling the truth when he is under the impression
that it is an untruth is, or is not, a liar; and whether
megalomania is, or is not, the only form of sanity. . . .
Leaving these abstractions and coming back to more
easily grasped matters, Mr. Hayes then referred to Mr.
Churchill's visit to Nice in 1922, to Sir Edgar Speyer's
degradation, to a watch given to Mr. Churchill by the
late Sir Ernest Cassel's family, and to a conversation
with Lord Haig at a civic luncheon in Dundee.

Mr. Churchill emerged unruffled from the ordeal.
He was then re-examined, and eventually left the box
at ten minutes past three and took a seat beside his wife.

He must have been glad of a rest. He had been in
the box the previous afternoon and the whole of that
morning.

An admiral gave evidence; so did a permanent under-
secretary for the Colonies, so did one of Mr. Balfour's
private secretaries. And the next day Admiral of the
Fleet Sir Henry Jackson and Sir Edward Packe, his late
assistant private secretary, were examined and cross-
examined. Later, Mr. Geddes, who had been Sir Ernest
Cassel's secretary, added his quota to the accumulation
of evidence, refuting the allegation that Sir Ernest
Cassel and Mr. Churchill, in collusion or not, made any
money out of selling British or German War Stock.
(The modest total of " The Syndicate " referred to in
Plain English was £54,000,000.)

Mr. Hayes's cross-examination of the witnesses for
the prosecution had from the first an inconsequence
that might have been borrowed from *Alice in
Wonderland*.

Apropos of War Stock he said to Geddes : " You
don't suggest that Sir E. Cassel gave £2,000,000 as a
present to a war fund or anything else?"

Mr. Geddes said " No."

" It was what every poor person in the middle-class

was advised to do at the time," pursued Mr. Hayes. Mr. Geddes, naturally dazed at the prospect of every middle-class person subscribing £2,000,000, could only murmur an assent.

"Do you know how much Sir Ernest subscribed to the funds for the Kaiser's Jubilee?" asked counsel a moment later.

"That," said Mr. Geddes, at last on safe ground, "I could not tell."

"What," Mr. Justice Avory interrupted, "is the date of the Jubilee you speak of?"

"I have not the faintest idea," said the witness.

Counsel's speech for the defence included a word-picture of Mr. Churchill which deserves to be retrieved from the oblivion of old newspaper files, if only for its remarkable English.

"In the witness box," said Mr. Hayes, "he frowned like a sphinx, rasped out a bitter reply, and the next moment he would smile a blandishment almost large enough to swallow you all." Later on Mr. Churchill became "a Napoleon who directed the destinies of our country in a frock-coat from London. . . . Nelson and Napoleon," asseverated Mr. Hayes, rising to yet greater heights, "would have been like mere cyphers in history compared with him." He concluded his speech with a passing reference to Macaulay's New Zealander.

Douglas was called to give evidence. Almost at once a passage of arms took place between him and the judge.

Avory objected to certain questions put to Douglas by his counsel as irrelevant.

"Lord Balfour," retaliated Douglas, addressing Avory, "was allowed to give evidence for many minutes without being interrupted, and I think a man on his trial should be allowed to speak in his own defence."

The story, or at least part of the story, of *Plain English* was told, and it followed Douglas's statement that a certain army officer had given him some information about the Battle of Jutland.

Douglas, who had drawn a salary of £50 a month as editor of *Plain English,* ceased to hold the post from October 16th, 1921. The officer had taken his place, and shortly afterwards became proprietor as well.

When he left, said Douglas, he was very angry, and the proprietor and he had a violent quarrel. His action against *The Morning Post* became entangled in the story, because it was after that action that he printed the pamphlet. Forty thousand copies were ordered before he was arrested, said Douglas, who had written to the printers telling them that he would probably require a hundred thousand. He could, he added in his evidence, have easily sold a million. An undischarged bankrupt since 1913, he had not made enough out of *Plain English* to get his discharge. He had always been a very poor man, and was left very little by his father.*

In a letter published in *Plain English* on March 19th, 1921, Douglas had issued a typical challenge. He was not, he said, in the least afraid of the Public Prosecutor, " backed up by the evil forces of the present Government." " If he fondly imagines he will be able to obtain a conviction," wrote Douglas, " in the absence of Mr. Churchill, he is making an even greater mistake than the Government made when they put up Darling in a vain attempt to convict Pemberton Billing."

The reading of this letter in court provoked an outburst from the defendant.

" I haven't been able to put my case before the court at all," he said. " I have been treated grossly unfairly. Every time I have tried to put my case to the jury, I have been prevented from doing so. It is the most abom-

*It was £20,000, according to his own account in the *Autobiography.* (See page 156.)

inable piece of unfairness I have ever seen in my life!"

Reference was made to another article which appeared on June 4th, 1921, suggesting that there should be a film exhibition of the British Admiralty recalling the destroyers and allowing the Germans to escape, and another film showing Balfour and Churchill reading a list of Jutland casualties and deciding to withhold them until the correction of the false report might safely be issued without disturbing Sir Ernest Cassel's peace of mind. Douglas, it appeared, was not the author of these ironic suggestions. But he admitted that as an editor he had passed the article for publication. It was, he said, written " in a more or less jocular way."

Avory asked acidly : " Do you call that jocular?"

" It was," said Douglas, " written in a sarcastic way."

" That won't do!" said his Lordship.

The army officer gave evidence on behalf of the defence. His evidence was delivered with less excitement, but in the course of the Attorney-General's cross-examination he included details even more dramatic than Douglas's. He admitted that he had been told that there had been an order in *The London Gazette* depriving him of his rank. Also that he had been twice convicted by the civil power.

" By jobs that you put up," amended the witness. " You have had me watched for three years, and spent thousands of pounds on detectives." He had been sentenced to six months' imprisonment for libel in February, 1922, and in the current year fined forty shillings for insulting behaviour. Furthermore, he had been three times certified for delusional insanity.

" If I *was* certified, I did not know it," he said.

Plain English, continued the Attorney-General, had referred to him as a gallant gentleman who was a great friend of the Duke of Northumberland. It was unfortunate that the Duke himself had stated that he had never in his life seen or even heard of the gallant gentleman.

On Friday, December 14th, his cross-examination and re-examination was continued.

His evidence became less and less an asset to the defendant's case. Among other statements, he said that he had met Lady Randolph Churchill when she was living in a flat in St. James's Place. The prosecution proved that Lady Randolph had not had a flat in St. James's Place since 1883 — seven years before the witness was born. He further stated that, reluctant though he was to mention it, he had met Mr. Churchill coming out of Boodle's Club "in an unfortunate condition." There was loud laughter in court. Mr. Churchill, laughing as heartily as the rest, then explained that he had never been a member of the club and never entered it.

Followed a long and lurid account by the officer of his discovery of an organized assassination planned by Lenin, of the report of the plot that he made at Salonika, and of the unfortunate view that the authorities took of his story. For they had hustled him away in an ambulance and put him in a cell with a raving lunatic. From these embarrassments he had eventually escaped in pyjamas concealed by a Red Cross nurse's uniform.

Mr. William Sorley Brown, editor of *The Border Standard,* gave evidence of having printed the Memorial Hall speech from a typewritten copy supplied by Douglas. According to a newspaper report, Mr. Brown began by taking the oath at the top of his voice.

"Are you deaf?" asked Lord Avory.

The witness said he wasn't.

" He comes from Scotland," said Mr. Hayes, and the explanation was accepted as adequate.

There was a short speech for the defence, ending in

a quotation from one of the defendant's poems. There was a long speech from the prosecution, entirely in legal prose. There was a still longer summing up, in the course of which the judge said that he did not believe that any counsel in a court of justice had ever been allowed greater latitude than had been allowed to Mr. Cecil Hayes. And then the case, which had shown signs of following in the Jarndyce-*versus*-Jarndyce tradition, came to an end.

The jury retired and, after an absence of only eight minutes, returned a verdict of guilty.

The judge, addressing the prisoner at considerable length, sentenced him to six months' imprisonment in the second division, at the end of which time he would have to find £100 surety " to keep the peace and be of good behaviour to all His Majesty's subjects, particularly Mr. Winston Churchill." Failing to find such a surety, there would be a six months' extension of the sentence.

The jury were exempt from further service for five years. Once again one feels that they had earned it.

The Times published a leading article on the case on the following day.

It began: " There will be general agreement with the verdict of the jury who tried the case against Lord Alfred Douglas. To those who have watched the career of the man, it (six months' imprisonment) will be regarded as a moderate sentence. For years, in newspapers and in circulars and in pamphlets, he has conducted a campaign of irresponsible calumny regardless of facts and intrepid in defamatory invective. At last he has been laid by the heels in quite a gentle way, but in a way which we hope—not with great confidence— will teach him a lesson."

CHAPTER IX

THE LATER YEARS

AFTER the loss of his actions against Custance and against Ransome, Douglas's affairs seem to have suffered a general deterioration. As a result of his bankruptcy, his club, White's, was closed to him. He had, he states, only two friends in the world upon whom he could wholeheartedly rely—his mother, and George Wyndham, his cousin. His wife and son were living with Olive's parents.

But his deserted, half-empty house at Hampstead did not remain without a mistress, using the word in both senses. Before the Custance case was ended a young and beautiful girl, whose name he indicates only by the initials " D. E.," had arrived with a pearl necklace and other jewellery which she wanted to sell for his benefit. Douglas was properly grateful. But he did not accept the offer. He found her waiting outside the court to hear the result of the case, and after that they met daily, and, recounts Douglas with his usual naïveté, went about together in a perfectly innocent way. He could not, he told her, as a Catholic, lead any other kind of life. Later, however, his scruples dissolved, and for three or four months they lived together. The financial stringency was eased by advance royalties on *Oscar Wilde and Myself* and by selling the letters and books of Wilde.

The scarcely surprising result of this liaison was a still firmer conviction on the part of Colonel Custance that his son-in-law was not a suitable husband for Olive, and an even less suitable father for his grandson,

Raymond. Private detectives watched the comings and goings at the house in Church Row; Douglas, totally unimpressed, records that he and the beautiful " D. E." used to identify and laugh at them.

It was Olive, the wronged wife, his " Opal " who, whatever her divergence from Bosie's first idealistic conception, could nevertheless show loyalty allied to a robust common sense in her treatment of her temperamental husband, who ended an impossible situation.

She rang him up, and suggested a meeting. The mere sound of her voice acted magically. The reign of the generous, unconventional, beautiful " D. E." came to an abrupt end. That it was also a stormy end was inevitable. (Later she wrote to say that she had returned to her native America and was now well-to-do. Whatever her new career, it could hardly have been more exciting than life with Bosie. One hopes it had a happier ending.)

He and Olive made it up, though they never lived together again. They reached a placid plateau of friendship, but the landscape of their lives was never to be bathed in the lovely light of their early passion, or a later steadier glow of perfect understanding and sympathy.

Douglas says that the reconciliation was a " nasty knock " for Custance and Sir George Lewis, who had both taken up a campaign against him. It is a little difficult to see why. Custance may have detested Douglas as much as he disapproved of him, and probably did, but a quiescent son-in-law, however objectionable, is obviously a smaller thorn in the flesh than one who entails the constant nervous strain of receiving libellous post cards and the constant expense of employing private detectives. As for Sir George, eminent solicitors are not in the habit of frittering away their energies in a vendetta against a young man who is, at his worst, a mere nuisance.

The complications involved in his separation from Raymond continued to provide material for the Court of Chancery. The matter had originally been dealt with by Mr. Justice Eve. Douglas's version, which he states is curtailed because he does not wish to blame his wife, stresses the point that he was not deprived of the custody of his child. As stated elsewhere,* the terms imposed by the court were that Bosie should pay the costs of Raymond's schooling, also that during the holidays the boy should spend two-fifths of his time with his father and three-fifths of his time with his grandfather.

The inequality of the division exasperated Douglas. The decision included every quality guaranteed to exasperate him—legal finality, a bias in favour of his arch-enemy, and the suggestion, in itself a snub and a mortal insult, that he was not a proper person to be given the complete charge of a small boy, and that small boy his son, for more than two or three weeks at a time. He insists that he had done nothing at all to make himself unfit to have the complete custody of Raymond. If the Court of Chancery refused to accept that view, so much the worse for the Court of Chancery.

The blood of generations of raiding Douglases ran in his veins. If the law challenged his right to his own, he was more than willing to take up the challenge. He kidnapped the boy, and took him to Fort Augustus to be educated by the monks under their abbot, Sir David Hunter Blair, secure in the knowledge that the court's jurisdiction could not extend to Scotland, and that so long as they both remained there nothing could be done.

Colonel Custance was the last person on earth to accept such a *fait accompli* lying down. He sent a detective to the hotel in Fort Worth at which the two

*See page 249.

were staying, and, in the absence of Douglas, persuaded the boy to return to Weston Hall.

Douglas's riposte to that was an application to Mr. Munro-Ferguson, the Scottish Lord-Advocate, for a warrant to arrest the Colonel on a charge of kidnapping. The Lord-Advocate refused to grant one. Douglas's comment is that he was a friend of Mr. Asquith. Possibly. But the friendship is hardly likely to have influenced him as much as the fact that the applicant himself was the original kidnapper.

Custance retaliated by asking Mr. Justice Eve, the Chancery judge who had dismissed Douglas's previous application, to commit Douglas for contempt of court. Eve handed the matter over to Mr. Justice Peterson. Douglas—here, I think, on safer ground—suggests that by this time Eve had had enough of him and his affairs.

The committal order was issued. When Douglas was brought up for judgment, Peterson, doubtless anxious for a peaceful settlement of a painful and complicated family quarrel, offered to revert to the old two-fifths three-fifths division. In the interval, however, Douglas discovered that Raymond had been secretly corresponding with his grandfather and that, so far from being "kidnapped" from Fort Worth, he had left with the detective of his own free will. On learning this Douglas washed his hands of the boy completely.

He did not even see him again for nearly ten years. The reconciliation with his wife was a step in the right direction. But it was a short step, and one which had very little effect on his domestic affairs. Olive went back to her father's house; Douglas, having given up the Hampstead house of mixed memories, went to live with his mother at Chelsea.

After the second Ross trial, and the prolonged disputes in Chancery over the custody of Raymond, Douglas's life seems to have entered upon one of those quiet periods, so brief and so infrequent in the tempestuous years of his middle age. He continued to live with Lady Queensberry, but outside London, in the less stimulating neighbourhood of Lewes.

Douglas was over fifty when he went to prison.

He wrote afterwards of his six months there as " unrelieved misery all the time "; comparison with Wilde's prison days of a generation earlier is inevitable.

Wilde's was a two-year stretch with hard labour; Douglas's a quarter of that time and in the second division, which meant more letters and more visits. Apart from these differences, the whole conception of prison treatment had changed since *De Profundis* registered another poet's reactions and the son of another marquess, whose five years' sentence was almost contemporary with Wilde's two years', wrote that prosaic, far more factual documentary record, *Penal Servitude,* by " W. B. N."*

Douglas was entering upon the period when one sees, still distant, but nevertheless inexorably clear, the shadowy glades of old age. It is a prospect which, without terrifying the spirit, should make for cooler blood and an intelligent realization of the dark unknown in which that shadowy glade must end.

In 1911 he had been formally accepted into the Roman Catholic Church. He deals with his conversion at some length in the *Autobiography;* perhaps the only surprising aspect of it is that he lingered so long outside the fold. Among the many letters I have received was one rather touching one from a fellow-Catholic concluding: "We still pray for the repose of Lord Alfred's soul."

Douglas did not forget his enmities. He attacked less frequently, though with the old vehemence. But he avoided entanglement with the law.

A skilled amateur pianist, whose playing at a concert

* Lord William Nevill, sentenced in 1898 to five years' penal servitude for fraud.

so charmed Douglas that he wrote afterwards asking if he might call, has given me a pleasant little picture of their first meeting. Her maid brought in his card but, when a little later he appeared, her immediate impression was that Douglas had sent his secretary to apologize for his failure to keep the appointment. It seemed impossible, she says, that the slim, active figure with the fair hair and vivid blue eyes could be that of a man in the middle fifties.

That visit became the first of many; she recalls particularly his gay, high-pitched laugh, and, on one occasion, his leaping upon a chair when a mouse crossed the room. He had a lifelong aversion from mice, which had driven him nearly frantic when they appeared in prison.

There is another story of Douglas, told me by Mr. Peter Noble, a youthful protégé. He and a friend, both of whom were professionally interested in the circus, heard of one which was billed to appear in Hove, where Douglas was then living. They invited him to see the show, with the added attraction of being introduced to the proprietor and his wife.

But they omitted to explain that, since the days of "Lord" George Sanger, it has become an established and recognized custom, so far as this country is concerned, for the owners of all circuses to endow themselves with titles. In this case, the Cockney proprietor was a self-created French Count and his wife a Countess. As such—again strictly according to circus etiquette—they were introduced to Douglas. The lady accepted "Lord Alfred Douglas" at "Big Top" valuation. As he moved away, she inquired in a clearly audible voice: "An' wot show is 'e connected wiv?"

His friendship with Shaw lasted to the day of his death. Shaw's letters, a number of which I have been privileged to see, always began "Dear Boy." They contained advice, frequently ironic, always Shavian; their tone suggests a shrewd, amused, disillusioned elder brother addressing a youngster who still needs looking after.

To Mr. S. L. Allcorn I am indebted for the following vivid little sketch:

" I first met Lord Alfred in 1930. I had had the temerity to criticize his interpretation of a Shakespeare sonnet, an indiscretion which promptly brought three or four pages of what I then regarded as abuse, though when I recall the savagery of his attacks in other directions I suppose I ought to have regarded his letter as mere rebuke. He sugared the pill, however, by commending some of my work, and this, coming from one whose ear was one of the finest in English prosody, gave me some comfort. (Incidentally, he considered Rupert Brooke grossly overrated.)

"At the outset he lodged a double claim for his superiority—his ear, and the fact that from the beginning he had made the study of Shakespeare his chief intellectual business and spiritual delight.

" No scholar could have approached Shakespeare in a more reverent mood. He continually emphasized the permanence of Shakespeare and, with his customary lack of modesty, the probable survival of his own work. His detractors have often referred to his ' conceit,' but I do not think they understood him. It was not ' conceit ' in the generally accepted sense of the word, but rather an insistence on the fact that much of his work was good, and a refusal to adopt the childish self-deprecatory attitude so common in lesser minds.

" One point he made was that the craftsman displayed a greater conceit by belittling a good product, in so doing implying that he could do better if he'd been really trying.

" In those days I was living near Hove and, following a few letters, he called on me unexpectedly, and heatedly enlarged upon his theory as to the identity of

Mr. W. H. (later published as *The True History of Shakespeare's Sonnets**). He asked me to tea the following day, and, taking my acceptance for granted, walked out and slammed the door. So began a friendship which continued up to the time of his death.

" Regarded by normal standards, he was impossible, fiery enthusiasms changing to brooding gloom without apparent cause, but for me he was a constant helper, frequently ' boosting ' me with editors, and often causing me embarrassment (incidentally, he himself seemed incapable of embarrassment).

" I still recall our walks in the public gardens, where he unconsciously provided diversion for children by making a show of tearing his hair in impotent rage over some ' anti-formal heretic.'

" During the last few years he became almost fanatically religious. The accepted Della Robbia plaque was soon joined by a plaster model of an angel, suspended by a wire from the ceiling over his bureau, and clothed only in an ill-made madonna-blue garment that emphasized its original nudity. I became used to it in time, but I was often amused by the startled manner in which new visitors regarded the little creature. I wonder where it is now!

" His intolerance is well known. He would become inarticulate with rage and refuse to discuss the pros and cons of a question with which he was unsympathetic, lest he lent it a false importance by such discussion. Luther and Savonarola were as red rags to a bull.

" Of his youthful indiscretions we did not speak, although there was no conscious avoidance of the subject. I do not think this was due to any feeling of delicacy on his part, but rather to his attitude that he had repented long ago, and that his abnegation, and a life of piety and self-denial, had, or should have, eradicated any sense of guilt. Perhaps the theatricalism

*See page 282.

of this unconsciously appealed to a part of him, but, whatever the cause, his sincerity could not be doubted.

" He lived in the past. True, he interested himself in current affairs, but he was more often wrong than right in his forecasts. For example, he told me in the early days of the war that it would not develop into anything much, and would not be comparable with the 1914-18 one in duration or intensity.

" Living in a world of his own, and with his tastes so Catholic, his religion filled what otherwise would have been an empty part of his life. I think that it was only by regarding those last few years as a period of preparation that he found the present age endurable.

" I make no charge of insincerity when I say I think his devotion to his religion was a form of escapism, a retreat from an unsympathetic world. Understanding his complex character, one can sympathize with Alfred Douglas, although he himself would have fiercely denied such promptings.

"A short time before his death he begged me not to worry about him, saying: ' I shall not be long. It's my heart, and I feel so tired.' He *was* tired, tired by his battles, legal, verbal and journalistic—though these affrays had been of his own making. He did not merely join issue with adversaries; he covered three-quarters of the journey before they entered the field. Remonstrance was only a goad to further attacks. I once questioned the benefits of badgering the Press. He would have none of it. ' Keep bashing away at 'em. They'll get tired before I shall,' he said, but I'm afraid they did not demonstrate any prostration.

" Poor A. D.! I am richer by his friendship, for I have the knowledge of a generous man, much maligned —a terrible example of the difference between fame and notoriety; a consistent friend to the one who had nothing to offer but a deep appreciation of his qualities and, perhaps, a certain blindness to his faults.''

Mrs. M. A. Idiens has furnished me with the following:

" In February, 1937 I gave a lecture to the South Place Ethical Society Poetry Circle, Conway Hall, on Lord Alfred Douglas and his poetry, having previously sent Lord Alfred the paper I proposed to read. He returned it with very interesting marginal notes. These included particulars, previously mis-stated, of his kindness to Oscar Wilde after he had been released."

In a later visit to Hove she lunched with Douglas. During the meal they discussed Wilde, but chiefly Shakespeare. Douglas said that he had discovered and proved to be a fact that Mr. W. H. was William Hughes, the handsome boy who for years acted the part of Shakespeare's heroines. Douglas had traced the family of the boy to Canterbury, where he lived with his parents, and where Douglas obtained full particulars. He had not published his discoveries because his publisher had " packed up " and he did not feel sufficiently energetic to obtain another.

" I found Lord Alfred," adds Mrs. Idiens, " to be a man of tremendous bodily restlessness. He talked for hours, but did not sit still for a second. His mind was keen, clear, logical and brilliant in its grasp of his subject. He had a concentrated and vital enthusiasm in everything connected with Shakespeare. His entire interest seemed to centre round literature, and all the aesthetic and abstract beauties of life."

Douglas's corrections to the draft of Mrs. Idiens's paper have a personal touch. She had said that " the ostracization of his work still goes on."

" This is now scarcely true," commented Douglas. On the statement that " Douglas helped Wilde to write *The Importance of Being Earnest,*" he retorted: " This is not quite correct. I do not claim to have helped Wilde in the play except indirectly. The point is that I was in his company all the time when he wrote it, and that from the moment we met he never wrote a single thing except when I was with him, the only exception being *De Profundis,* which is a letter to me."

A reference to Wilde's leaving prison " broken in body and mind " elicited a good many further statements from Douglas on the renewal of their friendship and of their financial relationship. Douglas gave Wilde in the last years of his life £400 in cheques, and a lot of ready money, as well as paying for his funeral, at which Douglas attended as chief mourner, in the church of Sainte Germain du Prés, in Paris.

In the letter accompanying the revised typescript Douglas remarks that, while he himself has been neglected and boycotted up to quite recently because of his connection with Wilde, he has had larger sales during the last forty years than most English poets, and that his poems have sold at least eight thousand copies, " which is good for poetry." The pendulum, he added, after referring with disgust to the way he was treated, and his consequent refusal to allow his work to appear in anthologies, had now swung the other way, and he got a good deal of fame and appreciation.

CHAPTER X

THE MAN OF LETTERS

IT is always difficult to assess adequately the work of any contemporary writer whose name has been widely associated in the public mind with events having no connection with his literary work.

Prejudices warp the critical judgment, and justice is hurried and untempered.

How shall we arrive at the literary status of Alfred Douglas? (His name is not even mentioned, incidentally, in the latest edition of Cousins's remarkably comprehensive *Short Biographical Dictionary of English Literature,* though Wilde is given a paragraph. His serious poems provide nothing for *The Oxford Dictionary of Quotations.*)

He was born with many advantages, apart from genius or talent. His social status was incontestable—one which normally would have opened every door to him. The spectre of an inferiority complex never stood at his elbow, as it does with so many literary aspirants. Nor did the spectre of acute poverty. (Such as he knew was entirely owing to his own thriftlessness.) Nor the lack of education. And with his own physical beauty went a passion for beauty, a love of lovely things which was an integral part of him, which manifested itself particularly in his choice of words, and reached its greatest heights in his poetry.

Where prose was concerned, his work was often lamentably and incredibly different. His pen would run away with him in a flurry of foolish phrases, or sprawl in those twin abominations, clichés and journalese, emphasized disastrously with unnecessary inverted commas.

Excluding his journalistic writing, his published works make up a surprisingly large collection. In addition, there were his letters, written to a succession of protégés on verse-form, or to his multitude of friends concerning a multitude of grievances, with a speed and fluency which increased with the years. The smallest comment, the most casual criticism, might be relied upon to bring a prompt, explosively emphatic reply. He enjoyed enormously the rôle of advisory uncle-in-chief to young and stumbling poets and, if they were sufficiently diffident, he could be amazingly generous, not merely in his holographic advice, but in doing his active best to help them to get their writings published. His whole attitude towards the versifier who was immature or inexperienced—and he was generally both—showed Douglas at his best, provided that the versifier's attitude was traditional and that proper respect was shown for rhyme and metre. He had no patience whatever with the prose-cut-into-short-lengths school of poetry. Granted those things, Douglas was so kindly, so generous that he created many friendships as fervent as they were sustained.

1. POETRY

There are arguments, and always likely to be arguments, concerning the place to which Douglas's poetry in its own right entitles him. He himself was, perhaps mercifully, untroubled by doubt. As one stating an obvious and indisputable fact, he says that not only is he a great poet, but that he has always known it. Indisputably great poets—or, for that matter, great actors, painters or composers, or practitioners in any form of art—are not in the habit of so labelling themselves; greatness normally includes a capacity for detached self-criticism, and such self-criticism springs from humility and an abiding sense of the heart-breaking limitations of all human effort in comparison with human aspirations.

But apart from this childish vanity, he was quite simply not of the stuff of which great poets or any other class of great men are made, stuff that involves qualities inherent and unmistakable in Milton or Turner or Johnson or Michelangelo, whatever their human pettinesses or lapses. One quality in particular he lacked—a sustained power of absorption in his subject. He surrendered far too often and far too readily to the lure of ignominious, even despicable things. His sojourning among the heights was never more than brief, and in the depths no longer than it takes to express some poignant moment. The still inner life, the tranquillity which Wordsworth knew, whatever the clamour and restlessness of the outward world, lasted with Douglas rarely beyond the time involved in the construction of fourteen exquisitely passionate, fault-lessly rhythmical lines.

That much being granted, it is no injustice to label him nothing more than a minor and intermittent genius; rewarded with occasional flashes of inspiration that illuminated his poetry briefly, yet for long enough to secure for some of it a permanent place in our English anthologies. He had, at any rate, one hallmark of the artist. However foolishly he might fritter away money and energy and reputation on lesser things, what he gave to his verse was never anything short of sincerity and passion and nobility.

" He was," wrote Harold Nicolson, " an admirable poet, whom some good critics have regarded as a master of sonnet form. On the whole, his poetry is more academic than adventurous, but it always revealed a certain distinction of taste and a genuine literary sensibility."

It seems to me an admirably sound analysis. And I feel that either deliberately or instinctively in the knowledge of his own limitations, he chose the sonnet because it embodied, as no other formalized verse-form did, exactly what he was capable of doing best. All artists tend, of course, to grope their way towards the path along which they can travel with a minimum of effort and a maximum of appreciation, even if it be no more than a deep, narrow track.

Omitting the sonnets, by which he stands or falls, there remains among his serious verse his " Perkin Warbeck," a long narrative poem written in 1893 or 1894, based on Hollingshead's *Chronicles,* and in the opinion of more than one critic a self-portrait in its description of the hero; " Rejected," which, in spite of some distressingly utilitarian rhymes, is full-charged with emotion; " The Ballad of St. Vitus," "A Triad of the Moon," and " To Olive," to all of which the same comment applies. These and a handful of others are poetry as distinct from verse. But not great poetry. They are Swinburne at his second-best. The critical reader is too often uneasily conscious of unpoetic words inserted to produce a rhyme to some word which the writer is determined not to surrender, of high-sounding metaphors and similes that simply do not make sense. (The last verse of " To Olive " is a case in point.)

It has already been noted that Douglas's most intimate colleague after Wilde's death—Crosland—was also a writer of sonnets, and of little else which holds any certainty of survival. Was it the same specialized form of genius that bound together in brief and restless partnership two men so preposterously different in every other respect?

For the purpose of criticism as a whole it is convenient to take the collected edition of his verse, first published in 1928. With that is included a preface which sets out with didactic finality the Douglas theory of poetry. Apart from a sidelong snap at Walt Whitman it does, however, spare us the incessant intrusions of personal feuds which make much of his prose such exasperating reading.

But while his English is clear-cut and straightforward, his logic is indefensibly weak. He compares, for instance, the poet who writes decasyllabic lines with an occasional Alexandrine thrown in with the musician who deliberately plays a few false notes in the Chopin concerto in order to produce a certain effect. The comparison is entirely false. A poet is *entitled* to experiment, to produce variations in tradition if he considers the risk justified. If his assumption proves wrong, his work is so much the poorer. But, for better or worse, it is his own creation. The musician, genius or otherwise, is no more than the faithful interpreter of the work of the composer, also a genius or otherwise.

And the conversion of the first three lines of Wordsworth's " On Westminster Bridge " into deliberately bald and laborious prose proves nothing whatever.

In addition to the preface there are comments, very brief comments, at the end of many of the poems. These prosaic, purely personal interjections—" Poor stuff ! " and so forth—may have some explanatory value, but immediately following individual poems whose entire effect depends upon their delicately perceived, exquisitely described imagery are ruinously out of place. The effect is altogether too reminiscent of the gallery-ite's comment on Macbeth's " Is this a dagger which I see before me?"—" No, you fool, it's a putty-knife ! " They should have been in an appendix.

The collection falls into two groups—" serious " poems and those described as " light verse." The second section occupies rather more than half the book, 135 pages out of 230. It includes " The Pongo Papers,"

THE MIDDLE YEARS

" The Duke of Berwick," " Tails with a Twist " and " The Placid Pug." Also the preface to the first edition of " The Pongo Papers," issued in 1907.

The verses may be—indeed, are—" light." But the preface is massively analytical, spoilt not only by defective logic but by personalities. This time the victim is Mr. Hilaire Belloc, whom he accuses, at some length, of imitating, in *The Bad Child's Book of Verse*, Douglas's " very great success." He claims that his own poems are by far the most elaborate rhymes that have ever been attempted, nearly as difficult to write as sonnets, and that the fact that they are not *wholly* nonsense rhymes has demanded a technique which is both elaborate and perfect to excuse them.

Possibly. But if that be granted, the author should have known better than to employ as rhymes—I quote from the first page only—" be " and " Society," and " irritations " and " invitations."

All the light verses might have been written by an undergraduate of kittenish imagination and with a natural flair for verse construction. And a very considerable number of adolescents, not all of them undergraduates, are equipped with precisely those two qualifications. (Such versification does, in point of fact, demand less ingenuity than its even lower-brow brother, the limerick, with its handicap of achieving extreme brevity, and an effective dénouement in its third rhyming last line.)

In 1925 the American " Little Blue Books " included, as their 788th volume, *Perkin Warbeck and other Poems*.

This miniature paper-covered series, published in Gerard, Kansas, by the Haldeman-Julius Company, and edited by E. Haldeman Julius, covers an amazingly wide field, though the books themselves are of the cheapest possible type, and priced, one assumes, at about five cents.

Perkin Warbeck has a badly produced likeness of the author, and an introduction by George Sylvester Vierick. The latter begins discouragingly: " Better known to scandal than to fame, more often heard in the Law Court than on Parnassus, Lord Alfred Douglas is, nevertheless, one of the great English poets. His output is small, but his wares are never shoddy. . . . Most writers who practise literature as a profession carry too much ballast. Too often their wheat is buried under bushels of chaff. Too often their jewels are marred by inferior settings. . . . This," asserts Mr. Vierick, abandoning his extremely mixed bag of metaphors, " holds true of Milton. . . . It is even true of Shakespeare. But it is not true of Edgar Allan Poe or of Alfred Douglas. Each in the handful they gave us is precious. There are no pebbles in the lot."

One would be loath to chill the enthusiasm of so fervid an admirer, but if ever there was a poet who descended from the creation of pure poetry to the manufacture of the sheerest emotional shoddy, it is Poe. And Douglas's verse included a considerable proportion below the level of Keats's " Odes."

A few further extracts from the introduction may be given.

" ' The Ballad of Reading Gaol ' owes much of its perfection to the inspirational advice and arduous co-operation of Douglas. When all the world had deserted Wilde,* Douglas paid for his funeral and wrote ' The Dead Poet '—a sonnet so fine that it is almost worth dying for.

" Douglas, with his boyish vanity, his desire to defy the world, was undoubtedly responsible for many of Wilde's indiscretions. Nevertheless, he was also his inspiration.

" Douglas in *Oscar Wilde and Myself* assumes

---

* This statement is, of course, a fantastic exaggeration. Wilde's final descent was in spite of helping hands, and not because of their absence.

towards Wilde's exotic vagaries an attitude difficult to
reconcile with his ' Hymn to Physical Beauty.'

" In many of his poems Lord Alfred plays with Greek
fire. We need not, in spite of his contradictions, condemn Douglas as a hypocrite. He may not himself
realize that whatever may be his intellectual convictions, he is at heart a pagan. His paganism is more
joyous than Swinburne's. Wilde was an Irish Protestant
with a middle-class conscience and pronounced Catholic
leanings, who vainly tried to make himself believe that
he was a Greek. Douglas was a Greek who vainly
imagines himself to be a Catholic. The boot does not
fit. It is easy to discern under the monkish gown the
cloven hoof of Pan.

" The Devil himself finds no more convincing
advocate in all literature than Lord Alfred Douglas in
' The Legend of Spinello.' Moved by ambivalent
emotions, imprisoned complexities in his own bosom,
confused by the conflict between instinct and reason,
the poet complains that he has lost both the Nazarene
and Apollo. However, the fear is unjustified. Apollo
cannot disown so faithful a worshipper. And even Jesus
cannot but smile on the poet who comes to Him with
an imperishable garland of lyrics.

" Unlike Wilde, Douglas is never the showman, but
always the poet. Whatever may be his personal
eccentricities, he sublimates them to art. In spite of
public quarrels and public scandals, in spite of political
feuds and literary vendettas, malice cannot gainsay the
vigour of his diction."

Neither malice nor anyone else, Douglas's enemies
least of all, would attempt to gainsay the vigour of his
diction.

While I find it impossible to agree without qualification with Mr. Vierick's introduction—from which I
quote with his full permission—it does present the
personal point of view of a wholehearted admirer.

2. Prose

The prose of Alfred Douglas belongs, as already indicated, to an altogether lower literary level. Superficially it has only two points in common with his poetry—its vehemence, and its ingenuousness.

Apart from his books, his prose writings include his journalistic writing, his satires (later published in book form), a succession of letters to the Press on any subject which chanced to set the highly combustible Douglas heather afire; a " preface " to the *Life and Confessions of Oscar Wilde* by Frank Harris (which gives an exhibition of fiery and incoherence mercifully rare in English literature), and the pamphlets which at intervals he flung at the world with the gusto of a small boy throwing a stone through the window of an unpopular master.

There is no space to deal here with so large and so miscellaneous a collection. His books, however, obviously justify discussion.

The first of these possessed remarkable qualities at every stage of its development—in the reason for its being written at all, in the fact that the nominal author did not write all of it, in the details of its actual publication, in its subsequent repudiation, in Douglas's deliberately omitting it from his list of publications. It was his *Oscar Wilde and Myself*, written in 1913 in collaboration with Crosland, and published in 1914, coincident with the first day of the first World War.

It was inspired by the fury of exasperation that followed the production of the suppressed portions of *De Profundis.*

Wilde had been lying in his French grave for fourteen years. And on his deathbed he had been received into the same all-forgiving Church that had embraced his one-time comrade in 1911. But neither repentance nor death cancelled a debt, real or imaginary, where Douglas's grievances were concerned. *Oscar Wilde and Myself* is nauseating, not only in the poisonous and sustained vindictiveness shown towards a friend so intimate and so well remembered that the writer had the victim's entire range of faults and weaknesses at his fingertips, but in its spiritual pettiness. Obscure details, *any* details are dragged into the story if they can be used to cast a slur on Wilde's name—the fact that his father, though an oculist and aurist famous enough to be knighted, once kept a chemist's shop in an unfashionable quarter of Dublin, and was later involved in an unpleasant legal action; other facts about Wilde's colossal appetite for good food and his capacity for limitless drinking; and yet more about his snobbery—a snobbery, incidentally, nowhere equalling that of which the whole book is redolent.

Passing on to the trials, he accuses Wilde of whimpering, of being a coward. He accuses him also of possessing something of which he himself knew nothing. The phrase is ambiguous, but whichever meaning is read into the sentence, Douglas is lying. He not only knew Wilde's secret—he himself was a partner in it.

Then, abandoning Wilde's morals, he turns to attack his literary reputation. Apart from " The Ballad of Reading Gaol," and with qualifications " The Sphinx," there is nothing he can praise beyond giving whatever credit may be due to " a plagiarist, an impudent and unblushing cribber, a flagrant copyist, an over-sedulous ape." His " pot-boiling fleers," otherwise essays, were also cribbed, his short stories do not quite come off, his plays contain twaddling dialogue and feeble humour, and never succeed in rivalling those of Arthur Pinero or Henry Arthur Jones.

So every aspect of Wilde's life is surveyed; spite can no further go. It is an incredible book, the book of a Hyde who sustained his horrible rôle long enough to write over three hundred pages of vilification, vilification actually toned down by the publishers before it appeared in print. Later, far too late, Jekyll ousted Hyde, at least partially. A good many details, some of first-class importance, were branded by Douglas as lies. He explained at considerable length that while he personally " passed " *Oscar Wilde and Myself* as a complete book it was actually written (*a*) jointly by him and Crosland, (*b*) with Crosland's help, (*c*) by Crosland alone so far as certain portions were concerned, e.g. the episode, or series of episodes, which began with Lord Queensberry's card at the Albemarle Club. The precise degree of responsibility does not seem to matter.

" Every great man," wrote Oscar Wilde, " has his disciples. And it is usually Judas who writes his biography."

Douglas wrote his own—wrote it, with variations, several times over. And no biography written has more effectively betrayed its author.

The *Autobiography* was his second book, published in 1929, and subsequently translated into French, German and Spanish. As a mirror of the mentality of the author it is, to a reader sufficiently interested to read it at all, profoundly revealing. As a book nominally setting out to give a coherent account of a man's life and told in his own words, it must rank among the worst autobiographies in the English language. It is, certainly without exception, the worst I have ever read. Incidents occurring in his youth are jumbled with other incidents that happened in middle-age; there is no attempt whatever to carry the reader along from year to year. Douglas slips and slides and glooms and glances, scattering as he goes prejudices and hates and moralizings and compliments with childish and unconcealed delight in his own cleverness and good looks and the eminence of his family. The reader's only hope of getting any clear picture of anything is to track whatever he thinks worth while from page to page, via the index—incomparably the best-written part of the book.

The *Autobiography* was followed in 1933 by *The True History of Shakespeare's Sonnets*. Here, still emphatically and unmistakably the same old Douglas, he had something to say coupled with a capacity to say it without exasperating or exhausting the reader.

The contention, as already stated, is that the " Master (not Mr.) W. H." of the Sonnets was a handsome boy named William Hughes, to whom Shakespeare was deeply, though entirely innocently, attached; charges that Shakespeare was sexually abnormal are confuted by quotations from the Sonnets themselves.

In 1938 *Without Apology* appeared. He described the book as " Random Recollections of My Stormy Life." It is certainly that. It is also considerably more.

Here is a mellowing in his general attitude to the world, and a slight, regrettably slight, realization of his own part towards keeping the fires of its animosity alight from the time of the Wilde trial onwards. What one misses is a parallel change in his attitude towards those he had come to regard as enemies never to be forgotten; never, dead or alive, to be mentioned without a sneer or a venomous reference to their past.

His enemies, he says, he forgave because as a Christian and a Catholic he was bound to do so. But beyond formal forgiveness he draws the line. Anything in the nature of tolerance towards other men's lapses, and especially towards those whose failings have been cancelled by death, apparently plays no part in his conception of either Christianity in general or Catholicism in particular. His friend Shaw, with the unerring Shavian genius for summarizing a situation, once demanded why Douglas, who had been so unjust to so many good men, should expect justice for

himself, and went on to refer to Douglas's exploitation
of Crosland's phobia for calumny in *The Academy*.

Douglas, of course, was furiously indignant at the
statement. But fury notwithstanding, it is the simple
and literal truth, as anyone taking the trouble
to go into the relationship between Crosland and
Douglas in those hectic days can discover for himself.
And Douglas's attempt to explain it away are more
damning than a frank confession.

The Evening Standard quoted, as *The Daily Express*
did, Douglas's comments on Crosland. He deals first
with his private life. Stories are told of his drinking,
his fecklessness, his casual treatment of his wife, of his
being badgered by bailiffs (an almost incredible
example of the pot calling the kettle black). Douglas
further damned him as treacherous, and utterly
unscrupulous, and added that if ever there was a man
who deserved the appellation of a fair-weather friend,
it was he. " Had it stood at that," comments the
Standard's critic, " one would merely shrug the
shoulders and question a little the taste that rolls a
dead man in the mud. But this turned my stomach:
' I have forgiven him, of course, because as a Christian
and a Catholic I am bound to do that.' "

There are interesting references to his father who, it
appears, was reconciled to Christianity on his deathbed
(the phrase is not mine), having been very religious as
a boy. If this is so, the change in Lord Queensberry's
convictions must have lasted about thirty years, with
extremely unfortunate moral and financial results.
With this belated but entirely justified conviction of
sin went an entirely unjustified belief that he had been
reduced to poverty. In point of fact, when all the fixed
charges on his income had been met, he had still eight
thousand a year to live on.

Finally, in 1940, came *Oscar Wilde—A Summing
Up.*

In reviewing *Without Apology, The Daily Express* (May 19th, 1938) commented on some of Douglas's strictures on living authors and on literature in general. "There is no longer hardly [*sic*] a reasonable competent literary review which can be trusted to tell the truth between good and bad work in any branch of art " is one statement.

Wells is dismissed as " a third-rate fictionist." Yeats is " a very minor poet." T. S. Eliot and Auden are " simply not poets at all." Eliot's poems he compared with a leading article in *The Times,* adding that his words were meant to contain no aspersions on the newspaper.

The Evening Standard mentions David Low, Shaw, Dean Inge, Dr. Barnes and Epstein among his *bêtes noirs,* and in conclusion quotes sentences which it stigmatizes as " ghastly."

The adjective is deserved.

3. CORRESPONDENCE

The staggering number of letters which he found time and energy to write, particularly in the later years, has already been mentioned. Generally speaking, they run true to form, or rather to two forms—the charmingly avuncular and the explanatory-denunciatory.

Among the first class, there are amusingly frequent references to the number of volumes of his own poetry that have been sold, and to the praise that he has received. In the second, there is the same old intolerance of anyone whose views differed from his own, and the same undiminished hatred of his four or five special enemies.

The total number of letters he wrote must run into thousands, including entire collections which the sheer exigencies of time have made it impossible for me to examine. Even a selection from those I have examined would fill a volume. Here there is space for only a typical few.

I will begin with the correspondence sent me by Captain L. H. Green. In a covering letter he states that as literary executor of the late Charles Kains Jackson, editor of *The Artist* in the nineties, he inherited the letters. Most, though not all, are from Douglas to Jackson. They conclude with a copy of a letter from Captain Green himself to Jackson.

In the first, dated August 31st, 1893, Douglas apologizes for not answering Jackson's letter—he has no excuse, he is dreadful at answering letters. (He cured himself very effectively of the fault in later years!) He sends two sonnets, one inspired by the phrase "sugar lips," employed in a translation by Sir Richard Burton. He has also just finished translating Wilde's *Salome*; it is to be published in October.

But he is bored to death and very unloved, and surrounded by what is popularly known as a bevy of fair girls, which fills him with misery.

The second letter is written on September 10th at Datchet.

After discussing his own poetry, he passes on to Wilde. He agrees with Jackson that to a certain extent he overdoes the "jewelled style," but thinks he has a very dainty fancy, a great facility of expression, a sense of the phrase, and an enormous dramatic instinct—the latter apart from the plays. His best things he has never written; Douglas fears he never will write them.

The psychology in anything Wilde writes will always bear the closest inspection. Everything he writes grows out of an abstract psychological idea; in most people, Douglas thinks, it is just reversed.

The letter concludes with an outburst of passionate affection and admiration for Wilde. He is the only man he knows who would have the courage to put his arm

on the shoulder of an ex-convict and walk down
Piccadilly with him.

A year and a half later Wilde was to be the convict
and Douglas the man to exhibit that courage.

On April 9th, 1894, Douglas writes excitedly that he
is about to pay his first visit to Florence. He is going
alone. Will " K. J." write and tell him anything he
knows about it, with regard to the eternal quest for
beauty " to which I am bound!"

Almost exactly a year later (April 12th, 1895)
Douglas, now in London, is writing tragically to ask if
Kains Jackson can do anything or suggest anything at
this terrible moment? The writer has lived through
what seems like countless aeons of anguish since Friday
(the day following Wilde's remand in custody, Sir John
Bridge, the Bow Street magistrate, having refused to
grant bail). Does K. J. know no strong, fearless man
who will stand up?

The letter is signed " Yours in misery."

The final letter is a copy of one written by Captain
Green himself to Kains Jackson on August 11th, 1919.
The writer was staying at Linford Hall, Wolverton,
with a friend named Knapp. The discovery of some old
photographs of Douglas had reminded Knapp of his
friendship with Douglas and his brother Drumlanrig
when all three were at Oxford. Knapp also knew—and,
incidentally, liked—old Queensberry. He agreed that
all the scandal seemed now to have been a storm in a
teacup.

The letter continues:

> He recalled meeting Oscar at Naples soon after his
> release. Bosie came up and greeted him and said, " Oscar
> is here, do join us, or do you mind?" Knapp said of course
> he didn't mind, he should be delighted. He said Oscar was
> quite broken, and talked platitudes.
>
> He also told me that Bosie was quite infatuated with
> Oscar.
>
> Knapp puts down Bosie's astonishing attitude to the fact
> that he " got religion." He said that Drumlanrig got it, too.

The relationship existing between Douglas and Wilde when they were together in Paris after Wilde's release is revealed in letters written by the latter to Ross in the summer of 1898.

Douglas, states a letter written on May 1st, had not gone to his flat yet, but Wilde had chosen some nice furniture for him at Maple's, and he would be moving in on the following day. Douglas went to the races apparently every day, and lost, of course. He had a faculty for spotting losers, which, considering he knew nothing at all about horses, was perfectly astounding.

Another letter, dated a month later, was by way of an apology for a postscript, inspired by Douglas, in " a rather silly " letter to Ross. Wilde thought letters of that kind " quite stupid and witless," but " Bosie has no real enjoyment of a joke unless he thinks there is a good chance of the other person being pained or annoyed. It is an entirely English trait, the English type and symbol of a joke being the jug on the half-opened door, or the distribution of orange peel on the pavement of a crowded thoroughfare."

A third letter concerns a dinner at Maire's, to which Wilde had made Harris invite Douglas. The bill, writes Wilde, was terrific. Harris and his second wife were there; Frank was wonderful on the Greek passion of Christ and Shakespeare—especially Christ.

There is another batch of letters written between 1938 and 1941 to Miss Norma Reeves. In forwarding them she says:

> I knew Lord Alfred when I was eleven and lived in an adjacent block of flats at Hove. We met frequently in St. Ann's Well's Gardens.

They deal, in the main, with trivialities — the trivialities that a kindly, elderly gentleman believed would interest a young girl.

Written on August 28th, 1938, the first letter acknowledges a magazine she had sent him, and which he read with great interest, " especially as most of it was written by yourself." He goes on to describe his own journalistic work, with the comment that he had always thought that the best thing about editing a paper was that one could print as much of one's own stuff, in poetry or prose, as one liked. The letter is signed " Yours affectionately," and then embarks upon a long postscript, in the course of which he loves his love with an " N " because her name is *Norma,* she is *nice* (alternatively *naughty*), she lives in *Nizell's* Avenue, every time he sees her (though he has tried to propitiate her by giving her an autograph of Bernard Shaw, a cheap watch, some stamps, a subscription to her magazine and a copy of the selected edition of his poems) she gives him *Nothing.*

A charming effort, worthy of Barrie himself.

Later letters refer to a pamphlet he had written during the war, in which he advocated seizing bases in Ireland. (The pamphlet had been circulated in the House of Commons, and he was apparently expecting Churchill to act on it.) The last letter, from a nursing home in Hove, is written with pathetic shakiness in pencil. The date is October 12th, 1944.

He is glad to hear from Norma again. . . . He is ill in bed with a bad heart, and not suffered to write any letters. . . . In a day or so he will send her a copy of the lecture he delivered before the Royal Society of Literature in the previous September on " The Principles of Poetry." He had then attacked T. S. Eliot and his school of poets.

When (and if) he gets well he will write again.

Mr. John Press, sending three letters from Douglas attacking T. S. Eliot, writes :

> I began by saying that the lines he had selected for condemnation were in fact quotations from a prose sermon from Bishop Andrewes, and that this practice of incorporating prose into poetry was a perfectly reputable device, used by Shakespeare himself.

That was enough to set in motion the whole machinery of Douglas invective against Eliot. His justification for expressing any opinion is rather obscured by his admission that he did not profess to know Eliot's work.

But it is in his correspondence with Robert Sherard, from whom for years he was estranged, that perhaps most interest centres. As Mr. Montgomery Hyde comments: " If this correspondence adds little to our knowledge of Wilde, it does throw additional light on several incidents. . . . The letters also possess the merit of candour; indeed, Douglas is considerably franker in them than he is in his contemporary writings, notably his *Autobiography*."

The most interesting letters cover a period of just over ten years—October 17th, 1929, to October 31st, 1939. (Robert Sherard died, aged eighty-two, on January 31st, 1943.) The first letter was in response to a formal—a very formal—olive branch tendered by Sherard. " I really cannot undertake to answer yours in the third person," says Douglas. But his own letter is stiff; he deals elaborately and formally, chapter and verse, with the origin of their quarrel, the basis of which was Sherard's support—or alleged support—of Ross against Douglas, and inferentially taking Wilde's part against him.

Sherard's attempt to make out that he was really a noble and pure-minded person was too foolish to discuss seriously; to know what Oscar was really like Sherard had only to read the letters he wrote to Ross from Paris. They were full of spiteful and insulting references to Sherard.

The letter, extremely long, as they all are, concludes by saying that it was quite natural and right that Sherard should have disapproved of him in many ways; the only thing that was absurd was that he should have tried to whitewash Wilde at Douglas's expense.

The next noteworthy letter (September 17th, 1932) deals with an article Sherard had written on Wilde for *John o' London's Weekly,* and with Wilde's having had " serious thoughts about skipping his bail." Upon this point Douglas says he is quite positive. Wilde was, up to the last, quite undecided, though urged to go away. He himself had strongly urged Wilde to go; surely Sherard wouldn't have considered it dishonourable to bolt when he had the consent of Bosie's brother who had gone bail, and when he (Wilde) realized the fierceness and vindictiveness of the prosecution?

Most of the rest of the letter deals with Wilde's unashamed and unchecked depravity during the last three years of his life.

Surely, says Douglas, a few days later, after a reply from Sherard, Sherard ought to call him " Douglas " or "Alfred " and not " Lord Alfred Douglas "? (His own three letters are signed " Yours sincerely," " Yours most sincerely " and " Yours ever very sincerely.") The fourth letter again asks Sherard to " drop the Lord Alfred business."

He complains (April 14th, 1933) that his book continues to get splendid reviews, but does not sell. His attacks on Harris are forgotten for the moment in the fury of his onslaught against André Gide and his book, *Si le grain ne meurt.* In another letter, he denies a statement in Lord Birkenhead's life of his father that F. E. met Wilde in Douglas's rooms at Oxford. And on September 17th he says that he is consulting his solicitor about Birkenhead's book, and will probably start proceedings.

On December 8th he mentions that his reference in the *Autobiography* to the money Ross left when he died was purposely rather cryptic; what he had in mind, though he cannot prove it, was that he probably got it by discreet blackmailing.

On March 1st, 1935, writing from St. Leonards-on-Sea, he says that his nephew Queensberry, with great generosity, has presented him with a very nice flat in Hove, into which he is moving, with his own furniture, during the following week. His mother has just taken another flat in the same building.

On March 8th, 1937, he flatly contradicts Sherard's statement that Wilde did not sell the scenario of *Mr. and Mrs. Daventry* to several people. Douglas says that he himself was in the Café Royal with Harris when Leonard Smithers and Roberts, two of the victims, met him by appointment and produced the scenario. . . . As to Oscar's getting drunk in the last two years of his life (never before), Douglas saw him over and over again so drunk that he could not walk and had to be helped into his cab.

On May 1st, 1938, there is a heartfelt tribute to Shaw, who had written *the last ultimate defence* of Douglas, and the most extraordinarily profound explanation of everything that happened as far as he was concerned, " putting him right " for ever. Douglas had received six friendly and delightful letters, as well as a book by Einstein to cultivate the otherwise neglected side of an acute and efficient mind, and when Douglas jocularly reproached him by quoting the Scriptures, saying that he was like a man who " reached his son a scorpion when he asked for an egg," Shaw had told him to go to his bankers for an overdraft of £100, which he (Shaw) would guarantee.

On June 28th, 1939, Douglas writes that he is getting very little out of his new book—only £30 advance—that he wishes he hadn't taken it on, and that it worries him frightfully. He always goes through the stage of thinking that he can't write any book that he is going to do. . . .

The last letter to be mentioned here may fittingly be one that he wrote shortly before his death to his old antagonist Winston Churchill. As a dying man, he implored him not to let down Poland.

Churchill replied immediately, informing Douglas that the domestic freedom and full sovereignty of the country would be preserved.

The letter concluded: "I trust your health may be restored," and was signed "Yours sincerely." An old, very rusty hatchet had been buried.

But I like best his letters to the little girl he loved with an " N."

CHAPTER XI

FINALE

THE years passed swiftly, with the events that filled them etched more perfunctorily on the memory. Douglas grew older. But not willingly less youthful. His insistence on youthfulness was, I think, only partly a matter of vanity; it was more an attitude of defiance, increasingly difficult to sustain, towards Fate who had given him so much, and now, with something of the bored impatience of a father who is tired of supporting a prodigal son, gave him no more.

The second World War came. Douglas was seventy by the time it had reached its crucial phase, and the British Empire was facing all the Axis Powers could drive or lash or cajole into the firing line.

Forty years earlier he had offered his services to his country, and had been rejected; twenty-five years after that rebuff he had offered them for a second time, and been rejected by Kitchener. Now Kitchener was in his Atlantic grave, and there was nothing Douglas could do beyond accepting the best with gratitude and the worst with cheerful endurance, as millions of other old men and women were doing.

He had at last to face that inexorable corollary of survival—physical deterioration. The slim, sprightly figure now moved with conscious, almost conscientious briskness; the once-overflowing vitality had to be treasured for exhibition; fatigue came insidiously and too soon, as sleep comes to children. Photographs show him making a gallant but unavailing stand against old age. An enlargement of the last photograph ever taken reveals a myriad of tiny wrinkles in the skin that until he was past forty looked so incredibly smooth and boyish.

There was a further, perhaps heavier, penalty. He was a survivor, a lonely figure whose great moments had been in a past as vanished and almost as forgotten as the days of the Crimea and the Indian Mutiny. Of the multitude of friends and enemies who had peopled that past, whom he had loved and hated—particularly hated — with such thoroughness, the merest handful remained, remote and detached now from the common interests or antagonisms that had linked them. Shaw still lived, and Arthur Ransome, against whom he had never felt more than a nominal enmity, and Alice Head, his secretary of *The Academy* days, and Max Beerbohm with the gods' gift of eternal old age, and Gerald Hamilton and Moore Pim, and, of course, Churchill. But a great host had gone, beginning with Wilde in 1900, and the lovely, long-suffering Constance, and Robbie Ross, and Chris Millard, and Robert Sherard, and his incomparable mother, who, living to be ninety-one, ended her troubled life in 1935. Olive, the wife once so passionately adored, so idyllically proclaimed his mate, and then for a time estranged, had lived near but not with him until her death in 1944. Both had changed; both had realized it. The health of Raymond, an only child, precluded the boy from being the link that might have united the three of them as a family.

Of the many lawyers who had fought for and against him, or as magistrates or judges had done their best to demonstrate the infallibility of the law when administered by fallible human beings, Travers Humphreys remained, and Comyns Carr. But the faithful Cecil Hayes had gone, and Clarke and Ned Carson and F. E. Smith, and Avory, and Eve, and Paul Taylor, and George Lewis.

Mr. Hector Bolitho has kindly allowed me to quote from his personal reminiscences of Douglas, whom he met when on leave during the late war:

" I remember a big sitting-room, with grey shadows outside, and the miserable winter tide beyond the sea wall; Alfred Douglas walking in, slowly, with a sad face but quick, lively eyes. Then some naval cadets from H.M.S. *King Alfred* joined us and our hostess, Olga Tredegar, tried to manage a rather confused conversation; the boys on one side talking of war; on the other, Alfred Douglas talking of poetry. There was a tough little midshipman who had never heard of Alfred Douglas. He no doubt felt that his place was with the erudite, so he piped up: ' Oh, I know a poem right through. I learned it at school. Milton!'

" Instead of frowning at the interruption, Lord Alfred Douglas said: ' I love Milton. Which poem was it?'

" The boy began, but his memory failed. Alfred Douglas prompted him, line by line, so that the midshipman navigated his way to the end of the sonnet. After this, Lord Alfred Douglas turned the conversation to the Navy, so the boy would feel that he was in home waters. It was a charming gesture from an old, distinguished poet to an eager boy.

" We met several times during the war, and his one or two letters to me carried on the sad theme of bitterness from which he seldom seems able to free himself. He wrote of the ' atrocious and fantastic libels ' on him in Frank Harris's book on Wilde; of his being ' forced into litigation by persecution.' And I went to tea with him in the little apartment in Hove where the remnants of his story are gathered—drawings of himself when he was at Oxford, inscribed books in rich covers that smelled of the nineties. The scene was sad and frightening, especially with the noises of the present war making him seem like a wrinkled ghost. He told me of the time when Wilde was working on *The Importance of Being Earnest,* and of the original play being so different from the version finally produced by Sir George Alexander. When I left he walked with me to the bus stop; a lonely old man, who had certainly paid a big and bitter debt for being allowed to leave the world some of its greatest sonnets."

It was lonely in the little flat at Hove, especially when neither Olive nor his mother were near to counsel or help. But he still had two traditional, never-failing antidotes to boredom—the exercise of his religion, and letter-writing.

They could not occupy all the hours, of course. But they did occupy a good many. His passion for letter-writing remained with him until the end. It resulted in correspondence on an eighteenth-century scale. Nor was it the typewriter-private-secretary sort of correspondence, but informal letters in his own characteristically headlong script. Much of this probably sprang from his eagerness to keep in touch with the new generation, from his refusal to be left behind, to be relegated to the mists into which so many of the prominent disappear during the later non-productive days.*

His other interests included, unfortunately, gambling. He had been an inveterate gambler all his life, but it proved a hobby altogether too expensive for a man whose judgment of horses was on a par with his luck. And his luck was consistently bad. St. Anthony of Padua, so co-operative in materializing small and informative boys (and in eliminating mice in prison!) does not seem to have helped him here at all.

---

*To give a personal example, when I wrote expressing appreciation of his views on poetry, as expressed in a brochure he had issued, I received, practically by return, a charming letter of thanks, amplified by typically Bosie-ish comments on the modern school of poetry and running to four pages. And this when he was already failing, within a few months of his death.

Where his monetary affairs were concerned, it would be an understatement to say that they were in a state of chronic chaos. More than twenty years before his death he had been made bankrupt, and for not very clear reasons of his own he declined to take any steps to have the bankruptcy annulled.

From his books he received royalties from time to time. Largely through the instrumentality of his friend Lord Tredegar, he had been granted a Civil List pension. Finally, he could rely upon a considerable though unpredictable flow of help from a number of other friends who held, so to speak, a watching brief on behalf of his debts. In short, he should have had enough, and more than enough, to live upon in reasonable comfort.

But he never had. A realization of the exact number of shillings in a pound does not suddenly dawn upon a man who has reached the age of seventy without discovering that money is not something to be disposed of at the earliest possible moment on the attraction of that moment.

He decided to leave the flat in St. Ann's Court; the Hove sea-front should form his parade no longer. For a time he contemplated coming inland, and accepting the hospitality of an old friend, Miss Mary Grosvenor, at Hampstead. He had actually arrived at the house with his luggage when a discussion with his sister, Lady Edith Fox-Pitt, led to a change of mind. The last few months of his life were still to be passed within sight and sound of the sea, at Lancing.

For some time he had suffered from his heart. As he grew frailer, he saw less and less of the outside world. Daily walks were abandoned. Religion absorbed yet more of his thoughts. . . . He ceased to leave his room, his bed. But he could still enjoy his meals—he had always been a man to whom the right sort of food was a matter of importance.

He forgave his enemies, or perhaps it would be safer to say those who, at some time or other, more or less vehemently disagreed with him. He mentions some of them by name—his wife, his son, his father-in-law, Crosland, Ransome, Wilde. Even, perhaps, his arch-enemy, Ross (though this is probably going too far), and Lord Oxford and Winston Churchill, and Sir George Lewis and other lawyers whom at one time or another he " smashed " and in general made look foolish in the Central Criminal Court. He asked forgiveness of the Almighty (did it ever occur to him, one wonders, to ask forgiveness of any one of those people who endured so much?).

Douglas died on March 20th, 1945.

Just before he slipped into the long, merciful oblivion that preceded the end, Lord Tredegar called. To him Douglas handed a packet that he took from beneath his pillow, a packet to be kept separate and sacred from all his other papers.

When the packet was examined, it was found to consist of letters written long ago to her adored and adoring son by the " wonderful mother." Douglas had kept them there as a talisman, a consolation, and perhaps, indeed, as a passport.

From *The Times* obituary notice, which admirably epitomizes his personality, though I cannot wholly agree with its analysis of his poetry, I quote the following:

> To have been identified with the fallen playwright (Wilde) was naturally a misfortune for a young man on the threshold of life, but the world would doubtless have forgotten soon enough if Douglas had permitted it to do so. Unhappily for himself, however, he persisted in believing that his fellow-men bore enmity against him. . . . Thus he wasted a notable talent upon an episode which by then was scarcely known except by historical reference to the younger generation, and was remembered with but little interest by the great majority of his own contemporaries. . . . The Wilde scandal not only embittered his life but may well

have helped to warp his nature. Thus he became quarrelsome and almost fiercely litigious.

It was natural that the serious poems of his younger manhood should show the influence of his models, among whom Rosetti and Dowson were the most easy to detect. In " The City of the Soul " there is less soul than city—and a dainty and gracious city it is. A quarter of a century later the sonnet sequence " In Excelsis " (1924) shows the soul full-grown. . . .

In prison, Oscar Wilde wrote *De Profundis*. In prison, Alfred Douglas wrote " In Excelsis." The contrast was intentional, no doubt, but the sincerity of the poems is proved by the outbursts of arrogance, anti-Semiticism, and the like.

A graver cause for disappointment lies not in these sonnets, but in the poetry that followed them. Never again did Douglas fill his mould so richly with the fruits of his highest and most arduous thought. For delicate and subtle moods and feelings he always had the perfect word. " In Excelsis " suggests that great poetry was within his reach, but that he did not follow it.

For all that, he has left much more than elegant fancies and fragrance. His conversion to the Church of Rome in 1911 gave his mind stability and substance. With that background and support he could relax his distrust of " art for art's sake."

But there must be no relaxation of the rules of poetic form. To take him literally would be to condemn half the lines in English poetry as irregular, and he intended to be taken literally. This impossible correctness he not only prescribed, he also practised it. He was happiest within the most rigid limits that he could impose upon the most strict of forms—the Petrarchian sonnet. Thus he kept his poetry too small in volume for his powers, but as pure and firm as he could have desired.

Douglas was buried on March 24th in the little cemetery adjoining the Franciscan Priory at Crawley, in the Sussex that he knew and loved. His sister and other relations were present; so, too, were others, not of the Douglas clan, who had known him in the past days. Not all of those days were overcast; there had been many gleams of sunshine through the clouds. But he must have been glad, I think, when sunset came.

BIBLIOGRAPHY

Annals of Our Time. Irving.

Oscar Wilde and Myself. Lord Alfred Douglas.

Life of Lord Carson. Edward Marjoribanks.

Oscar Wilde—A Summing Up. Lord Alfred Douglas.

Autobiography of Lord Alfred Douglas.

Lord Alfred Douglas, His Life and Work. P. Braybrooke.

Without Apology. Lord Alfred Douglas.

The History of Shakespeare's Sonnets. Lord Alfred Douglas.

The Aesthetic Adventure. William Gaunt.

The Pre-Raphaelite Tragedy. William Gaunt.

Victorian Doctor. T. G. Wilson.

My Life. G. R. Sims.

Sixty Years' Recollections of Bohemian London.

The Beardsley Period. Osbert Burdett.

Savage Messiah. H. S. Ede.

Victorian Parade. Horace Wyndham.

Old Q.'s Daughter. Bernard Falk.

Mainly Victorian. Stewart M. Ellis.

The Hundred Years. Philip Guedalla.

Caesar Ritz, Host to the World. Marie Ritz.

Introduction to "Perkin Warbeck and other Poems." Geo. S. Vierick.

Oscar Wilde: Three Times Tried. Stuart Mason (Christopher Millard).

Oscar Wilde. Frank Harris.

Oscar Wilde. Arthur Ransome.

My Bohemian Days. Hy. Furness.

As We Were. E. F. Benson.

Victorians and Their Books. Amy Cruse.

The Life and Genius of T. W. H. Crosland. W. Sorley Brown.

Modern Paris. Robert H. Sherard.

Twenty Years in Paris. Robert H. Sherard.

Life of Oscar Wilde. Robert H. Sherard.

Oscar Wilde, The Story of an Unhappy Friendship. Robert H. Sherard.

Oscar Wilde. G. J. Reiner.

Oscar Wilde (Play). L. and S. Stokes.

Oscar Wilde and the Theatre. James Agate.

Aspects of Wilde. Vincent O'Sullivan.

New Preface to the " Life and Confessions of Oscar Wilde." Frank Harris and Lord Alfred Douglas.

Life of G. de Maupassant. R. H. Sherard.

The Sporting Queensberrys. Lord Queensberry.

The Quest for Corvo. A. J. A. Symons.

While Rome Burns. Alexander Woolcott.

The Delightful Profession. H. E. Wortham.

Some Victorian Women. Harry Furness.

Shapes that Pass. Julian Hawthorne.

Portraits of the 80's. H. G. Hutchinson.

INDEX